How Democracies Live

How Democracies Live

Power, Statecraft, and Freedom in Modern Societies

STEIN RINGEN

The University of Chicago Press
Chicago and London

The University of Chicago Press, Chicago 60637
The University of Chicago Press, Ltd., London
© 2022 by The University of Chicago
Published 2022
Printed in the United States of America

31 30 29 28 27 26 25 24 23 22   1 2 3 4 5

ISBN-13: 978-0-226-81887-0 (cloth)
ISBN-13: 978-0-226-81912-9 (paper)
ISBN-13: 978-0-226-81911-2 (e-book)
DOI: https://doi.org/10.7208/chicago/9780226819112.001.0001

Library of Congress Cataloging-in-Publication Data

Names: Ringen, Stein, author.
Title: How democracies live : power, statecraft, and freedom in modern societies /
    Stein Ringen.
Description: Chicago : University of Chicago Press, 2022. | Includes bibliographical
    references and index.
Identifiers: LCCN 2021042870 | ISBN 9780226818870 (cloth) |
    ISBN 9780226819129 (paperback) | ISBN 9780226819112 (ebook)
Subjects: LCSH: Democracy. | State, The. | Liberty. | Poverty.
Classification: LCC JC423 .R5158 2022 | DDC 321.8—dc23
LC record available at https://lccn.loc.gov/2021042870

♾ This paper meets the requirements of ANSI/NISO Z39.48-1992 (Permanence of Paper).

Also by Stein Ringen

The Perfect Dictatorship: China in the 21st Century, 2016

Nation of Devils: Democratic Leadership and the Problem of Obedience, 2013

The Korean State and Social Policy: How South Korea Lifted Itself from Poverty and Dictatorship to Affluence and Democracy, with Huck-ju Kwon, Ilcheong Yi, Taekyoon Kim, and Jooha Lee, 2011

The Economic Consequences of Mr. Brown: How a Strong Government Was Defeated by a Weak System of Governance, 2009

What Democracy Is For: On Freedom and Moral Government, 2007

Citizens, Families, and Reform, 1997 and 2005

The Possibility of Politics: A Study in the Political Economy of the Welfare State, 1987 and 2006

About the Cover

Pictured on the cover is the ancient Athenian stele of democracy. It is made of marble and is about a meter high, much like a gravestone, now preserved in Athens' Agora Museum. A relief shows the people of Athens under the protection of *dēmokratia*. A text is inscribed of a law forbidding the reintroduction of tyranny, both the act of rising up against the *dēmos* and collaboration with any would-be tyrant. This law was passed in 337 BC as the short-lived democracy was coming to an end when Athens was being overwhelmed by the Macedons. It was, sadly, a hopeless attempt to salvage what could not survive. In this law, its setting in stone and its aftermath, we see what the experience of democracy taught the Athenians. Democracy gives protection. It is always in peril and itself needs protection. When the foundations have eroded, it is too late to repair the house.

Contents

We Need Democracy

". . . in order that men might not fear each other, there was a natural benefit to be had from government and kingship, provided that they are able to bring about this result."
EPICURUS, ca. 300 BC

Times have not been kind to democracy. This book is in its defense. That defense grows out of a conviction that if we and our children cannot live under reasonably well-functioning democratic rule, our and their lives will suffer for it. It is not a book of predictions or doom and gloom, but a reminder, a sober reminder, I hope, of the majesty, albeit imperfect majesty, of the democratic enterprise.

The shock of the real

In early 2020, a deadly virus spread across the world to bring down upon peoples and governments the ultimate crisis. In a matter of weeks, the contagion had reached pandemic proportions, as if out of a horror movie. Every country and territory was touched, and within countries every region. Within a year, there were more than one hundred million recorded infections worldwide, and more than two million deaths, both without doubt undercounts. National economies were sinking into deep recession.

Although a full analysis of the COVID-19 pandemic and its management will have to wait, much has been learned, and was learned quickly once the gravity of mayhem was recognized. The calamity for most people brought an unexpected gift to the analyst. Matters that in ordinary times are fuzzy present themselves with crystallized clarity.*

---

*I follow "COVID politics" to the end of 2020. My purpose here is to elicit lessons, not to do an analysis of the epidemic as such, and the lessons relevant for my purpose were learned early and quickly.

America and Britain, the core democracies, responded poorly, failing to contain the epidemic and allowing contagion—and death—to spread. That was a tragedy, which in the American case, however, is not difficult to explain. The initial response there was extreme in its ineptitude. That the nation's high political command was unable to grasp the severity of the crisis and failed to mobilize the population into a collaborative response was to prove costly for many Americans, but there is no mystery for the analyst that a failure of leadership results in a failure of policy.

The British case was different. The government did respond with much force but was still unable to provide the population with such protection as should have been expected. From that paradox, there is much to learn about power and statecraft, about people and government, about democracy. Britain presents itself as the ideal laboratory for the observation of the politics of crisis management.

What COVID-19 brought home with shocking brutality was that we are not safe. We were going about our business as usual: children to school, parents to work, friends to bars, couples to restaurants and theaters, families on vacations. Then suddenly, overnight, it was all dangerous, literally, tangibly, deadly dangerous. Businesses and jobs were on the edge of an abyss. Life is not safe.

That should have come as no surprise. This was not the first epidemic scare, even in recent times. In 2002, an epidemic that became known as SARS-CoV erupted in China and spread across Asia, Europe, and the Americas, but without causing pandemic-like damage. In 2009, an influenza epidemic that became known as "swine flu" erupted, probably originating in Mexico, again spreading globally before being contained by the next year. In 2013, an Ebola epidemic erupted in West Africa but was prevented from spreading beyond the region. There were ample warnings from health workers that epidemics were likely to strike again and that we all, under global connectedness, were much exposed.

All the while, we had been living under the threat of global warming and environmental destruction. News had been reaching us in a steady flow of rising oceans, violent storms, floods, and wildfires. It should have been easy for all to see. Life is not safe.

In 2008, the world economy crashed, with a ferocity similar to the crash of 1929.[1] Jobs, businesses, and savings were destroyed. Wages widely stagnated or fell. Homes were lost. Old industries failed, and with them their communities. In Europe, the eurozone fell into a further crisis of unsustainable debt. Again, life is not safe.

It is difficult to fully grasp that modern livelihoods are precarious, not only for poor people in poor countries, not only in civil wars, not only for refugees or desperate migrants, but for all of us, even the comfortably off in affluent and well-organized countries. We want to think that pandemics are of the past and the stuff of science fiction or that "someone" will take care of it. We want to think that climate change is far away in time and distance and that we can carry on as usual. We want to think that markets absorb the effect of economic fluctuations and that households for the most part cope. Always, there are self-proclaimed know-it-alls who tell us not to worry: We live without problems with reoccurring flu epidemics. Temperatures rise and fall; that is nature's way. Markets self-regulate. We want to believe those who reassure us.

It is difficult for governments as well to take in, partly because consequences follow in unpopular and expensive policies. In Britain, following the crash of 2008, the government cushioned the banks while otherwise, in disregard of historical experience and good economics, sat out the slump by cutting back on public finance and investments. On health planning, in Britain again, a simulation exercise had been conducted in 2016, code-named Exercise Cygnus, on preparedness for a possible influenza epidemic. It had revealed the kinds of shortcomings that would materialize in the response to COVID-19, such as inadequacy in the supply of necessary equipment and meager testing and laboratory facilities, but the findings had been classified and not made public knowledge, and had not been followed up on.

The pandemic, however, was something else. This or that political leader, a Trump in America or a Bolsonaro in Brazil, may have preferred the path of denial, but, delusion discounted, what COVID-19 did, and did quickly, was to get it acknowledged as an inescapable fact that we are not safe.

From the recognition of precariousness follows a need for protection. That, again, was immediately apparent. Ordinary people, workers, entrepreneurs, free-lancers, businesses, banks, rail and bus companies, bars and restaurants, sports leagues, gyms, airlines, arts organizations, unions, charities—all overnight demanded protection. They called out for information, guidance, direction, coordination, and economic support.

The imperative was to bring the epidemic under control. The virus that causes COVID-19 works through the respiratory system to produce a severe flu-like infection. The disease is highly contagious and, once active and if not controlled, it is likely to strike a large part of the population. The infection spreads from person to person when anyone who has the disease breathes, speaks, laughs, coughs, or sneezes and leaves droplets with the virus in the air to be inhaled by others nearby. In the absence of a vaccine, suppressing the contagion requires people to maintain enough distance from each other to prevent droplets from traveling from one person to the next. Holding the epidemic under control, therefore, depended on behavior, on people adopting cautionary habits of daily life, habits they found alien and distasteful. In that interest, they were in demand of information, facts, analysis, statistics, guidance, encouragement, even coercion.

For protection, it turned out, there was one place and one place only to go, to the government. All those in need of protection, from the mightiest corporation to the humblest family, called on the government for protection, for financial support, for regulations, and for information, explanation, and guidance. In terms of behavioral adaptation, they called for explicit instructions, and then, for everyone to be able to trust that others would do likewise, for a backup of coercion that failure to comply might trigger punishment. On financial support and regulation, it no longer mattered how much anyone had earlier wanted the government off their backs. Now it was government involvement that was wanted, everywhere and by everyone. The kinds and magnitudes of protection that were in demand can only be forthcoming from governments. No other agency has similar resources or similar society-wide authority, and no other agency can back up action and authority by law.

The need for protection should have come as no surprise, nor should the turning to government. Previous epidemic outbreaks had been contained by determined government action. In the mobilization of protection against global warming, the effort goes to leadership by coordinated government interventions. In responding to the economic crash, at issue was more or less of the governmental visible hand in economic enterprise. In the United States, government stimulus helped the economy to recover relatively quickly and probably saved the auto industry. In Britain, the absence of stimulus aid caused the recession to be prolonged. What public policy is basically about, mostly if not exclusively, is protection. Defense, police, and criminal justice are protective policies. Education is a protective policy, protection against future deprivation. Business regulations are protective policies, against cheating and unfairness. Daily life regulations, for example, health and safety or building regulations, are protective policies. Health and social care are protective policies, as are pensions, social services, family policies, and welfare programs. Protection is what governments deliver—or do not deliver. Governments fail when they fail in protection.

The governments that everyone called on responded in most cases with brazen activism. In Britain, a Conservative government was in charge, firmly committed to an ideology of restrained public policy. Now, however, overnight, this government set itself to assume control of society and the economy in a way that would have been unthinkable only weeks or days before.*

---

*The British Chancellor of the Exchequer, Rishi Sunak, in a speech on March 17, 2020: "This national effort will be underpinned by government interventions in the economy on a scale

SOCIAL CHOICE

The epidemic has the structure of being massively dangerous for a population but not massively dangerous for many or most individuals. If not contained, it will inflict unacceptable morbidity and mortality. But if you are not elderly or impaired in health, you are pretty unlikely to be infected and if infected, pretty unlikely to suffer serious consequences. (Even in a high-prevalence setting, unless you are in a superspreader bubble, the statistical risk of infection to any individual on any day is unlikely to be more than about one in a thousand.) For most people, therefore, it would make good sense to disregard the virus and go about ordinary life. But if most, or even many, individuals continued to circulate in society as usual, the aggregate effect in the population would be unacceptably high rates of morbidity and mortality. It would seem that in the epidemic, individual rationality might undermine the possibility of collective (social) rationality.

In fact, however, what transpired, at least initially and in most countries, very much so in my British laboratory of observation, was that most people were perfectly able to understand the dilemma and the necessity of restrictions in their own behavior in the interest of other people's protection. Restrictive behavioral guidelines and rules from the government were wanted and by and large complied with. It seemed that most people accepted that the common good depended on restrained self-interest and saw no irrationality in following up in their own behavior. That is encouraging up against what some theoreticians have thought of as the difficulty, or even impossibility, of collective rationality.

However, the experience was also that the readiness to accept restrictions on oneself was not spontaneous. It did not come directly out of the individual's own understanding. It rested on information, guidance, and clear rules from above, from the government. Where that kind of straight information and guidance was not forthcoming, nor was the ability of individuals to rein themselves in for the benefit of others. That was the story in the United States, where at least the central government did not encourage behavioral restraint with the use of authoritative information and messaging.

It would therefore seem that collective rationality, where that requires compromises in individual behavior, is indeed possible, but possible only with the guidance of a superior authority, for society as a whole the authority of government. Social rationality, then, in more or less demanding situations, is dependent on leadership, society-wide on government leadership.

---

unimaginable only a few weeks ago. This is not a time for ideology and orthodoxy. This is a time to be bold. A time for courage. I want to reassure every British citizen, this government will give you all the tools you need to get through this."

Simply—and this was the story from one country to another, at least in Europe, if in variable ways and degrees—the government took over. It did that quickly, and with little or no opposition, not from inside the state apparatus nor from society at large. Later, when the emergency dragged on into the next year, some of the early consensus started to crack and some opposition to be voiced against the hard hand of government, but even then it was still the degree of support for and acceptance of restrictions that was conspicuous.

Here is the astonishing list of main government emergency policies in the British case, following immediately from the acceptance of the health scare:

- The country was put into lockdown. Except for essential workers, people were ordered to stay home. Essential outlets, such as food stores and pharmacies, remained open but were told to control entry and avoid crowding and to make shoppers as much as possible keep a two-meter distance from each other. Schools and colleges were closed, except schools for children with exceptional needs and those with parents deemed essential workers. Churches and places of worship were shut, as were restaurants, bars, cinemas, theaters, and gyms. Travel over any distance for pleasure was banned. When the lockdown started to be eased, in late May, it was under a general instruction to people to continue to maintain social distance. At train stations, security officials and police with experience in crowd control were in place to monitor the behavior of people returning to work. Later, when the wearing of face coverings became mandatory on public transportation, police patrolled stations and trains to enforce compliance.
- The stay-at-home population was ordered to not go out except when absolutely necessary: for essential work, for food or medicine, for medical care, and for one, but only one, daily exercise, at which a two-meter distance from others was to be maintained. Family members not living together were not allowed to meet or to visit relatives in care homes or hospitals; grandparents were not to see grandchildren, and only a minimal number of people could attend weddings and funerals. People with second homes were forbidden from using, even visiting, their own property.
- Only minimal transportation services were kept operating. Railways were put under public management. The government absorbed most of the cost of running transportation services with virtually no revenue.
- Public sector workers were kept on salary. Pensions continued to be paid.
- A furlough program was introduced to keep private sector workers employed, the government absorbing up to 80 percent of the wage cost. At least 70 percent of private employers eventually furloughed some or all employees, at the peak putting about nine million workers on the state payroll.
- Loans, tax relief, and cash grants were made available to businesses.

- The self-employed and freelancers were offered grants of up to £2,500 per month. By the time the first lockdown started to be eased, in early June 2020, there were about two and a half million recipients.
- Homeowners were offered mortgage holidays, or deferments.
- A scheme in support of business start-ups was introduced in which private sector backing would be matched with equivalent state-backed loans.
- Support totaling in the hundreds of millions of pounds was made available to theaters, orchestras, museums, and other cultural institutions, and eventually also to sports clubs and recreational facilities.
- Income support for families was ramped up. The integrated system, known as Universal Credit, for years mired in logistical chaos, suddenly worked without friction. In the second half of April alone, 950,000 applications were processed, as compared to an expected normal of 100,000, as 10,000 additional staff were recruited for front-line management.
- The Bank of England cut its interest rate to 0.1 percent, bought up the bulk of government debt, provided banks with funding to increase their lending, provided debt relief to big businesses to enable banks to support smaller businesses, and "helped" banks with liquidity by forcing them to not pay dividends to shareholders or bonuses to staff.
- The National Health Service was reorganized top to bottom to create COVID capacity. Private hospitals were integrated into the national system to maintain nonpandemic care. The military was mobilized to manage the logistics of personal protective equipment provision. An emergency "Nightingale" COVID hospital was created and equipped in a London convention center in two weeks, for a capacity of 4,000 patients. Similar emergency facilities were built in six other locations across the country (a backup capacity that in the end mostly did not need to be used).
- Additional funding was provided to local governments for COVID-related work. In London and elsewhere, local government authorities and charities joined to take the homeless off the streets. Countrywide, 14,500 people were moved into emergency accommodation, mainly to budget hotels.
- Fast-track research funding was made available from various government sources.
- The government gave information and instructions to the public in daily briefings, effectively mobilizing the entire media system into an apparatus of government communication.

All this capacity depended, obviously, on money. That proved to be no problem. The government announced early on that finance would be available and that it would provide whatever was needed. It did not know what the cost would add up to but committed to whatever was necessary and to covering costs as they arose. Original programs were intended for limited duration, more or less three months, but were soon extended, the package above roughly still in operation into the next year. It would all be funded from borrowing. Before our eyes, the impossible magic was performed of plucking unbelievable amounts of money from out of thin air. When economic expertise started to estimate what the bill might add up to, the guestimates were in the order of hundreds of billions, in sums beyond meaning to the ordinary mind. The cost of the furlough program alone in its first months was the equivalent of the country's annual defense budget. By the end of 2020, from the launch of emergency policies in March, the government had incurred about £400 billion in additional borrowing.

Power and capacity

The immediate clarity that resulted from the management of the epidemic can be summarized in six brief lessons: We are not safe. We need protection. We need government. We need to be governed. We need leadership. We need to allow our governments power.

However, the combination of government and power is a deadly brew. We were entering into a Faustian pact in which we for our own good signed up to governance that came back to us with dictatorial force. Autocratic governments, we know, are monsters. Now we were learning, as a practical reality, that so are democratic ones, at least ultimately. Inside the edifice of mild, benevolent, democratic government sits a beast of fearsome power. What came on display in the extraordinary public policy of pandemic and economic management is the near unlimited force that is available to a modern government. It can legislate, including to award itself emergency powers. It can order people how to live, down to the minutest detail, down to obliging them to wait in a regimented socially distanced line for a guard to allow them into a supermarket to buy a loaf of bread. It can communicate those orders in a relentless barrage of instructions day in and day out. It can remove from ordinary people elementary and inalienable rights, down to the right to go in and out of one's own home or to meet up with family and friends. It can take over businesses and put them under public direction. It can mobilize the armed forces into the management of domestic administration. It can make itself the employer of last resort for the entire national force of salaried and self-employed workers. It can make itself the funder of last resort of the nation's banks and direct their lending policies. It can create near to unlimited finance. All of this it can do overnight. We may well turn to our governments for protection and guidance. We may well get them to unleash their awesome powers. But we may not think that action on these understandings comes at no cost. If our governments are to do what we ultimately ask of them, we finally have to let the monster out.

The purpose of democracy is that we be well and safely governed. We citizens deputize the job of governing to a small group of representatives whom we trust because they are beholden to us. We can allow them into positions of power because we know that they know that we can remove them if they abuse our trust. By the same token, we expect them to use the power they are allowed productively because they know that if they don't, we will deputize someone else in the next round. We are in a nexus of power, effectiveness, and control.

It is elementary, democratically elementary, that governmental power must be under the control of those who are governed. Otherwise, we have dictatorship. Is all that governmental power we have recently seen at work under democratic control? We might hope that once the pandemic is over, emergency powers will be put back in the box for governance to revert to normal. But that is an unlikely hope. Powers once mobilized get held on to. Once the emergency is over, we should expect to be in a new normal of more, probably much more, assertive governance than we have for some time been used to. At the very least, we must be prepared again for big-power governance. A further lesson from life under this pandemic is therefore that we should look carefully into the vitality of our democratic systems in their ability to hold fearsome power under control.

Has power been used effectively? Looking to the British laboratory again, the government had mobilized unprecedented force, at least in peacetime. There were achievements. Jobs and businesses were saved. Not all, by any account, but jobs survived that would otherwise have been lost, as did businesses and other ventures that would otherwise have gone under. More money was distributed to families in need. Again, not to all, there were cracks in the safety net, but to many. The health care system coped with rising demand, not without some treatments being sacrificed, but it held up under severe stress and was to do so throughout the emergency. When vaccines became available, beginning in late 2020, the rollout was quick and well organized. That was in contrast to earlier failures, such as in testing, tracing, and quarantining, and is explained by the kinds of prior preparations and plans now having been made that were not in place when the epidemic first hit.

However, if the government had managed to some degree to cushion the economic recession, less was achieved in keeping the health contagion under control. The National Health Service performed admirably in the delivery of treatment, but outside of the NHS, prevention was a failure. In the East, many countries did contain the epidemic, both democratic ones, such as South Korea, Taiwan, New Zealand, and Australia, and autocratic ones, such as China and Vietnam. In Europe and the Americas, we managed less well, nowhere achieving the containment that proved possible in the East.*

The British government took pride in the measures it rolled out as second to none in terms of resources, scope, and ambition. It was justified in thinking so. It was an awe-inspiring display. But it did not carry through to putting Britain in the first rank among even European countries in successful emergency control. Far from it, the epidemic ravaged through British society with consequences more devastating than in most comparable countries. By the end of the first hard emergency lockdown, in May and June 2020, the consensus among epidemiologists was that the government had responded too late and that if a lockdown had been imposed only a week earlier, the number of COVID deaths three months later would have been only half of the actual incidence.[2] During that same period, Britain held the unenviable top spot among European countries in excess deaths relative to population size.[3] While by summer it looked as if the epidemic was being reasonably contained, that turned out to be a mirage. The regime of lockdown and social distancing had brought infections down to a small number, but when restraints were relaxed, the numbers quickly shot up again, the case numbers by autumn far exceeding the highest numbers during the first spring wave. The number of COVID deaths also rose again, if less so than the number of cases, reflecting improvements in medical treatment. A year on, the total number of reported infections was approaching four million and the number of deaths passed 100,000, which, along with that of Belgium and Slovenia, was the highest death toll relative to population size among European countries, and higher than in the United States. The government's emergency measures, which had been thought of as short and temporary, were prolonged into the next year.

---

*In a comparison of COVID management in almost one hundred countries by the Lowy Institute (as of mid-January 2021), the best performer is New Zealand and the worst Brazil. The method used combined six outcome measures into an index with a scale from 0 to 100. New Zealand's score was 94.4 and Brazil's, 4.3. Two countries had scores in the 90s, New Zealand and Vietnam, and three below 10, Columbia, Mexico, and Brazil. Reasonably successful countries such as Finland and Norway had scores around 70, Sweden, less successful, at 55, and poorly performing European countries, including Britain, Belgium, and France, had scores in the mid-30s. The United States was near the bottom of the index range with a score of 17.3. On average, smaller countries performed better than larger ones and authoritarian regimes slightly better than democratic ones. China was not included in the study. Taiwan was the third country in the ranking, just below Vietnam (https://interactives.lowyinstitute.org/features/covid-performance).

Why did power prove ineffective? Much turned out to work poorly: the provision of protective equipment in the care sectors, testing so as to follow the spread of the virus, tracing so as to detect carriers of the disease, isolation and quarantining so as to prevent spread. The government was obviously blamed on a charge of incompetence, but that is hardly the full explanation. There had, as we have seen, been inadequate preparations. When the epidemic occurred, the necessary governmental apparatus was simply not there. Because plans and provisions were not in place that the government could mobilize, it found itself having to improvise and run after the unfolding disaster, catching up as best as it could. There was no established division of labor between central and local authorities, resulting in excessive centralization of the emergency response as an exercise run from London with minimal input and participation from localities. There was no plan of protection for care homes, initially leaving this sector ignored and to itself. All that might be put down to incompetence on the part of previous governments, and that may well again be part of the story. But the final explanation should be sought in shortcomings not just in the political leaders of the day but in the British system of government itself. For example, follow-up from Exercise Cygnus had fallen victim to a culture of secrecy in Whitehall. As with so much else, these shortcomings came into sharp view in the COVID experience. We will explore some of them in more detail as we move on.

It is, again, elementary that when we see the kind of power that is latent in democratic governments, we need a matching capacity of control. However, the slap-in-the-face, sit-up-and-take-note lesson from the mixture of success and failure in emergency management, as observed in the British laboratory, comes down to *effectiveness*. Governments cannot do for us what we ultimately ask of them if we do not allow them power. But power, we are seeing, is only a necessary condition for effective governance, not a sufficient one. The translation of power into effective rule, it turns out, is a *big* problem. Power is one thing, the *use* of power something else.

Rise and fall

It had looked so good. The twentieth century was a long lap of victory for democracy. The First World War, horrible as it was, had put an end to the European near-absolute monarchies. The League of Nations was formed, as a forerunner to what later would be the United Nations. Although democracy failed in many countries under the advance of Fascism and Communism, it survived and took hold in "the West," western and northern Europe and in North America and Oceania, even riding out the Great Depression. In the

Second World War, Fascist totalitarianism was defeated. The United Nations family of organizations emerged as a blueprint for global government. In Europe, Germany and Italy reinvented themselves as democracies and joined in the creation of the European Union. The colonial empires of Britain, France, Belgium, and Portugal dissolved. The remnants of Fascism faded away in Spain and Portugal. In Asia, independent India established itself as the world's biggest democracy and has, miraculously, survived as such. Other countries in Asia and Africa followed suit. In 1989, the Berlin Wall fell, and Communist dictatorship came to an end on the continent. In Latin America, military dictatorship all but ended. The Soviet empire disintegrated, the West having won not only the Cold War but also the competition for affluence. America stood supreme in the world in wealth, might, and cultural influence. Liberty became so much the dominant language that even dictators had to dress themselves in that cloak. When Mao Zedong reluctantly agreed to a written constitution for the People's Republic of China, the resulting document was framed in the language of democracy and human rights.

But it did not last. Toward the end of the century, the global advance of democracy stalled, as did democratic assertiveness.[4] Into the vacuum left by the Soviet Union stepped China to challenge the West in economic and military might, and with an alternative model of state-capitalist authoritarianism for which it claims superiority in the delivery of order and progress, a claim many saw to be credible.[5] Russia rejected democracy and invented its own brand of neo-authoritarianism, and turned to antidemocratic aggression in its international relations.[6] Following through from perceived international disorder and economic failure were further impacts on attitudes, beliefs, and outlooks, finally in a crumbling of confidence. In revived democracies in Central Europe, new elites, even many of those who had been on the barricades to bring down the old dictatorships, turned against "western liberalism" and reverted to muddled ideologies of nationalism, anti-Semitism, and "illiberal democracy."[7] In the established democracies, revolts from below, often, but unhelpfully, branded "populism," gained strength to shatter an illusion of harmony and rip democratic cultures apart in conflictual polarization.[8] In America, the heartland elected Donald Trump as president. In Britain, a majority in the 2016 Brexit referendum rejected European integration.

Twenty years, then, of dramatic decline. Yesterday democracy was the only game in town, the form of government everyone would naturally and obviously wish for and aspire to. Today it is entirely standard, even in polite company, to dismiss democracy as ineffective and having had its day. Add to that the failed stress test, in some democratic countries, of pandemic management. If not now, when would be the time to reexamine? If not now, when would be the time to go back to first principles?

Revolt

In November 2020, America held presidential, congressional, and local elections in the most volatile of circumstances. The campaign was aggressive and undignified—but democratically "correct." The Republican and Democratic parties offered starkly different visions in both substance and style, giving the voters real choice. Four years earlier, a presidential candidate had been elected on an antiestablishment ticket. Now he was up before the voters again, who assessed what he had offered and delivered, and by a majority rejected his continued rule and offered the mantle to the challenger. The spectacle of the campaign had been so ugly that it was easy to lose sight of this being democracy at work as democracy is supposed to work. The elections were conducted under the cloud of the COVID epidemic, yet the turnout was the highest for a century. Because of the epidemic, an unusually large proportion of votes were cast early and by mail, making the administration of the vote and the counting process exceptionally demanding. In contrast to the unruliness of the campaign, the election itself was safe, smooth, and efficient.

This election put on display the polarization of American society. It is easy to think it was about Trump and his unorthodox, to put it mildly, presidency. But it was not. It was a clash of "tribes" with irreconcilable worldviews. It is easy to think that Trump had stoked divisions in the population. He had, but he could do that only because the divisions were already there. It is easy to think it was about shortcomings in the Constitution, but constitutional provisions proved robust. What pushed through the surface, to stare anyone in the face who wanted to see, was the breakdown of democratic culture.

Around and following the election, shenanigans came to play which amounted to an attempted coup d'état against the lawful electoral outcome, a clumsy attempt, perhaps, but an attempt nevertheless. Trump refused to accept the result, branded it a cheat, and declared himself to have won. Allies both in Congress and around the country followed suit by refusing to acknowledge the vote. A raft of lawsuits were filed in courts, including the Supreme Court, for some of the vote to be disqualified. In at least three states—Georgia, Michigan, and Pennsylvania—attempts were made to remove sections of the vote from the final count. In a last-ditch effort, the sitting president, after having been defeated in the election, called a mass rally of followers and extremists in Washington, DC, on the day of Congress's formal ratification of the vote and incited a mob, some armed, to march on and attack that same Congress. None of this succeeded. That speaks to the robustness of the Constitution. But it was attempted. It was thought valid to seek to get parts of the vote rejected by litigation and administrative maneuvers. It was thought that a revised outcome would have been legitimate. There can be little doubt that had the attempt succeeded, large sections of the American population would have applauded it and embraced the defeated candidate as their rightful president. All this speaks to the shattered state of democratic culture.*

Polarization is not unique to America. It lies at the heart of the general democratic decline over the past twenty years. In Brexit Britain also, and in France, Italy, Germany, Central Europe, and elsewhere, tribes stand against each other, in sometimes hatred of each other, in distrust of "the system," in distrust of "the establishment," in distrust of democracy itself. Above, I have called it a "crumbling of confidence."

Why? Why have we fallen back into cultures of anger and mutual hostility? The shock of the pandemic contains lessons on this question as well. It taught us about risk and the necessity of protection. But there was more. We would also see that risk is not randomly distributed. That again should come as no surprise, but was brought home with much clarity. It would be said of a virus that can strike rich as well as poor that "we are all in the same boat." But we were not. We were soon to see that the virus footprint followed the normal fault lines of inequality and stratification. Poor people were more exposed to risk than the well-off, members of ethnic minority groups more than those of the majority population, Black people more than white. In Britain, even among workers in the National Health Service, who were, generally speaking, not more at risk than the rest of the population, doctors and nurses of ethnic minority backgrounds were more likely than others to be struck down by the virus.[9] If hospitals were well protected, a totally different story unfolded in care homes. Long neglected of government organization and investment, these institutions found themselves at the end of the line in the availability of

---

*Perhaps Trump's maneuvers did not amount to an attempted coup. It might have been tantrums by a bad loser or a deranged man. It might have been scheming toward a post-transition political platform for the outgoing president or a perverse money-raising exercise. But that a defeated sitting president refused to concede and engaged to get parts of the vote disqualified, even inciting insurrection against lawful institutions at lawful work, was sufficiently dangerous to merit being called by its rightful name. It is usual to take it as an operational criterion of functioning democracy that transitions of power are orderly and peaceful. By that criterion, democracy in America was in the balance. For my own part, I found myself physically shaken by being in the position of writing, in earnestness, about an attempted antidemocratic coup d'état in America.

testing of caregivers and residents, in the distribution of protective equipment for workers, and otherwise. Privately run care homes fell through the cracks in the government's business support programs. From March 2 to June 12, according to the Office of National Statistics, there were just over 66,000 deaths among care home residents in England and Wales, compared to just under 37,000 in the same period the year before.

The causes of deprivation are many and complex, but we may think of current entrenched inequalities and their consequences as in some or large measure resulting from previous neglect in protection. It is not supposed to be this way in democracies, grounded as they are in a principle of equality, that sections of the population are systematically left behind so that when misfortune strikes, these are the people to again fall by the wayside.

In the advanced economies, we have been through a second economic revolution of entry into the information economy and exit out of (some) traditional manufacturing economies. While entrepreneurs and high-skill workers have thrived, workers in the old manufacturing economies have lost jobs and status and slid into downward mobility in pay and pride. We have been through the most devastating economic crisis since the 1930s, bringing further deprivation in economic standard and social standing to the same people. And now we are in the midst of a combined health and economic crisis, which again is falling with disproportionate weight on the already left behind. The stubborn persistence of deprivation has finally lifted the dispossessed out of silence and pushed them to speaking out and into revolt. The crash of 2008 was a turning point. Financial markets had been deregulated, notably Wall Street and the City of London. Free market ideologists had promised economic safety, and that the secret of stable economic growth had been elicited from market rationality so that growth would continue undisturbed.* Everyone was to benefit. It was only that everyone had not been benefiting. Instead, inequalities had widened to obscenity.[10] It was only that the secret of economic stability had not been found. Instead, it all came crashing down. When it did, it was the small folks at the end of the line who, again, suffered the indignity.

Thus understood, the crumbling of confidence is not an accident, not inexplicable, not unreasonable, not "populism." It is a loss of confidence where loss of confidence is deserved.

---

*When it did not, the former chairman of the US Federal Reserve, Alan Greenspan, famously described himself as "shocked" when "the model I perceived as a critical functioning structure that defines how the world works" turned out to be "flawed."

It was understandable that people in the American heartland rallied behind the radical candidacy of Donald Trump. He was promising to take on the establishment that had relegated them to the standing of second-class citizens. It was understandable that they continued to rally behind him in the next election, however unpalatable a person he was, since the establishment he had dethroned had spent four years heaping contempt and abuse on those who had had the impertinence to lend their support to the insurgent. It was understandable that people in the British heartland rallied behind the cause of Brexit. "Europe" was just a code word for Londoners, middle-class success, and lives of plenty, travel, and cosmopolitanism. It is not the fault of the dispossessed that unprincipled seekers of power exploit their unhappiness and ignorance.

So the trouble for democracy is not disenchantment but *revolt*, straight and simple, revolt from below. There is class-based revolt by the dispossessed, deep into the middle class in response to stagnant standards of living. There is geographically based revolt by people in neglected regions. There is ethnic revolt by people who have long suffered discrimination. There is race-based revolt by people who have been on the receiving end of entrenched racism. There is gender-based revolt by women no longer prepared to tolerate exclusion from equality and abuses of power. There is identity-based revolt by people who have suffered disrespect, such as those of the LGBTQ communities. What unites these revolts is a determination on the part of those who in their various ways have suffered neglect to no longer accept exclusion in silence.

In fact, if the waves of revolt reflect a loss of confidence, it is not a loss of confidence in the system but in the establishment, in those who have been in charge of the system. Those no longer willing to suffer in silence are turning *to* the system rather than against it. They are opting in, not opting out. The economist Albert Hirschman, in a remarkable book called *Exit, Voice, and Loyalty*, explained that when people respond to dissatisfaction with a system, whether economic or political, by voicing that dissatisfaction, they are expressing loyalty. If they did not have hope that the system might respond, they would not see it worth their while to fight their cause. It is when people turn their backs and exit in silence that they are expressing genuine loss of confidence.

These revolts, then, are a good thing. They represent a push for correction, a warning, an opportunity. It is not a problem in democracies that people speak up and give voice to their interests, even when it is frustration they are voicing. *Particularly* when it is frustration they are voicing. It is silent frustration that would have been a democratic disaster.

Faced with revolt, justified revolt, it is up to the men and women who happen to be in power, the establishment, to take charge. It is not for the dispossessed to shut up, but for those charged with governing to step up. They may respond by blaming the victims, by dismissing the warning, by disqualifying the discontents as populists. Or they may listen and seek to repair the damage and offer the disenfranchised inclusion. If there is a crisis of democracy, it sits at the top in the form of inadequate governance, not at the bottom in the form of demands for betterment. If we are to lift ourselves out of crisis, it falls on the establishment to start the lifting.

What they say

Into this maelstrom of convulsions have stepped the political analysts with their own despondency and loss of confidence. In times of trouble, the story of decline is seductive. As Europeans after the First World War were enraptured by Oswald Spengler's *Decline of the West*, now observers are again predicting that "our world" is in decline and that the future is elsewhere, in the East, under more forceful modes of government.[11] Questions long thought to have been resolved are again open. Does democracy work? Is it at all viable?[12] Liberalism itself is to blame.[13] A swath of works warn of or predict the death of democracy.[14] There are fears of a return to Fascism.[15]

In this literature we are in the terrain of excellent works that add up to a failure of the collective imagination.* It is quite wrong to think that democracy is *now* in danger. Democracy is *always* under threat and *will* fail unless it is cared for and maintained. It is praiseworthy to sound alarms of warning, but there is something distasteful in all this delight in death and gloom, like predators feeding off the soon to be cadaver of a dying horse. The detached cynicism of the death-of-democracy literature is unattractive. Some ability to idealism, even in hardened political scientists, on behalf of one of humanity's greatest inventions would be gratifying.

Democracy lives as long as we who live under democratic rule believe in it, and dies when we turn our backs. What it takes for democracy to thrive

---

*The term *failure of the collective imagination* I have taken from here: On a visit to the London School of Economics in November 2008, Queen Elizabeth asked why the economists had not seen the economic crash coming. She received no answer then, and when a group of economists about a year later sought to reply in a letter, they could do no more than concede that "the failure to foresee the timing, extent and severity of the crisis and to head it off was principally a failure of the collective imagination of many bright people, both in this country and internationally, to understand the risks to the system as a whole."

is that leaders and citizens understand it and want it. It is as the Athenians learned. If the foundations are solid, the house stands; if the foundations crack, the house falls. It is what the Americans are learning. Even if the American Constitution is robust enough to rebuff an attempted coup d'état, democracy withers if the culture withers. Democracy can tolerate tensions, but it cannot tolerate being abandoned.

As for what is to be done, the recommendation now, predominantly, is to rethink democracy, to reinvent and redesign it, to find a new and better form. Democracy plain and simple is not enough; there should be more to it. The better democracy comes with add-ons: democracy should be deliberative, participatory, monitory, and so on. Citizens should reengage and be more involved. There should be more direct democracy and more referendums. Planning and budgeting should be participatory. We should move on to post-democracy.[16]

This reinvention-of-democracy literature, however, is yet another case of collective confusion. Since democracy as we know it has run into trouble, let's just consign it to the scrap heap of history and start all over with something new and better. It is another way of blaming the victim, as if democracy is in peril not because it is failing citizens but because they are failing it. That is a dangerous line to take at a time when democracy is in need of being defended. It is not only plain wrong, not only in disregard of how much has been achieved, it also gives succor to the autocrats in Beijing and Moscow who trash democracy and boast superiority for autocracy precisely because they are able to claim that western democracy has proved impotent.

Furthermore, it is based on a misunderstanding of the nature of the trouble the established democracies have come up against and to underestimate how deep it sticks. These schemes for doing democracy better go to fixes upstairs while overlooking that it is the foundations of culture that have been weakened. There are no doubt shortcomings in constitutional provisions in many democracies, but no more than the Athenians 2,300 years ago can we today legislate ourselves out of cultural disintegration.

A recent review of the state of democracy in the world by a group of esteemed scholars convened by the Hertie School of Governance in Berlin, finds that it is in a bad way.[17] It has become infested, they say, in a term that runs through their report, by "malaise." Citizens are dissatisfied with the way they are governed, voting participation is low, political parties are not trusted, and voters are flocking to populist agendas and candidates.

The scholars are right to be concerned. The historical experience is not encouraging. "On more than seventy occasions [in the twentieth century] democracy collapsed and gave way to an authoritarian regime."[18] When we look out over the European and American landscapes and see polarization, anger, distrust, and confidence draining, it is not frivolous to ask if democracy is possible on such foundations.

The remedy, the Hertie scholars suggest, is to look for innovations to make democracies more democratic. The way to do that is to get citizens to do more. They should participate more, vote more, for example, in more referendums, decide more in various forms of direct participation, engage more in staged forms of formalized deliberation, and so on. The argument is for more direct democracy and less assembly democracy.

It is true, as we know from masses of survey evidence (comprehensively reviewed in the Hertie report) that more than for some time, and across the democratic world, citizens tend to feel that governments and elected representatives do not work well or on their behalf. However, if citizens feel that governments are not working on their behalf, that is probably because governments *are* not working on their behalf. Citizens *feel* dissatisfied because they are right to *be* dissatisfied. There is a sleight of hand in the Hertie analysis: in their expression of dissatisfaction with their governments, citizens, it is said, are demanding more of a role for themselves in the form of direct participation. But that connection is not obvious and is not supported by much evidence, if any evidence at all. There is a lack of logic. If citizens have turned off, the remedy cannot be that citizens turn on. More likely, citizens who are dissatisfied with governments that do not work on their behalf are demanding governments that *do* work on their behalf.

If citizens have it right, the prophets should not blame them for not doing enough. Citizens are doing what democratic citizens are supposed to do; it's their representatives who are not doing their share. If they did, they would have loyalty, and "malaise" would be the least of anyone's problem.

In *The Life and Death of Democracy*, John Keane lays before us a grand history of continuity in the many ways the people (in some meaning) have found of exercising checks from below on those who govern from above. There is a tradition of oversight by assembly that goes back to Mesopotamia prior to Athenian democracy. There is a republican tradition that goes back to ancient Rome. There is a Muslim tradition from the management of the Arab conquest of the Middle East, North Africa, and Spain. There are the British and Spanish parliamentary traditions. There are various strands of direct democracy. In this history, the way we do it now, with elections at the core, is but one among many possible ways.

Keane also envisages a future where elections may play a minor role and government is informed and checked by a myriad of citizen groups and social movements that snap at the governors' heals, not only at election time but day in and day out and never leave the toffs up high in peace. He calls this "monitory democracy," which he thinks of as the third stage in democracy's long evolution, following assembly democracy and representative democracy. He finds shoots of monitory democracy in strange places, not only in the established democracies where young people are turning away from politics as usual and taking their engagement to single-issue activism, but also in dictatorial China. There he sees a vibrancy of democracy-like experimentation at the local level, an experimentation that is permitted and even encouraged by the formal custodians of state power.[19]

But in this story line there is something missing, and that is *power*. It is suggested that if people engage, they will be listened to and that governance will in that way be democratically responsive. It is true that there is a great deal of continuity in the evolution up to present-day democracy, but it is also true that there have been two, and only two, big-bang inventions in that long history, that of direct (more or less) popular (more or less) rule in ancient Athens and that of electoral representative government in the American Constitution. These inventions were *different*. They were not arrangements for putting ways of engaging into the hands of the people, or only that, but for putting *power* into their hands. In Athenian democracy, that was done by the people making themselves their own governors. In representative democracy, it is done by the people electing governors. These inventions were based on the understanding that we the people cannot trust governance unless we have power.[20] It is not enough that we have say; if we do not also have power, we are exposed to autocracy and in risk of tyranny.

If monitory democracy is offered up as one alternative to representative democracy, a second alternative that is making the rounds in the literature goes under the name of "deliberative democracy."[21] The idea here is that the making of public policy should respond to such demand from below that emerges as a more or less consensus view from carefully orchestrated processes of deliberation. This way of thinking shares with the idea of monitory democracy a skepticism about the effectiveness of elections as a democratic method. Deliberation is a more sophisticated way for citizens to find a shared view of what should be done by way of public policy.

Now, deliberation is obviously a good thing, certainly in my way of thinking, and I will have much to say about it as we move along. But it does not follow that deliberative democracy stacks up as a credible form of government. The idea has the same defect as that of monitory democracy, of not dealing with the problem of power. It must be a good thing to give the demand from below the authority that comes from it having been honed through careful deliberation, but that cannot be instead of an arrangement that puts not only demand but also power into the hands of the people.

All forms of government contain propensities to autocracy. Observed the political theorist Robert A. Dahl: "Perhaps the most fundamental and persistent problem in politics is to avoid autocratic rule."[22] If we the people are to trust that governors work in our interest, we must ourselves have power. It is no doubt right that there is democracy-like experimentation afoot in many places, but that in itself does not mean power. In the China Keane has been observing, for example, power is monopolized from above, and the direction of movement in the political system is not to encourage power from below but to tighten the dictatorial grip ever harder. Where there is local experimentation, that is as permitted from above, and as may be beneficent for control, and in such parts of the country where Beijing has things under control. The power to crush influence from below sits above and is unleashed against such influence as is seen to be a threat, whether from now decimated communities of human rights lawyers or champions of women's rights, or from the predominantly Muslim population in Xinjiang, which is experiencing that ultimate danger in nondemocratic government of outright police-state tyranny.

What I say

My method is to converse. I converse first with my contemporaries about our present condition. Some of them I find to be false prophets who lead us astray.

I then turn to some of the most eminent relevant thinkers over the ages, starting with Max Weber, Niccolò Machiavelli, Aristotle, Alfred Marshall, Alexis de Tocqueville, and Robert Dahl, and, in the way of the classics, to discoursing with them for wisdom. I have not intended to analyze their works in any complete way, but, in my own mind to sit down with the masters and engage in conversations, starting from some of their basic teachings.

Finally, I turn to my contemporaries again, but now to "the people." It is preposterous, of course—and I am well aware of it—to want to make oneself a prophet and teach people about themselves, about how they should live, even how they should think. But I have sought the guidance of the greats. I believe they have taught me something. I believe much is at stake. I believe I should let others know what I have learned. I will do that in a series of recommendations in the postscript, only prefacing all that with a single recommendation here.

I *recommend* that we resolve to salvage democracy, not to reinvent it.

We have behind us a new industrial revolution, economic crises, inequalities that keep being reproduced, and the shock of the real in a deadly pandemic. Before us the issues and questions are laid out: freedom, risk, protection, government, power, uses of power, controls over power, media, leadership, effectiveness, rationality, trust, confidence, inequality, exclusion, polarization, revolt. And underlying it all are the vexed matters of governmental performance and democratic culture.

This book speaks to all these matters. It does that by restarting from scratch in five essays on core concepts in political theory. These are autonomous treatises—I call them "books"—each seeking to add insights to the state of theoretical knowledge. They also aim to feed into a road map for how to respond to revolt and the crumbling of democratic culture. The essays are followed by a postscript in which the threads are pulled together in the form of recommendations for shoring up the democratic project.

We start, as we must, with power, the necessary fuel of government, democratic no less than authoritarian, and at the same time the force that threatens our freedom. What is it, what is it made up of, where does it sit, how does it work, how can it be made to work well? Political science is the science of power but has, strangely enough, not found a robust definition, or a definition at all, of its own core concept. I will produce the much-needed definition. Perhaps for want of anchoring themselves to a firm definition, those same scientists have obsessed over power. At least as far as effective governance goes, they have exaggerated the power of power. I will bring that extravagance down to earth.

We move on to the use of power, to the big problem of translating power into effective rule, to statecraft. What, practically speaking, *is* a government, and what do governments *do*? What do governors do, the women and men who are in charge? What does it matter that they are skillful? What does good leadership amount to? Governors, we will see, are up against sundry *others*: bossed, servants, courts, citizens. Those others are sometimes friends, sometimes enemies. Governments are never in charge. Day in and day out, they do battle with those they depend on to subdue them to their will.

Then to freedom. Not only is there the dilemma of freedom and power, freedom is also the ultimate value that gives meaning to democracy. What does it mean to live a free life? What is unfreedom? Who is the free citizen? It turns out to be demanding, to depend on the ability to reason. Freedom of choice comes into it but does not take us far. The term *rationality* is abandoned, having been contaminated by a destructive influence in the social sciences that has gone under the name of *rational choice*. Freedom is instead taken to be a child of reason. A decades-old debate between "positive" and "negative" liberty is laid to rest.

At stake is also exclusion, or the avoidance thereof. As freedom is the good that democracy is meant to promote, exclusion is the bad it is meant to prevent. That is dealt with as a problem of poverty. Not all exclusion is material, but if we could collaborate to rid our communities of the scourge of poverty, which is possible, much would be done toward achieving democratic harmony. It is not ambition enough to reduce or modify poverty; we should determine to *eradicate* it. It is not enough to help the poor; we should prevent their degradation. This essay revisits the foundations of neoclassical economics to salvage its original honor as a moral science that has taken meaning from an ambition to rid the world of the evil of poverty.

The final essay deals with democracy itself. It will answer on the difficult question of how to define it. Current definitions generally start from free and fair elections. That approach is abandoned in favor of a new definition that makes no mention of elections. Elections are a way of *doing* democracy but not what democracy *is*. I will praise the election method for its "unexpected smartness," but I will not take it to be the meaning of democracy.

My definition will instead be built on the three Cs of culture, conversation, and contract. For now it is sufficient to say that "culture" enters into the definition as part of what democracy *is*. The conventional wisdom is that a well-functioning democracy is more likely where it has the support of a democratic culture. But that in my opinion is too weak. A democratic culture is not just an advantage, it is indispensable. Nothing is perfect, of course, but there is no well-functioning democracy without democratic culture.

There is culture, and there is constitution. The postscript deals with both, and with their interactions. The culture is the foundation upon which sits the constitutional architecture. There is a dilemma: while constitutional provisions can be reformed—and I will be making various recommendations to that effect—such reform is both difficult to implement and unlikely to be effective unless there are improvements in the cultural foundations. Those foundations, in turn, cannot be much reformed by legislation or other constitutional means. A culture must repair itself. Someone like myself, who wants to speak in defense of democracy, can do little more than feed into that repair by explaining what is at stake and trying to excite confidence in the many advantages of democracy compared to any conceivable alternative. Robert Dahl, in his exploration of the American Constitution, found that its ability to guide America forward depends on how Americans think about their Constitution and understand its logic and function. In that spirit, and from an explanation in some detail of the benefits of democracy, I will recommend how we, leaders and common folk, should endeavor to think about the democratic form of life.

America and Britain are the core democracies, the homes of the American Constitution and the Westminster model. I gravitate to these cases in my commentary. I look beyond them and into the global vista of democratic variations, but my attention drifts back to these two countries. I think that as democracy goes in America and Britain, so it goes in the world. It matters for all of us that the Americans and Brits are able to reform at home.

In the case of the United States, I identify "an American Predicament," a radical reconfiguration of power and decline in democratic culture that has occurred over the past half century or so. There are many causes, a main one being the free-for-all in the use of private and corporate money as a political resource. I recommend a cure that is new relative to previous proposals and more practicable. I suggest also a way of taming the excessive power the Supreme Court has been able to usurp.

In the case of Britain, I identify an "English Delusion," a mindset that glorifies adversarial governance at the cost of good government. Here, big gains can be made with surprisingly simple reforms in elections and the working order of Parliament's House of Commons.

The counterfactual to democracy is autocracy. Autocracies, like democracies, come in many forms, more or less hard, more or less dictatorial, some totalitarian, some grounded in crude military might. Out of this landscape, a reconfigured People's Republic of China has emerged with a combination of state capitalism and autocracy to challenge, as no other previous autocracy, our combination of economic capitalism and political democracy. Assertive dictators dismiss freedom of speech and faith, and a free press, as "western" ideas and claim to be the custodians of a different set of "Asian values" that does not contain the "western" notion of liberty.

I have studied the Chinese model carefully and have learned much about democracy from looking into its nemesis.[23] The China that presents itself to the world comes to us through the filter of history's most imposing propaganda machine. If you look behind the fog of obfuscation, you will see that there is less beauty than the men in Beijing will have you believe, and more of ugliness. Still, there is a mystery. We who live under our model are likely to live in material comfort and without the danger of tyranny. Those who live under their model are less affluent and more exposed to tyranny. Yet it may look as if there is less assertiveness on our side than on theirs, possibly less contentment. That perception may not hold if we dig beneath the surface. We can be critical because we have the freedom to express ourselves. The Chinese may profess satisfaction because they are not free to object. Certainly, the Chinese leaders never trust that they have the trust of their people and subjugate them to "a gargantuan security and information control apparatus."[24] But there is still a mystery. There is, now as at previous junctures of self-doubt, a lure of authoritarianism, both for those who look in from the outside and those who live on the inside. There is a battle raging over ideas, and the idea of democracy has come on the defensive. Having looked carefully into what the competition represents, and its ability to present itself as attractive, I believe it is desperate that we regain confidence in the democratic alternative.

Democracy is not a cuddly business. It is about power, battle, statecraft, leadership, obedience. It heaps expectations on those who govern and those who are governed alike. It is not enough for those who govern that they have legitimacy; they must deal with the problems and deliver. It is not enough for those who are governed that they have rights; they must engage and obey. Finally, what I have been exploring is not just democracy, but the *understanding* of democracy.

BOOK ONE

The Problem of Power

Max (Maximilian Karl Emil) Weber was an old-school German academic aristocrat of the early twentieth century to whom contemporary political and social thinkers continue to defer. He is usually described as a sociologist but has monumental contributions to his name as much to the study of politics, economics, history, religion, and more. He dealt extensively with power and with the state, and with the combination of the two. What finally makes a state, in his analysis, is that its custodians hold the ultimate power of physical violence. No sentimentality there.

We citizens should be as unsentimental. We should recognize that if we live with order around us, it is because power is exercised over us. We humans have a wonderful capacity for doing good, for friendship and loyalty, for tolerance and involvement, for fairness and justice. But that same intelligence can also be used for bad, for inflicting evil on others and doing harm to ourselves. And so it is that we wretched beings need guidance and protection. Left to our own devices, we are hapless and easily succumb to selfishness, irrationality, or violence. We need encouragement to not give up on liberty. It does not come of itself and is in some ways burdensome. We need to be taken by the hand and led from the path of least resistance where we are only for ourselves to a place where we engage with others as citizens. We need togetherness.

Governments must have power in order to deliver for us. If we don't allow our governors power, we will not have order. But governments with power are a threat to our liberty. Citizens must therefore have the power to check those who exercise power over them. If we don't control the governors, we get autocracy. This is the crux of democratic government, that they must lord it over us and that we must lord it over them. The *basic* merit of democracy is that it solves the problem of power.

About power itself, Weber was realistically cautious. He explained it as "the probability [or chance] that one actor within a social relationship will be in a position to carry out his will despite resistance."[1] That is, as would be expected from the towering social theoretician of his age, a very smart analysis. But it is also a surprisingly unfinished one that leaves many ends not tied up.

It is smart because it pulls power down to earth. Here is the careful observer who sees the limitations of power. Power does not get you what you want; it just gives you a go for the prize. How it all works out depends on the social relationship. There is always a context. That's the strength of Weber's definition.

Others have been less cautious. A big misunderstanding in later political theory has been to overstate the power of power. My aim is to correct that mistake.

The weakness in Weber's definition is that it is unfinished on two accounts. Whatever power is, it cannot be a probability or a chance. At the very least, it must be what makes for a probability or what gives you a chance. But just what that is, Weber does not tell us. Furthermore, although he locates power within a social relationship, it is the elementary confrontation between will and resistance he for the most part deals with, more than the intricate social webs that actors operate within. My aim is, further, to tie up those loose ends.

His followers initially stuck so close to the master that they failed to bring the analysis much forward. On the contrary, some regressed in that, while failing to correct what was wrong, they also ignored what was right. Raymond Aron defined power as "the capacity to do, make or destroy," Talcott Parsons (with unfailing destruction of language) as the "capacity to secure the performance of binding obligations by units in a system of collective organization," James Coleman as an actor's "control over valuable events," and Robert Dahl as "the ability of A to get B to do something he or she would otherwise not do."[2]

All these definitions preserve what is failing in Weber's: they do not identify, describe, or define the thing "power" as such. They do not *distinguish*. Aron does not distinguish at all. For him power and capacity are one and the same. But that makes no sense. Somehow, capacity must flow from power, and if so, power must be separate from and prior to capacity. If power is capacity, we just have a nondefinition of two words for the same thing. Coleman and Dahl are much in line. Power is the same as control or ability. Parsons is twice mistaken: capacity grows out of power but is not the same as power and, since it gets you only a probability, does not secure anything.

Furthermore, these definitions are even weaker than Weber's on the social context, which here pretty much disappears. In their different ways, they all say that power does and set aside Weber's warning that it can take you only so far. In reality, power is only an input into a convoluted process with many impediments on anyone getting their way. What those who put power in get out of it, if anything, depends on the process and context. To understand how power works, we must get a grip on the thing itself and then move into the intricate machinations that play out on the road to outcome. In technical language: power is the independent variable and outcome the dependent variable, with process and context between as intermediate variables.

The failure to distinguish is a failure to deal with power separately as a thing in itself. If we define power as control or capacity, we end up in the tautological short circuit that power is identified by success in the outcome. But the relationship between power and success is a mystery, and we cannot unravel that mystery unless we define power as something that is prior to its use. Power is obviously beneficial for anyone who wants control over people or events, but such control depends on many things in addition to power itself. Power increases the probability that you may be able to control events, but it does not give you control.

Some of this shortcoming has been rectified in more recent work but not all of it. Steven Lukes includes in his analysis the ability to influence other people's mindsets so as to not only get them to do something but get them to want to do it. Pierre Bourdieu, in his concepts of symbolic power and habitus, sees power as an aspect of social interactions, including language. Joseph Nye has classified power as hard, soft, and smart—hard power is the ability to command, soft power the ability to persuade, and smart power the productive combination of hard and soft—and kept reminding us that the use of power and its outcome is never a mechanical matter but always depends on the context.[3]

These later approaches broaden the analysis from the confrontation between will and resistance to bringing in also the wider setting within which such confrontations unfold and thereby rescue and develop Weber's "social relationship." But they do not overcome the failure to distinguish. Pierre Bourdieu pronounces on power without bothering with any definition at all. Lukes and Nye are carefully aware that the use of power depends on social conditions, but for them too power equals ability. But influencing people's mindsets is not a kind of power, it is a way of using power. So too with the hard and the soft. These are not different kinds of power but different ways people with power use it.

The big distinction that needs to be salvaged from the blur, and to be always kept in mind, is between, first, power and, second, the use of power. Power itself does nothing. It takes effect when actors use it. Power follows through to outcomes by the way it is *used*.

Influence

The reason power can give you no more than a probability is that you can do no more with it than to influence people and things around you. You cannot determine what others will do or what is to happen. You may have the power to torture a prisoner to talk, but you cannot know if the confession you force out of him is true. The slave owner can force the slave to work, but hardly to efficient work. The employer cannot set any wage he wants; he must consider what the worker is willing to work for. The union cannot enforce any settlement; it must compromise with what employers are able and willing to accept. China has overwhelming power relative to North Korea but can do no more than influence the North Korean leaders (and not even much of that).

When power is put to use, it is influence that is released. The holder of power cannot just sit back and let power work. He must use the power he has to make himself influential. It is misleading to think of power, as Coleman will have it, as control over events. Actors with power have influence over events. Power sits further back, as a source of influence. In technical language again: influence is another intermediate variable between power and outcome.

There is obviously more or less power and more or less influence. Weber singled out a strong form that he called *Herrschaft*—we might think of it as the power to coerce—but defined even that as a probability: the probability that a command will be obeyed. That probability can be very high. If your boss orders you to a job, you are likely to do as you are told—but if the context is against him, you could refuse, or only pretend to obey, in which case he might get something that looks like obedience but not get the task done or done well. Power grows out of the barrel of a gun, said Mao Zedong, and so it does. If you have a gun, you can command me to hand over my money, and the probability is that I will—but I could gamble that you do not have the guts to fire and stare you down. The United States has more gunpower than any other country and therefore much influence. Still, in its dealings in the world, from China to the Middle East to Africa to Afghanistan, it is the limitations in its capacity that are conspicuous. If you think the US has as much capacity as it has power, you are blind to obvious facts in world affairs. What flows from power is influence, sometimes a great deal of it, but never, irrespective of the amount of power, more than influence.

Resources

Power, says the philosopher Leszek Kołakowski, is "everything that allows us to influence our surroundings."[4] Note *allows*. Kołakowski makes the distinction that escaped Aron and others. Your power is not in your influence over your surroundings, but in what might allow you to influence them. It is prior.

Power comes to play (using the standard terminology) in "games" between "actors." People become actors when they enter into games in which things work out so that some dominate, more or less, and others are dominated, more or less. If you are going to play that game in any other way than as a victim, you need to bring with you something that might enable you to stand up to others, something to bang the table with. Power grows out of resources, such as Mao's guns. You must be in command of resources that you can use to establish a standing vis-à-vis others. It turns out, then, that power is, after all, not the independent variable but another intermediate one. Power is prior to influence, but there is also something prior to power. The analysis starts not with power but with resources.

That brings us a step forward. It tells us something about what makes for Weber's probability but not everything. There is no power without resources, but resources are not all there is to it. Your power depends on resources but is (usually) not equal to your resources.

Resources are personal and institutional. In *The Jungle Book*, the tiger Shere Khan dominates the jungle by force of his physical strength. He is stronger than the other animals, who live in fear of him.[5] Physical strength is a resource. A parent can grab a child by the ear to enforce obedience. But as the child grows up and the parent grows older, power relations change. The child can now deny the parent the domination of strength, or even turn the tables and threaten to beat up the father or mother.

Physical strength is a personal resource; it belongs to the person. He or she owns it and does not get it from anywhere else. Other personal resources are, for example, money, property, knowledge, competence, reputation, charm, and persuasiveness. If you inherit a fortune, you become a more powerful person. You can use your new wealth to buy yourself more influence. You may not do that, you might hide your money away, but you could if you wanted to—you have the resources. The power of wealth is not something that emerges only when the holder uses it for influence. It sits in the wealth as something the holder could mobilize, if and when she wanted to. So, too, with, for example, competence. I have spent five years undertaking a study of the Chinese political system. That has given me a competence that I can use to influence the way others think about China. They listen to me (if they do) because I have a documented competence behind me when I speak. If you have a reputation for wisdom, or ruthlessness, you can get others to pay attention. If you have charm, you can use it to influence people you deal with. It does nothing for you unless you turn it on, but it is because you have it that you can turn it on. When you use power, you put to use something that is already there, some kind of resource that is available to be used.

"McCain now has the power to either destroy the president's national security policy or shape it constructively." So wrote the *New York Times* on January 13, 2015. What had given Senator John McCain that power was that he had become chairman of the Senate Armed Services Committee. McCain had thereby become a holder of power (in addition to the power he already had as a senator and committee member). That gave him a new platform from which to influence things (until he fell ill and died on August 25, 2018).

The way McCain became a holder of power was that he took up the office of committee chairman. The power in question sits in the relevant office. It is *used* by the holder of the office, but it is in the office it resides. If it is not already there, there is nothing to use. Again, power is prior.

This is the logic of institutional resources. McCain was the actor, but the resources he was able to deploy belonged not to him but to the office of which he was the holder. He was, as committee chairman, not an operator by force of resources of his own but as the manager of institutional resources.

We can think of resources as akin to money in the bank. The money that sits in an account is what the account says, so much and no more, and is available to be used or wasted by the holder of the account. The military resources of a nation sit in the fighting assets of its land, sea, and air forces. Corporate managers have behind them control over capital and jobs. Union managers represent a workforce and can threaten industrial action or promise industrial peace. There are more resources to play with in a global corporation than a local company, which is why the global president has more power than the local director. McCain's committee is endowed with certain rights of action and certain rights to be consulted. The chairman can use those rights to get into the game with the president in the shaping of national policies.

Is there, using Nye's terminology, a distinction to be drawn between hard and soft resources and in that meaning between hard and soft power? Yes and no. There are clearly hard resources. The guns out of the barrels of which grows power are hard resources. The right of a slave owner to whip his slaves is a hard resource. Personal charm is a soft resource. But there is no mechanical link so that hard resources equals hard use and soft resources soft use. Hard resources can be used in both ways. The slave owner who whips his slaves uses hard resources in a hard way. His plantation neighbor who does not is softer in his use of the same resource. When the United States engages in war, that's a bit of a failure. It is more successful when it can let its hard might speak softly and get others to comply without military action. Soft resources, too, can be used differently. Reputational resources, for example, can be used aggressively, by showing off and bullying, as in the case of President Trump, or modestly, by letting reputation speak for itself, as in the case of President Dwight Eisenhower. China has proved itself inept in soft use of power.[6] That is not for want of relevant resources but because of inexperience, which gives the Chinese leaders a tendency to boast, to overdo their display of excellence, and to be excessively tetchy about slights to themselves and often offensive to others—by being too hard in the use of soft resources.

Rules

Power grows out of resources, but the use of given resources is (usually) regulated by rules. Rules say which actors have access to what resources and what they can do with them. Shere Khan's power is, unusually, pretty equal to his strength because there are no rules in the jungle to constrain his use of it. A boxer in a regulated match has less power than strength because he cannot use his strength in any way he wants; for example, he is not allowed to hit below the belt.

Whereby we can now define power. The power of an actor is a function of the resources that are in the actor's reach and the rules that regulate his use of those resources.

Hard-core theoreticians think that power is all material, for example, a matter of weapons or economic strength, and that the weight of material facts settles it. But that is not right. The transition from resources via influence to outcome depends strongly on the rules of the game. When it was uncovered in late 2017 that there was a permissive culture in and around the British Parliament of some (mostly male) members of Parliament using their position to extract sexual favors from (mostly female) juniors, the response was to impose rules of conduct to make that usage of power unavailable. Of course, there is no guarantee that all seniors would always obey the rules, but the imposition of new rules nevertheless changed power relations and made juniors less exposed. America's military power grows out of the conventional and nuclear weapons in its arsenal. But the commander in any theater, say, the Pacific, cannot appeal directly to the power of nuclear weapons, which by the rules of military management can only be put to use by the president. The constant tug-of-war between emperors and popes in the Holy Roman Empire was about rules: who appoints bishops, who elects emperors, and who is eligible? When the Duke of Brandenburg captured the bishopric of Mainz in 1514, it cost him bribes for which the repayment of loans was on a scale to release the Reformation. What made the office so valuable was that it had authority over the meetings of imperial electors and their agendas, over the rules.[7] When Persia was seriously threatened by Rome in the third century AD, it responded, successfully, with a political revolution in the rules governing the management of power resources: "A new ruling dynasty, the Sasanians, emerged around 220 AD, offering a strident new vision, one which required the removal of authority from provincial governors, who had become independent in all but name, and a concentration of power at the centre. A series of administrative reforms saw a tightening of control over almost every aspect of the state."[8]

One power-relevant rule is ownership. If you own a bank account, you have access to the money that sits in it. You can use that money in various ways, such as to buy influence. However, there may be other rules that regulate how that money, although yours, can be used. Most democracies, for example, regulate the use of private money for political purposes. If those regulations are strict, no amount of money in your ownership can buy you political influence. When the US Supreme Court, in the *Citizens United* case in 2010, scrapped regulations on the political use of corporate money, that increased the traction of money as a power resource in American politics by removing restrictive rules on its use.

Another category of power-relevant rules is rights. In a democracy, adult citizens have voting rights and are able to take part in the political game with the power of the vote. Not all citizens do, but they have the power that comes from their right to vote. In the United States in 1965, the Voting Rights Act removed rules that in some parts of the country had denied Black voters effective access to the right to vote. The right to strike enables workers to stand up to employers. During Margaret Thatcher's premiership, new labor laws imposed restrictive rules on unions for the calling of strikes, thereby limiting their power of action.

Rules are formal or informal. Formal rules exist in writing in appropriate documents. They can be constitutional provisions or given in laws or other documents of procedure that regulate the workings of public or private organizations. In a patriarchy, the power of the husband-father will in part be given in law, for example, when he is the legal owner of all family property. A surgeon's power comes from the combination of his personal resources—his medical competence—and his certified rights to practice his trade. Say a surgeon is caught having prescribed illegal drugs to sports competitors and is prohibited from further practice; he is then without the power he used to have, although he still has the same resources of competence.*

Informal rules—often called conventions—are understandings that are not necessarily written down anywhere or legally binding. There are conventions about how formal rules are to be understood. In the American Constitution, for example, the power to declare war is vested in Congress, but the president still has relatively wide powers to engage the country's armed forces in warlike operations. What the president can do without Congress's explicit approval is regulated by "understandings." Then there are further conventions about how things should be done that are not grounded in formal rules. The British prime minister meets the Queen once a week to inform her about government matters. There is no law that obliges the prime minister to do so; he or she does it because that's what prime ministers do. After the political difficulties of the second Iraq war, it became accepted that Parliament should be consulted ahead of similar warlike operations, a convention that in 2013 prevented the government from intervening physically in the civil war in Syria (until Parliament revised its opinion in 2015). The power of parents over children is determined in part by conventions of filial respect.

Conventions are social or political. Social conventions are shared (more or less) understandings that have evolved through experience about how things are done in these parts. In the British political system, it is a convention that members of Parliament usually return to their constituencies once a week or so and hold "surgeries" in which constituents can meet their MP and offer opinions or information, seek advice, or voice complaints. An MP who fails to hold regular surgeries will be considered to be failing in her job. Political conventions are imposed from above. In the Chinese case, for example, the laws, including the state constitution, list a range of civil rights for

---

*The body of rules that regulate political activity is typically called a constitution. The use of that word in English is sometimes confusing because of a peculiarity of the English language. In America, the Constitution is the document adopted by the Constitutional Convention in 1787 and later amendments. Britain has no similar constitutional superlaw and is therefore often said to not have a written constitution. But that is not correct; it is only that formal constitutional provisions are found in a range of different laws rather that in a single document. However, when someone refers to "the constitution" in Britain, he is likely to have in mind both formal rules and informal conventions. Also in America, political life is regulated by many other provisions than those in the Constitution, from both ordinary laws and informal conventions. In German (and Germanic languages), there are two words for what in English is covered by one: *Grundgesetz* (basic law) and *Verfassung* (the body of formal and informal rules). Writers in English sometimes distinguish between a constitution (formal rules) and a constitutional system (the body of formal and informal rules).

citizens, but it is an accepted fact that the will of the Communist Party stands above the letter of the law and prevails in disputes, including in court cases.

Why would actors with resources obey rules that constrain them in making use of their resources for their own benefit?

Well, they may not. They may use their resources to avoid the rules that bind most people. In Moscow, and no doubt elsewhere, the owners of limousines can purchase blue lights for their cars that enable them to use the hard shoulder on motorways, as if they were police vehicles, and avoid traffic jams.

If they do obey, that may be because the prevailing rules are good for them. The resourceful may have been able to shape rules to their benefit, in which case it may make sense for them to obey even if it looks as if they are constraining themselves. For example, modern states depend on extracting huge taxes from their citizens, something that is extremely difficult. To make it more palatable (to the rich), there is a tendency to shift the burden from direct to indirect taxation. Indirect taxes, such as sales taxes and value-added taxes (VATs), have the virtue of appearing to be fair although in reality being heavy on the poor and light on the rich. The rich, having won the battle over the rules of taxation, have an interest in then paying up what the rules say in order to not rock the boat.

Or it may be because of social pressure. In my home country, Norway, the tax records of all taxpayers are published annually in each municipality for all to see what others—neighbors, acquaintances—have declared in income and paid in taxes. Taxpayers then know that they cannot easily withhold (much) income from taxation without suffering social shame. In countries in which charities play an important role in society, such as in the United States and Britain, it is a convention to make charitable contributions, and those who do not are held in disrespect.

Finally, obviously, the law is the law, and those who do not obey are in risk of prosecution and punishment.

Offices

Personal resources are real enough and matter, but power of substance sits in institutions, and in real power games it is usually institutional power that really counts.

Businesses are not content to influence public policy each with the force of their own economic power. They merge their powers into, say, the National Federation of Industries and work collectively through that office. Even political leaders who have established great personal standing tend, if they continue to want to be of influence, to establish new offices from which to work once they give up their official positions. Nelson Mandela did not rest in retirement on his very considerable laurels but established a foundation from which to work. So did, for example, Jimmy Carter, Bill Clinton, Tony Blair, George W. Bush, and Barack Obama.

Offices are of many kinds, such as the office of king or emperor or president or prime minister, or party chairman, or member of cabinet, or chairman of the board, or national bank governor or private bank president, or company director or director of finance, or union steward, or military commander (high or low), or police constable, or dean of a university faculty, or head of the English department in a secondary school, or chairman of the neighborhood committee, and so on endlessly. For that matter, parenthood is an office. Parents have power over their children because they are parents.

Whoever is King or Queen of Britain holds the power that sits in the royal office. Previously, that was a great deal, more in some periods than in others; now there is not much left. When King George III, against whom the colonists in America rebelled with the Declaration of Independence, was incapacitated by illness and unable to govern, the power of the monarch was still in place. When he recovered (temporarily), he could take it up again. The power that came Senator McCain's way was already there in the committee and would come into the hands of whoever would become chairman. When someone is elected president of the United States of America, that person becomes the commander in chief the moment he or she is sworn into the office in which the power of supreme command sits. Ahead of that, between the election and the inauguration, the successful challenger becomes the "Office of the President-Elect." When someone is appointed president of a bank or head of a union or manager of a sports team, they take up the power of their respective offices. When Jorge Mario Bergoglio became Pope Francis, he overnight became a man of world power, not because he had changed personally (except for his name) but because he took up a new office. When Xi Jinping became Chinese leader in 2012, he acquired the power of leadership by being installed in the office of general secretary of the Chinese Communist Party, which is where the power of leadership sits. He rapidly made himself a very powerful leader by taking up more offices. He became chairman of the Central Military Commission without delay and also national president. He then consolidated his power by taking control of additional offices, some of his own making. He became chairman of the core leading group on economic policy. (In the Chinese system, the leaders work through "leading groups.") He established new leading groups with broad remits of which he made himself chairman: a leading group on reform, a leading group on national security, and a leading group on internet security. With each of these offices Xi became the holder of additional powers, and in two years he had made himself the most powerful leader in China since Mao.

In Italy by 1929, Benito Mussolini had fortified his position of power by making himself head of eight government ministries, including those of war, navy, and air force. In Germany in 1934, when President Paul von Hindenburg died, no new president was appointed, and "[Adolf] Hitler himself took on the authority of head of state. With this move, his total power was cemented. State power and Führer power were one and the same." That consolidation was denied Mussolini in Italy, where the king remained in office as head of state. In France, in June 1937, a new prime minister, Camille Chautemps, "empowered by parliament to legislate by decree [powers that had been refused his predecessor], raised taxes and ended social reform."[9]

When Aung San Suu Kyi and the National League for Democracy took up power in Myanmar in March 2016, after having won the fall elections, she was for constitutional reasons prevented from holding the office of president. Her position as national leader was instead established by the creation of a new office of "state counsellor" and by her assuming four cabinet positions, including that of foreign minister (until she was dismissed in a military coup in 2021).

In 1993, in Britain, some Euroskeptic members of Parliament in the Conservative Party formed what they called the European Research Group. This committee lived a quiet life until the aftermath of the referendum on Britain's EU membership in 2016, when it mobilized as a pressure group for what became known as a hard Brexit. The existence of the group enabled members to speak not only in their own capacity but as representatives with the authority of an office behind them. Their most prominent spokesman, Jacob Rees-Mogg, was able to operate not only in his own capacity but with the title of chairman, and others cropped up with the title of deputy chair. Giving themselves the backing of an office, if in reality a pretty virtual one, was immensely effective for a relatively small faction and enabled those who spoke for it to exercise disproportionate influence within the Conservative Party as well as in Parliament and in public discourse. Subsequently, other Conservative Party factions have taken to calling themselves "research groups."

All of which brings us to another definition. An *office* of power is a position in society in which is vested certain controls over resources or certain procedural rights. Such controls and rights allow a holder of the office to take actions of consequence and to make himself heard or consulted and have his interests considered and respected when others contemplate action.

Uses of power

Power can be used to dominate from above or to stand against from below. It is not that there are actors on one side who have power and others on the other side who can only cower. There is power on both sides of the exchange, behind both Weber's will and resistance.

The tendency in the definitions I have started from is to treat power as that which comes down from above. In Weber's definition, it is the top dogs who are "actors," while others are pretty anonymous. But that's to underestimate the force of resisting. Those who resist can sometimes utterly destroy those who are supposed to be in command. On February 4, 2015, the then British home secretary, Theresa May, announced (technically reannounced) an inquiry into historical child sex abuse and the appointment of a New Zealand High Court judge, Lowell Goddard, to lead it. The home secretary has the statutory power to appoint commissions of inquiry, but this was her third attempt to get one going. The first two attempts failed because they met with resistance that would have disabled the inquiry had it gone ahead as planned. The resistance came primarily from the National Association for People Abused in Childhood. Their resistance was based on objections against the commission of inquiry's original specified area of authority and leadership and was backed by a threat of not accepting the inquiry on its original terms as legitimate and of not collaborating with it, acceptance and collaboration the inquiry was dependent on if it was to be effective. This forced the first two leaders appointed to the commission to resign and the home secretary to go back to the drawing board on the commission's authority. The result was that it was given additional powers, notably to compel witnesses to attend and give evidence and to oblige them to provide documentary evidence. Furthermore, a leader was appointed who was accepted as neutral. One of the concerns to be investigated was the alleged previous existence of "pedophile rings" in high establishment circles and the possible cover-up by establishment figures (a concern, it later turned out, based on entirely bogus evidence). The commission's first two leaders were themselves establishment insiders, and their appointments were resisted on the argument of potential conflict of interest. When Justice Goddard was appointed, Home Secretary May said that Goddard "was as removed as possible from the organizations and institutions that might become the focus of inquiry," and the chief executive of the National Association for People Abused in Childhood said that her appointment "would enhance the whole credibility of the inquiry." (But it was not to be. After just over a year in the job, its third leader abruptly resigned, apparently because of internal conflicts in the commission and its secretariat, and a fourth leader was appointed.)

Let's call that which comes down from above "order-influence" and that which can be countered from below "resistance-influence." A hierarchy is a system of offices of power. The more explicit the hierarchy, such as in a military organization, the clearer the rules of command and obedience and the more likely an order will be followed. The higher up in the hierarchy, the more we are dealing with ordering; the lower we get down, the more actors are confined to resisting.

The business of the top office is to give orders. There is no one further up the line with a right to tell the holders of this office what to do. Offices further down the line give orders downward and have other orders imposed on them from higher up.

At the bottom of the line are people who have no other outlet for power than to resist. However, hardly anyone is totally without power to resist, if only an increment. Even North American slaves, who lived in extreme disempowerment even by the standards of slavery, could with some effect resist. Their masters depended on their labor, and slaves could use that dependency to extract concessions, or sometimes to subvert or sabotage.[10]

Resisting is real power use, but still it is not of the same kind as ordering. There is power on both sides of the exchange but not equivalent powers. The top dog has the initiative. Resisting is reaction. America is top dog internationally with plenty of power to call the shots. The question for smaller countries is how to respond and maneuver.

The aim for those who give orders is to be *obeyed*. The aim of those who resist is to be *heeded*. Most actors in the power game play both roles, at one and the same time working on those who are weaker to get their obedience and protecting themselves against being bullied by those who are stronger.

What enables underdogs to resist is *dependency*. Top dogs issue orders but are dependent on the acquiescence of underdogs. Even the tiniest bit of dependency is a source of power. In David Hare's play *Behind the Beautiful Forevers*, about a community of rubbish scavengers at Mumbai's airport, a character says, "The fact that they want to get rid of us is our power, it is our only power."

The higher up in the hierarchy, the more concentrated the power to resist. For example, government ministers are strongly dependent on their top officials to get their policies implemented. The permanent undersecretary in a ministry represents the sum total of resistance-influence that resides in the bureaucracy of which he is in charge. Say the minister of finance has some idea for a tax reform, but his and two or three other relevant undersecretaries get together and agree that it is a bad idea and discuss how to brief their respective bosses to that end. That would normally make the policy dead in the water. (If you think this kind of thing does not happen in government, you have not worked there.)

Lower down the hierarchy, the power of resistance is more dispersed. There are more offices and actors who are each relatively less powerful.

At the bottom of the line, again, the power to resist is extremely dispersed, spread out among the mass of ordinary people. It is there, though, and may in the right circumstances be effective. Even the lowly worker is in some control of at least one asset, his own labor. Václav Havel, the Czech author and dissident who later became president, called it "the power of the powerless."[11] He predicted that the silent workday subversion of the people would eventually wear down the Communist regime's ability to rule.

The collapse of the Communist regimes in Europe might seem to have confirmed Havel's prediction, but it is doubtful that it was dispersed resistance-influence that did the job. The regimes were never able to make their people dedicated workers in the Communist orchard, and the people did deny them economic efficiency, but it took more than dispersed resistance to deny them control. When the Berlin Wall fell in 1989, something had happened to the constitution of resistance. Suddenly, people who had been used to dragging their feet individually in pretended obedience shifted into a tacit agreement of acting collectively. It was when that happened that the apparatus that until that day had maintained control found itself unable to prevent people from merging their powers and tearing down the wall behind which they for years had been imprisoned.

The difference here is between anarchic and organized resistance. As long as power at the bottom of the hierarchy is broadly dispersed and disorganized, it can yield only very limited influence. What may give it more effect is that it is organized into a collective force. We can say that it is gathered into offices of coordinated power. This is the logic of labor unionization. In a confrontation between employers who hold concentrated power and employees who have only their individual increment of power to lean on, the employees are helpless. By joining together, they can merge their many small increments into a stronger force. In *The Jungle Book*, the "law of the jungle" is that the strength of the pack is the wolf, and the strength of the wolf is the pack: each wolf brings his resources to the pack, and the collective resources of the pack protect each wolf.

A brilliant illustration of the difference between anarchic and organized resistance is in Hans Fallada's Second World War novel *Alone in Berlin*. A husband and wife find themselves in opposition to the Nazi regime. Their only son had been drafted into military service and killed in action, meaninglessly as the parents saw it. They decide that the regime that had committed this crime should be opposed. There are others in the husband's workplace who are opposed to the regime, and they try to form a cell—an office of organized power in my language. But the attempt fails: it is too difficult, too dangerous, and too unlikely to matter. The husband and wife are on their own and, in a pathetic display of powerlessness, can find no other outlet for their resistance than to write anti-Nazi messages on postcards, which they leave here and there in Berlin to be found and hopefully read. Inevitably, even that fails, and they are caught.

Skill

The influence an actor can acquire depends, first, as always, on the power he holds. If you become prime minister, that power is a great deal; if you become head of the neighborhood association, not so much. But it depends also on how you work the power you have. If you use it well, you will have more influence; if you use it badly, you will have less. Influence, then, is not given by the stock of power alone but also by the actor's skills in using it. A president holds the power of the presidency which for him is a given. He then applies his skills to the use of that power, as did, for example, President Lyndon Johnson to great effect. The National Association for People Abused in Childhood was able to break the home secretary's first two inquiry initiatives by skillful use of not very much power. Shere Khan is in command in the jungle thanks to his strength, but not only that. He also has a very specific skill for the use of power: total ruthlessness. When the wolves demur, he grabs the head of the pack by the throat and throws him to his death over the edge of a cliff. The equally strong tiger with less ruthlessness might have had less influence. Genghis Kahn was able to establish a conquest in the thirteenth century more extensive than that of Alexander the Great fifteen hundred years earlier thanks as much to skill as to power. He certainly had power but also the same total ruthlessness as Shere Kahn, if on a bigger scale, accepting no rules to limit his use of force. But although totally ruthless, he also had the ability to use force strategically. "Peaceful submission was rewarded; resistance was punished brutally." In one city, "every living being—from women, children and the elderly to livestock and domestic animals—was butchered as the order was given that not even dogs or cats should be left alive. All the corpses were piled up in a series of enormous pyramids as gruesome warnings of the consequences of standing up to the Mongols. It was enough to convince other towns to lay down arms and negotiate."[12]

Skill, then, in the game of power, is the ability of the actor to maximize the probability that she will be obeyed or heeded, given her power. As power is a function of resources and rules, influence is a function of power and skill.

Power is a fact on the ground that tells its holder that it is pertinent for him to impose his will on those around him and those others that it is prudent to pay attention to what he wants. If there are no facts of power, there is no basis for either influence or obedience. Still, we need to ask just how it comes about, if it does, that A influences B and that B obeys or heeds A.

It is obvious that someone with more power may threaten someone with less with reprisals if he does not obey. On a day in late 2013, hundreds of North Korean officials were gathered in the Gang Gun Military Academy in the country's capital to witness the execution of two officials from their own ranks, Ri Ryong-ha and Jang Su-gil. They were executed by antiaircraft machine guns, with the effect that their bodies were torn apart. The remains were incinerated by flamethrowers. Shortly after, Jang Song-thaek, Kim Jong-un's uncle and until then thought to be second only to Kim himself, was convicted of treason and executed in the same way.[13] Obedience within this system is then not difficult to understand.

The threat of reprisal is a constant in the use of power. One reason soldiers are likely to obey their officers is that the officers have the power to punish them. One reason you are likely to do as your boss says, is that she can otherwise fire you, or demote or sideline you, or deny you interesting jobs in the future.

The fact of reprisals notwithstanding, neither influence nor obedience is obvious and do not necessarily correlate directly with power. Actors who want their will carried out generally depend on more and better influence than they can get from threats.

You are the holder of power. You want to use it for influence. You depend on getting others to listen and oblige you. Your power may be a fact that others are obliged to accommodate to, but "obliged" is the most flexible principle in the book. Lawmakers have a right to impose taxes that citizens then have a duty to pay, but many who can will cheat on those obligations. A boss may have the right to fire workers, but remaining workers may not accept it if he does and may have ways of taking revenge, such as to undermine the company by working to rule. A parent is entitled to tell the child to do her homework but will not necessarily prevail.

No holder of power can just appeal to his power and expect others to cave in. More or less, those who want to be obeyed or heeded must get others to accept what they want of them. Even in systems in which power is said to be absolute, it turns out to be relative: "[F]ear alone is not enough; even after killing millions, Stalin grumbled that still no one obeyed him. Autocracy 'is not as easy as you think,' said the supremely intelligent Catherine the Great; 'unlimited power' was a chimera."[14] Top dogs must lead. They must apply skill and work on those who are supposed to obey. They must exercise leadership.

Leadership is the use of power from above. Effective leadership is the use of power that gets results. Wise leadership is the respectable use of power for worthy causes. Good leadership is the combination of effective and wise use of power for order-influence.

The definitions I have started from, those of Aron, Parsons, Coleman, and Dahl, are not of power at all but of leadership. Lukes's making people want to obey is not power but leadership. Nye's hard and soft are different ways in which holders of power exercise leadership.

A leader is not a good leader unless he is effective, but effectiveness alone does not make for good leadership. Leadership is likely to be more effective the more it is wise because it is through respectability and worthiness of purpose that leadership can gain respect. The biographer William Ewald, who spent half a lifetime endeavoring to establish Eisenhower's reputation as one of America's great presidents, argued that he merited that distinction because he was "a man not only effective in leadership but ethical in character."[15]

Effectiveness in leadership depends crucially on the power the leader can lean on. The more power you hold and the more unambiguous it is, the more you are a leader and the more you will normally get others to obey. But not even effectiveness is a straight product of power. If you are unwise in the use of your power, you will fortify resistance and forfeit obedience.

If those who give orders are leaders, let's call those people leaders depend on "followers."[16] Leaders own the initiative, but followers can resist. Leaders and followers are up against each other. The leader wants something done but is dependent on followers to make it happen. He needs to make them react in his favor if his will is to be carried out.

Followership is the use of power from below. Effective followership is the use of power that gets results. Wise followership is the respectable use of power for worthy causes. Good followership is the combination of effective and wise use of power for resistance-influence.

Power is not a bad thing. Order-influence is a necessary energy of social, political, and economic efficiency. Resistance-influence is a necessary force to check the use of power from above so as to prevent excess, abuse, and autocracy. Socially beneficent outcomes depend on how leaders and followers act and interact.

The combination of good leadership and good followership is difficult and elusive, so much so that Robert Dahl, for all his deep understanding of how democracy works, had to resort to "luck" in explaining it: "Lucky the country whose history has led to these happy results!"[17]

The leaders have the initiative. It falls on them to offer good leadership and to elicit good followership in return. Followers must respond, and it falls on them to resist sensibly and to comply sensibly with good leadership. This kind of beneficent covenant, in which leaders and followers collaborate out of habituation, I have elsewhere called a "settlement of order."[18]

Order in this meaning fails to emerge or breaks down if power is misused on either side of the exchange. If power from above is overused, there is tyranny and inevitable repression of even legitimate resistance. That is the situation, for example, in the People's Republic of China. If power from above is underused, there is inaction, disrespect of authority, and free-for-all self-serving indulgence in resistance. This is pretty much the recent state of affairs in American politics, with gridlock in Washington and alienation in the country. If power from below is overused, necessary rule breaks down with social chaos the likely outcome. That was the state of misery in Britain during the 1970s period of extreme industrial unrest and economic disintegration. If power from below is underused, there is a danger of drift toward despotism.

In Joseph Nye's analysis, the use of power is to command or persuade. The more power a leader can lean on, the more she can enforce obedience. The more the power of followers, or the more limitations on the use of power from above, for example, by safeguards in democratic constitutions, the more he must rely on persuasion. The leader's dilemma is that the more he needs to use persuasion, the more that is because followers hold power. But how can you persuade others to do as you want when they do not want to do it and have the power to resist?

Now, persuasion *is* possible, and leaders are often very persuasive. But leaders who need to persuade followers to dance to their tune need something to back up their persuasiveness, something that will make followers comply even when they are inclined not to and make them change their minds and behaviors in ways they do not spontaneously see to be in their best interest.

They cannot rely only on power, because the reason the leader has to turn to persuasion is that he does not have enough power to enforce obedience.

Power on the side of the leader makes others obey commands. What makes them accept persuasion is *authority*. A leader with authority can persuade reluctant others to go along with his wishes, or, to take up Lukes's argument again, make them believe that what he wants of them is really what they want too. Said Catherine the Great: "One must do things in such a way that people think they themselves want it to be done in this way."[19]

Power comes to the leader from his resources. Authority is a more elusive commodity. It appears to sit in the person. Some people, it is often said, have natural authority. George Washington was a natural leader who had authority in abundance (and was so aware of it that he hardly spoke in the Constitutional Convention in 1787 because he knew that if he did he would stifle further debate).[20] Otto von Bismarck ruled Prussia and Germany from 1862 to 1890 as chancellor and engineered the unification of Germany, without any conventional political base and mostly due to his forceful and complex personality—but also the king's backing.[21] By the end of his tenure, President George W. Bush had so little authority that when a reluctant Congress in 2008 was forced to bail out the American banks, they did so more in spite of than because of his efforts at persuasion. Tony Blair started his premiership with authority in abundance, which, however, was gradually worn down by bad policies, excessive spin, and plain wear and tear.

Contrary to power, which sits behind the actor as an objective fact, authority is in the eye of the beholder, in this case of the followers who are asked to obey. When underlings see that spark, it works wonders. If servants acknowledge their superiors as "their lords," said the observant Niccolò Machiavelli, they bear "natural affection" for them.[22] They then go along with leadership, said Weber, by virtue of "habituation."[23]

Authority is contained in the willingness of followers to listen and be persuaded. No leader has any other authority than that which followers see in him. He has the authority he is able to extract from those he wants to lead and that they are willing to award him. Authority, then, enables leaders to get followers to do for them, but at the same time the leader is at the mercy of followers for the authority he needs in order to lead them. Although appearing to belong to the leader, his authority is really in the gift of those he wants to lead. The ultimate power of followers is that they can deny the leader the authority he needs to be able to affect them. That, again, is Havel's "power of the powerless." Some power is held, as we have seen, even by those who appear utterly powerless. They may not be able to oppose visibly, but as long as the leader is in any way dependent on them, they can always subvert.

To see the workings of authority, consider a symphony orchestra.[24] There is no system on the surface of the earth with as clearly defined a structure of power, at least at the point of performance: the conductor decides, the musicians do. But for all his power, the conductor cannot decide that the orchestra will play well. He has the power that rests in his office, but the musicians have the power that he is completely dependent on them for performance. The orchestra produces sound, but the conductor is the only member who himself has no sound. If he cannot get the musicians to play as he wants, he does not get the performance he wants. If the musicians drag their feet, the orchestra will not perform to capacity. If his power is accepted, he will conduct, and the musicians will play, but if he wants excellence, he needs to translate his power into authority. He needs, with Machiavelli again, to get his musicians to see him as "their lord" for whom they bear the "natural affection" that they do for him not only out of acceptance but out of enthusiasm. He needs good followership. It is power that makes the conductor the conductor. But once his power has put him before the orchestra, it is of very little further use to him. The will he wants to be carried out is good performance from his musicians. To obtain that, to move the orchestra from playing to playing well, he is totally dependent on authority. Once he is in office, power is nothing and the use of power everything.

Leaders have to extract authority from followers, but just how does that happen? What are the magnetic forces that pull authority out of followers and attach it to leaders? There are two: first, as always, power itself, and, second, a wondrous magic called *legitimacy*.

Power and authority, we have seen, are different things, but they are nevertheless related. When powerful people speak, others listen because the speaker is powerful. Leaders speak with authority when they speak from a platform of power. They are in office, hold power, and can use that base to make themselves authoritative.

However, the authority that springs from power is crude and fickle. It rests, ultimately, on force, threat, and sanction. It is extracted and therefore resented. It is authority that leaders cannot trust, that is not firm, and that followers will revoke if they can. It *pushes* followers into settling with their leaders, but people who are only pushed are not happy.

The authority that sits on legitimacy is something else; it is elegant and given freely. It gives the leader the authority that followers believe that the leader has the right to lead. This is the jewel in the crown in the power game that makes for stable, strong, and reliable authority. It *pulls* followers into a settlement that they see as rightful.

According to Weber, legitimate authority rests on law, tradition, and charisma. He should have added a fourth source: the always necessary component of power itself.

Power contributes to authority, as we have seen. It also contributes to legitimacy, but now indirectly. The link between power and legitimate authority is
not power as such but the way power is used. Underlings incline toward obeying a leader when they believe not only that he is in office rightfully but also
that he uses the power of his office well, when he displays good leadership.

Legality breeds legitimacy. A legal government has the authority, for example, to get people to pay taxes because any government needs revenue to
operate, and a legal government has the right to collect it. When the colonists
in New England said, "No taxation without representation," they were claiming a right to withhold from an illegal (as they saw it) government the authority to tax them. It had the power to tax them, but the colonists set about
undermining its authority.

Tradition breeds legitimacy. The reason George W. Bush was never completely without authority was that he spoke not only in his own capacity but on
behalf of the Office of the President of the United States of America. Hence,
even during the financial crisis of 2008, when his secretary of the treasury,
Hank Paulson, was the doer, it was still essential that the president put the
authority of the presidency behind the Treasury's policies.

And charisma breeds legitimacy. Jimmy Carter ran out of authority as
president but was able to rebuild impressive personal authority for himself
once he was free from the burdens of office.

Any leader will try to present himself as charismatic and will call on legality and tradition with as much effect as he can. But these influences are by and
large beyond his control. A leader is either exercising power lawfully or not,
traditional authority is attached to his office or not, and leaders are as they
are—unattractive ones are unattractive and attractive ones attractive.

The great variability in the quest for legitimacy is the way power is used.
Skillful leaders who are seen to use power for good purposes and with wisdom gain legitimacy in the eyes of their followers. Those who use power arbitrarily or recklessly forfeit legitimacy. They are seen as someone who should
not be in office. When followers allow leaders power, they know they are in
danger. They are in danger of being abused, and they are in danger of being
ignored while others, friends of the leaders, are privileged. To get followers to
award them legitimacy, leaders need to reassure them about the way they use
their power.

The reassurances that followers need are of two kinds: the restrained use
of power and the fair use of power. Leaders who exercise restraint show the

ruled that they do not use power abusively. The greatest of Roman emperors, Augustus, gained respect by being seen to deploy less power than he had under his command.[25] A later effective leader with great power who also had the gift of restraint was Otto von Bismarck, not quite the "iron chancellor" he has been made out to be: "The key to his success lay in a marvelous combination of strength and restraint. He built up positions of great power only to disarm his opponents with carefully graded concession that made them feel relieved and secured."[26] Leaders who govern fairly show that they use power for the public good and not to the benefit of some at the detriment of others. One of the (few) mistakes the autocratic but shrewd Park Chung-hee, the Bismarck-like leader of South Korea from 1961 to 1979, was to pamper his home district with government money and investments. That caused lasting resentment in other parts of the country so that when the authoritarian regime weakened under his successors, this simmering resentment contributed to igniting the revolts that eventually brought it down.[27]

Influence, we now see, is shaped in the main by three forces. First, *power*. It is power that defines the game and the force that leaders and followers can put behind their interests.

Second, *the use of power*. While power is more or less a given for its holder, what is up for grabs is the way he goes about using it. This is the force behind his influence that is regulated by his own doings. A leader with much power but with little skill in its use will pay the price in the forfeit of influence.

And third, and decisively, by *authority*, in particular the authority that comes from *legitimacy*.

Context

This is where we have come to so far: The starting point is resources. The power of an actor grows out of the resources she has access to as mediated by rules, and is in turn converted into influence through the mediation of skills. What now remains of analysis is the step from influence to outcome, which brings in the final mediating factor, that of context.

The context is made up of the facts of the world, the rules (again) of the game, and people's perceptions and understandings of their world and the games they play. As power is a function of resources and rules and influence a function of power and skills, outcome is a function of influence and context.

The world is as it is and there is in it a march of history that presents itself to even the most powerful as a pattern of imperatives. In Shakespeare's *Julius*

Caesar, Brutus says, "There is a tide in the affairs of men. . . . And we must take the current when it serves, or lose our ventures." Bismarck, the greatest of German chancellors, said of statesmanship that it consists not in aspiring "to control the current of events, only occasionally to deflect it: the statesman's task is to hear God's footsteps marching through history and to try to catch on to his coattails as He marches past."[28] At the end of Francisco Franco's regime in Spain, when "the last of the pre-war European dictators" died in 1975, the attempt to engineer a dictatorial continuity disintegrated. "Crucially, though not plainly to be foreseen, the king, if at first cautiously, placed the weight of his popular legitimacy as the monarch on the side of the forces pressing for democratization. He was not an instinctive democrat. But he recognized the way the wind was blowing."[29]

The economy is strong or weak, growing or stagnating, puttering along or collapsing into crisis. When Lehman Brothers, the global bank, fell into bankruptcy in 2008, economic policy in the United States, and soon in other countries, changed overnight as a way of responding as best as could be to uncontrollable and rapidly moving events.

Military technology is where it has come to. Alexander the Great's *sarissa* (or was it his father, Philip, who made the innovation?), a long spear used by his infantry, changed the nature of military engagement, as did President Obama's drone warfare. Transport technology (from Roman roads to the jet engine), production technology (from the spinning jenny to robotic factories), communications technology (from the telegraph to the internet)—such evolutions change the terms of what can be done and who has the means to do what.

A technological innovation of not insignificant effect on power relations was the paperback revolution in the 1960s and 1970s. Books became cheap and easy to produce, and political and economic literature was spread widely. The reading of such material, complicated material, became fashionable, notably among young people, notably students. Knowledge, or at least the feeling of knowledge, was democratized, and young people felt empowered. This was hardly the only cause of the waves of upheavals in Europe and America that people of my generation think of as "1968," but it made up a part of the setting.

Another new-technology effect is that of real-time war reporting, in particular on television. That has changed the circumstances of warfare, at least in democratic countries, again through a redistribution of knowledge. Ordinary people know more about the realities of war, and government elites are less able to control and dominate relevant discourses. This was a contributing factor in the collapse of America's war in Indochina. That war was lost partly on the battlefield and partly at home as a result of a draining away of popular acceptance. During the First World War, in contrast, the reality of trench warfare was not collective knowledge on the home fronts until well into the war, and decision makers did not have the same assertive and shifting public opinion as is now breathing down their necks.[30]

Today, the big issue is modern information technology, the internet, social media, and big data analytics.[31] These tools are putting the exercise of power from above under more scrutiny and is enabling new forms of organized resistance. One effect is to more or less undermine the role of traditional political parties and to augment the role of single-issue and ad hoc organizing. Grassroots organizations have new resources and take on a new confidence in claiming a right to participate. While democratic politics was once a matter of fighting elections and then getting on with governance in the periods between elections, it is now more a matter of continuous battle.

The same tools are also new means of political manipulation. The information that is spread through social media can be engineered and manipulated both in content and distribution. That can be done by deliberate design. Those who can buy the kit—and businesses selling big data competence are mushrooming—can get information systematically slanted to their benefit, and get it slanted in different ways to different audiences, all by the analysts' knowledge of what kind of slanting works for which audiences. We on the receiving end may see what looks like good information and have no awareness of how it has been designed and for what purposes. It can also be done in spontaneous networks, by the spreading of rumors, lies, conspiracy theories, and such. We are better informed than ever but also more at risk of being misinformed. Instruments that with one hand improve on the freedom of information, with the other hand distort the job done under the ideal of a free press. Media manipulation is nothing new, but the capacity in today's social media landscape for slanting what comes to us as facts of the world is on an entirely different scale.

When asked by a reporter what a prime minister most fears, Harold Macmillan is said to have answered, "Events, dear boy, events." In politics, as well as in business, stuff happens, and suddenly the world is different. Events can be dramatic: a political leader is assassinated, the stock market crashes, there is a blowout on an oilrig in the Gulf of Mexico. Or they may be trivial: the Australian prime minister Tony Abbott made the silly decision (in January 2015) to award the Duke of Edinburgh (the Queen's husband) a knighthood and found himself suffering a revolt in his own ranks. The day-to-day business of a leader is much about putting out fires. Accidents, friction, and luck are the day-to-day facts of politics. A battlefield accident in a war, for example, of "collateral damage" by "friendly fire," can change the way the war can be conducted. The arguments for waging war, or for waging it in a certain way, are weakened, and the case for alternative strategies strengthened. Events in this meaning are generally unpredictable, or unpredicted even if they should have been predicted. For leaders they are often problems, in part because for followers they often represent opportunities.

Games have rules, and rules condition what actors do and can do, what avenues are open to them, what they are prevented from doing, and what the benefits and cost are of alternative actions. But rules also represent opportunities. Those actors who understand the rules and how to work or manipulate them have an advantage over less skilled operators.

National-level operators are equally subjected to regimes of rules, but with the difference that some operators on this level are also the main makers of formal rules, if not to the same degree of informal conventions. The lawmakers have the power to make and change the rules that others are obliged to obey.

When the First World War broke out in 1914, there was a conspicuous absence of international institutions in Europe through which governments could have exchanged information and negotiated collectively. There was a mesh of mostly bilateral treaties and lines of communication, some secret, but next to nothing by way of collective arrangements (except for an ineffective Conference of Ambassadors in London). Subsequent analysis holds that the war broke out partly as a result of misunderstandings by the European powers about each others' intentions and capabilities.[32]

One hundred years on, the international setting is completely different. International law has been expanded hugely, as has the body of multilateral treaties. International courts and tribunals are established to uphold law and treaties, with the power to make decisions that are binding on nations and national actors. There is a network of multilateral organizations—from the European Union with substantial supernational powers, via the organizations of the United Nations family and a range of regional political and trade organizations, to talking shops such as the G7 and the G20. These jointly make up a layer of global governance that surrounds nations and conditions the way they behave and can behave, and the way they deal with each other. There are also effects within nations in that citizens, businesses, and organizations on the one hand are bound by international rules and on the other hand have resorted to supernational authorities that can control and override national authorities. This system of global governance is in continuous evolution, whereby the international context in which nations and their citizens operate is ever evolving and changing.[33]

Contextual effects reach into the power game through the beliefs and ideas that sit in people's minds as signals to behavior—through their mindsets. "Ideas," said the economist John Maynard Keynes, "both when they are right and when they are wrong, are more powerful than is commonly understood. Indeed, the world is ruled by little else."[34]

Beliefs go to the state of the world, to our understanding of how things are. Is Russia a danger to neighboring countries? Are women by nature emotional beings, less capable than men of rational logic? Is there global warming? Is the UK's National Health Service in a crisis of capacity?

Ideas go to questions of what can and should be done. Should Russia be punished for perceived aggression? Can women have equal rights with men? It is not long ago that it was generally thought, and not only by men, that they could not. Should we use less energy to reverse warming—and would it work? Should NHS budgets be increased?

We form beliefs according to the facts of the world and ideas about action according to a calculus of how problems should be solved. The way we see things reflects our understanding of where we are, here and now, in the ever-moving march of history. We analyze our situation and obey the facts of our world as it is.

However, between the world as it is and our perception of it are various filters that color what we see and how we think. One such filter is language. No one who lives in Britain can fail to know the correlation between language and power. When a Briton speaks, you know very soon if she belongs to the upper or lower reaches of the social hierarchy. The establishment has its own dialect that speaks horizontally to establishment peers and vertically, downward, to others. It is a dialect that claims superiority and that works as an instrument of domination: *we* speak, *you* listen; *we* explain, *you* learn. There are dialects within the establishment dialect that position the users higher or lower within the elite.

Another filter is what is broadly referred to as "media." The world does not come to our attention directly but is brought to us with the help of some medium or other. This includes newspapers, magazines, television, radio, internet, blogs, pamphlets, literature, films, reports from government agencies and national and international think tanks, corporations' annual reports, scientific studies, official or unofficial statistics, and so on endlessly. The new world of social media is radically transforming the ways in which the world presents itself to us. We know more, we are better connected, the spread of information is more rapid. But this brave new world is also, again, one of more sophisticated manipulation and deceit.

Also, beliefs and ideas are formed with the help of metabeliefs that we, so to speak, already have implanted in our minds. These are, for example, religious beliefs, ideologies, values, norms, understandings of human nature, and more intangible worldviews. For my own part, I tend to look at the world without any, as I think of them, ideological blinkers, with confidence in ordinary people's capacities but also our need for guidance from laws and social interaction, and to see the world of today, its many problems notwithstanding, as an arena of great ongoing progress. These are beliefs and ideas, naive some might say, that lead me to political engagement, but not party political, and to confidence in the force of information and knowledge as vehicles of human progress.

At any point in time, these filters and how they operate are shaped by the legacy of what has gone before. The language that is available to us today has evolved through the human experience up to now and is all but neutral with respect to today's facts of the world. The media setting is changing with dramatic speed, but there are also more or less constants, such as in Britain the authoritative influence of the always excellent BBC, the British Broadcasting Corporation. In the sphere of metabeliefs, there seems to be a divergence in the world between some areas of ever more secular cultures and other areas where religious beliefs, some extreme, are gaining force.

Out of these filters and legacies come, at any point in time, a pattern of more or less prevailing beliefs and ideas. These, if not necessarily agreed upon without question, in the aggregate carry more weight than competing ones. Those who have prevailing beliefs and ideas on their side own the narratives and the agendas of discourse and politics.

Strategies

Power on its own does nothing; it just sits. It is unleashed when actors put it to use. There must (for those who like theoretical language) be agency. Power games can be limitlessly complex, but at their core they are still, as Weber explained, about actors maneuvering for influence and effect. Always, the understanding of what power does is a matter of understanding how actors operate up against each other and what shapes and constrains their thinkings and doings.

Actors may operate with the powers they have, within the prevailing context. Let's call this Strategy D, for direct: using influence directly to shape outcomes.

In this strategy, the context is a given. Actors who are to be successful need, in Joseph Nye's words, "contextual intelligence."[35] They need to understand the facts of their environment and how others think about themselves and their world. They need to understand what is possible and what is not, and where and how they can act with effect. The context offers opportunities and puts down constraints. If you are to be of consequence, you must go with the flow of the possible and understand which avenues are viable and not set off down roads that will take you nowhere.

But actors can also use their resources to influence the context itself. That gets us into the metagame of shaping the arenas where will and resistance meet. The context is now not given but something to be worked on and rigged. Actors need a different kind of contextual intelligence, not just an understanding of the context as it is but a grip on how it can be changed. Let's call this Strategy I, for indirect: using influence indirectly to condition contextual settings.

I have interpreted Steven Lukes's argument, and possibly also that of Pierre Bourdieu and Joseph Nye, to be, in the language I have now adopted, that power theory has been too narrowly geared to Strategy D thinking and that the theory should be broadened so as to give adequate attention to Strategy I logic. Indeed, I think that what these theoreticians suggest, certainly Lukes, is that Strategy I is the real game: dominate the context, and you dominate everything else; work within the context as it is, and you can achieve no more than others allow you.

Some Strategy I examples: Say banks want certain regulatory strictures to be relaxed. They might try to bring that about by using their influence to put pressure directly on the lawmakers, for example, by threatening to move their business abroad. But if this is a period of animosity against the banking industry, they may conclude that the context is against them and that they have to tread with caution if lawmakers are going to be persuaded that their cause is valid and if they are to avoid further backlash against their industry from an already hostile public. That being the setting, they may decide that this is not the time to invest their influence in putting pressure on lawmakers directly and fall back on Strategy I, for example, by launching a public relations campaign to improve the standing of the industry in public opinion. If successful, that might have the result that lawmakers decide on their own to relax regulations for a now more trusted industry, or it might create a new climate in which it is possible for the banks to bring influence to bear directly on the lawmakers.

The German presidency offers another illustration. This is often described as a mainly ceremonial post. The constitution gives the office of the president very little power, but there is some. The president has various prescribed roles and therefore certain rights of presence and participation. That is enough power for the holder of the office to attain not insignificant influence, if he uses his limited powers with skill. The holder of the office at the time of this writing is Frank-Walter Steinmeier, who is disposed to using such influence as he has productively, as he sees it, in German public life. But how can he do that? Strategy D is not available. The constitution does not allow the president to influence government policy or legislation directly. But Strategy I is available. It is legitimate for the president to seek to influence public opinion, if not so much on specific issues at least on public thinking more broadly. President Steinmeier decided to use this opportunity to orchestrate a process of nationwide deliberation on democracy, in the hope of stimulating better understanding of and respect for democratic procedures and values in the German public. This was at a time of widespread unease in public life, and it was no doubt the president's hope that his initiative might be helpful toward encouraging trust in German politics. In obedience to the constitution, he was not seeking to influence political decision-making directly but rather to improve, in his eyes, the context of political culture.

In recent elections in the United States and Britain, as well as Britain's Brexit referendum, it would seem that preelection campaigns have been subjected to orchestrated interference from Russia and possibly elsewhere—China? North Korea?—through systematic social media manipulations. These manipulations appear to have been geared to influencing public beliefs, for example, with the help of rigged news stories and biased understandings of issues, priorities, and what was at stake. They may also have been geared to creating confusion and lowering public confidence in democratic procedures and to the destruction of democratic culture. The historian Timothy Snyder calls it the policy of "strategic relativism: Russia cannot be stronger, so it must make others weaker."[36] For which purpose, social media manipulation is a godsend tool.

The contextual setting is a battlefield. Formal rules are subject to being changed. Conventions evolve, in part under determined pressure. The march of history can be deflected. We are subject to being influenced in our beliefs and ideas. The filters through which the world comes to most of us are to some degree under other people's control; certainly the media are, certainly social media. Context is king, or at least kingmaker.

The most visible current metagame of power is that unfolding in American democracy. While elections and election campaigns run their course, the real action has been in battles over rules, conventions, media, ideas, narratives, and agendas, in what I have elsewhere called the "backstage" arena.[37] The systematic creation by monied and corporate interests of offices of institutional power in media outlets, data engineering, lobbying organizations, super-PACs (political action committees), and the like, and the combination of gridlock in Washington and polarization in the country, has enabled a reconfiguration of influence in the American system. While previously there was at least some balance between corporate interests relying on economic resources and labor on organizational resources, capital has advanced in power, while labor has declined. Monied interests have accumulated power by corporate actors embracing organizational capacity with a new determination and adding that to the force of their economic power.[38] This has given capital, through the network of friendly offices of influence, a near hegemony in the game of shaping the agenda of what issues are to be pertinent for political action. How deliberately coordinated this enterprise has been is an open question. There are no doubt big and determined actors in the game, but no conspiracy is required. All it takes is for the idea to spread that if you have money to spare, a good investment for some of it is to put it into politics.

The influence flowing from this network of offices has been used to change the rules of the game. Formal rules restricting the use of private money as a political resource have been relaxed, mainly through rulings by the Supreme Court, culminating in the *Citizens United* case in 2010, which lifted most restrictions on campaign spending by corporations and struck down one hundred years of regulatory legislation. Conventions have changed so that political candidacy has been made forbiddingly expensive, to the degree that it has become impossible to run for national or state office, other than exceptionally, without big economic backers. As a result, money has come to rule. Laws and budgets are obviously still decided in the normal constitutional way in the federal and state legislatures, but more than previously, much more, it is laid down outside of those institutions what can be decided—that which is acceptable to the economic backers lawmakers depend on—and who the decision makers are to be—those acceptable to potential economic backers.

It has also been used to change the political culture of beliefs and ideas. Corporate interests have grasped that influencing legislative and budgetary decisions with the help of economic power—Strategy D—does not give them control and that to be effective they must get into the act earlier with organizational power—Strategy I—to dominate the narratives and agendas that shape the decision game. If we go back to the parade of presidents from Franklin Roosevelt through to Lyndon Johnson, politics was fought predominantly onstage and with less powerful organized interests. The political question was what governments could and should do, with taxation a constraint. The eight years of Republican rule under Eisenhower did not challenge the prevailing consensus. He was a fiscal conservative, but one for whom taxation was still a function of necessary action. Gradually, starting with the presidency of Ronald Reagan, the political question, the narrative, has been reformulated so that taxation has become the primary parameter and government action the consequential one. That has created an entirely different political setting, with different prevailing understandings of the meaning and role of government—the fear of "big government"—with different agendas, even a different language of politics.

This battle has been fought in the backstage arena. Onstage, the rules of democracy apply, and the equalization of political power through the vote is a reality. Backstage, in the battle over beliefs, ideas, narratives, agendas, and language, a minority can hold sway thanks to its dominance in economic and organizational resources. Hence, corporate interests have won not only, or even primarily, by dominating the competition onstage but also, or rather, by attaining dominance over the terms of the competition backstage.

Weber again

Political science is the study of power, but the science of power has failed to find a robust definition of its core concept. To understand government, we must understand power, and to understand power, we must understand the long trajectory from resources to things happening out there in society. To this end, the macho language of doing, making, and destroying does not help much. When actors start operating, things get complicated, and anything can happen. Power matters but is not in command.

I have started from Weber's caution about the limitations of power. I have identified power as a thing in itself, prior to its use, and explored how very much more than just power comes into play for those intent to impose their will on others. I have noted Weber's observation that the impact of power depends on the social relationship. That has led me to a reflection on the mediation of rules, skills, and context along the road from power to outcome.

I have argued the following:

- The aim of power analysis is to understand how outcomes in society are shaped by power.
- The analysis needs to *distinguish* between power and the use of power.
- The analysis needs to identify power as such, prior to and independently of its use by actors.
- Power is grounded in resources.
- Resources belong to persons or institutions, and actors operate either with their own resources or as custodians of resources that reside in relevant offices.

- The use of resources is regulated by rules.
- Rules are formal or informal (conventions).
- What flows from power is influence, sometimes more and sometimes less, but never more than influence.
- Actors are sometimes leaders and sometimes followers, and power sits on both sides of the exchange.
- Leaders depend on followers, and that dependency gives followers power.
- Leadership is the use of command-influence, and followership the use of resistance-influence.
- The aim of leadership is to be obeyed, and of followership to be heeded.
- Actors bring, and must bring, skills to the use of power.
- Skill is the ability of the actor to maximize the probability that she will be obeyed or heeded, given her power.
- The tools of leadership are to command or persuade.
- Persuasion depends on authority.
- The authority of the leader is in the gift of the followers on whose obedience or acquiescence he is dependent.
- The more effective authority is that based on legitimacy.
- Legitimacy depends, in addition to Weber's classical criteria, on the way power is used.
- The exercise of power and influence takes part within contextual settings.
- Contexts are made up of the facts of the world, the rules of the game, and people's understandings of their world.
- Contextual effects work through beliefs and ideas in people's minds.
- The context is a battlefield, and this is the metagame of power.
- The main strategies of influence are to work directly on outcomes within a given context (Strategy D) or to work indirectly by rigging the context (Strategy I).
- Strategy I is the real game: those who truly dominate are those who control agendas, narratives, and ideas.

I have explained the stages of power analysis:

- Power is a function of resources and rules.
- Influence is a function of power and skills.
- Outcome is a function of influence and context.

The final difference between the standard post-Weberian approach and my recommended one is in the relationship between power and capacity. The standard approach equates power with capacity (or control, ability, or the like). I distinguish between power and its use, whereby capacity depends on a range of factors of which power is only one. Does it matter? What difference does my approach make and is it significant?

A *first* difference is in the very understanding of power. Here I remain faithful to the strength of Weber's definition and pull power down to earth. The power-is-capacity approach inflates the power of power. It assumes that power gets things done. I insist that power is only the starting point for things getting done.

A *second* difference is that my approach resolves what Weber left hanging in the air, the meaning both of power itself, of the thing, and of his "social relationship" and how it conditions the use of power.

A *third* difference is in the role of rules. Rules matter. The use of power is regulated by formal rules and informal conventions. Those who hold power and want to use it can get no more out of it than the rules allow them.

A *fourth* difference is in the relationship between power and influence. I insist that what flows from power is only influence and not control, that influence is the intermediary between power and outcome. Hence, actors can have much power and little influence or little power and much influence.

A *fifth* difference is in the understanding of power and action. In the power-is-capacity approach, actors have power and bring it to bear on others. I insist that there is power on both sides of the exchange and that leaders have power over followers and followers power over leaders.

A *sixth* difference is in the role of agency. I insist that power works by the way it is used and hence that the understanding of power and consequence depends on an understanding of the persons that operate in the power game, crucially on their skills in managing the power they have. In my understanding it is not power that does things but persons.

A *seventh* difference is in the crucial importance of authority for leadership. Leaders cannot just lean on power for effect but are usually utterly dependent on authority for the conversion of power into influence.

An *eighth* difference is in the understanding of legitimate authority. To Weber's classical sources of legitimacy—law, tradition, and charisma—I add a fourth source: the way power is used.

A *ninth* difference is the understanding of the power game. The elementary game is between actors engaging with each other with their respective resources. But because that game is conditioned by contextual circumstances, there is also a metagame of control over those circumstances. There is competition over the terms of competition. The big winners are not those who prevail in the game but those who own the game itself, the rules, the language, the narrative, the agendas, the prevailing beliefs and ideas.

In the process of which, to my delight, I have been able to add something of meaning to Max Weber's analysis. One addition is in the understanding of power, where I have been able to pin down the definition of the thing itself.

Another is to get further into the meaning of "social relationship" by exploring how contextual influences work through beliefs, ideas, and mindsets. A further addition is in the understanding of legitimacy, where I have extended the range of sources from Weber's classical ones of law, tradition, and charisma to including also the way power is used.

BOOK TWO

The Problem of Statecraft

In *The Prince*, the most famous how-to about governing ever written, Niccolò Machiavelli speaks to the man set to govern the state of Florence. His message is straightforward: if you want to govern, you better be effective.

Well, exactly to whom he was addressing himself, and why, and what he meant, is not easily said. He does preface his tract with a letter to "the Magnificent Lorenzo de' Medici," but when he started to write it (in 1512), he did not know that Lorenzo would be selected by the pope to be the new Florentine leader after the collapse (in all but name) of the republic. Perhaps he wanted to flatter the young and inexperienced prince to get himself a job, but it is likely that his friends advised him to hold back and that he never presented his text to Lorenzo. Perhaps his thinking was not at all useful advice but rather to confuse the autocrat with inconsistent and counterproductive ideas and thus entice him to failure. Machiavelli was a man of the republic who had every reason to resent the new ruler. Or perhaps not. He had been high up in the city, as second chancellor (but was not of good enough family to aspire to the top of Florence's hierarchy). Although a man of the republic, he was also desperate for job and position and in need of money. He had had to leave the city for the village of Sant'Andrea, with only the tavern for community. His father had died in debt, and now, lonely and seeing himself unable to pass anything on to his own children, he was probably ready to compromise on his principles if he could get himself back into government service and the city life he loved. He wrote the tract quickly, finishing it the year after he was deposed, having endured a spell in prison and under torture. Could it be that he wrote it in anger or to get resentment off his chest? We do not know. It does not much matter. The text has been in front of us since it was published shortly after his death and has spoken to practitioners and thinkers of government ever since. It says many things and points in many directions, but there is a consistent message through it: those who presume to govern, of whatever kind they are, need to deliver.[1]

Effectiveness is not an issue of much passion in modern political science, except in a strand of writing that holds delivery to be more a problem of implementation than of decision-making, such as in the inspiring works of the late Aaron Wildavsky. Governments are nowadays mostly judged by whether they are constitutional, legitimate, democratic, rule by law, and so on—all important matters. But I think a fair reading of *The Prince* should be taken as an encouragement to get back to basics. We should of course be concerned with how governments do things, but also, and very much, with what they get done. It's what they get done they are thanked for, and what they don't get done they are blamed for.

Machiavelli had good reasons to occupy himself with effectiveness. Italy in general and Florence in particular were in decline, suffering from internal disarray and threatened and to some degree subjugated by foreign powers, the French king and allies. So when he reflected on the doings of the new prince in the hope that he would deliver effective rule, what he had in mind might have been less the glory of the prince and more the standing of the state. Even if no longer a republic, Florence was still Florence and needed to be governed. His message was one of effectiveness for a purpose. He thought that effective rule was necessary if the ruler was to have any chance of winning the goodwill of the people. It is in the interest of those who are ruled that the rule they are exposed to works. Otherwise, not only the state but also citizens suffer.

For Machiavelli, then, effective rule is a noble ambition. But it is also, in another piece to his puzzle, a difficult ambition. From this awareness comes his many recommendations for ruthlessness on the part of the ruler. There is no escaping his cynicism on the use of devious means, but was he an apologist for tyranny? The reason, at least one reason, he was a man of the republic was that, under republican rule, where there is a division of power and where those in office are answerable to at least some of the people, there will not be tyranny. He also thought that kind of rule was the best basis for a stable state. But in the setting in which he reflected and wrote, republican rule was no longer available. The problem was how to secure effective rule when power was in the hands of a ruler whose position rested not on the institutions of the state, but on a foreign authority (in this case the pope). The prince had been parachuted in by the enemy, yet that same prince was the only hope for the state. It is to rule under those circumstances, or so we may think, that Machiavelli's hardest recommendations apply.

However that be, he was ready to recommend very hard means indeed, and his book for that reason has been condemned as a tract of the Devil. He himself thought it a lesson of history that the ruler who is to be effective must will the means. The times he lived in were brutal. When hard means are necessary, some ability to ruthlessness on the part of the ruler is in the interest of both the state and its people. In today's language we might say that Machiavelli was alerting the new Florentine prince to contextual intelligence, to the imperative of understanding the situation he was up against and the means that would work in that setting.

Those of us who are concerned today with the future of democratic government have much the same reasons to occupy ourselves with effectiveness. Democracy is challenged. Movements of antipolitics and anger are taking hold. The institutions of the state have been unable to spread protection through society. Cohesion of the rulers and the ruled is much wanting, as is goodwill from people to governors. Admirable constitutions are falling into disrespect and weakened by internal divisions, lack of confidence, and poor leadership. External powers of nondemocratic persuasions are asserting themselves. In Europe, authoritarian Russia, with customary paranoia, is busy stirring up disorder in the democratic part of the continent and winning admiration for "strong government," in particular in some of Europe's fresher democracies. In China, a reconstituted People's Republic is on a mission to make totalitarianism work, racking up followers who either admire authoritarian force or hate democracy, or both.[2] However you read *The Prince*, it is a reminder that the elementary condition of good government is effective government. We today need to be reminded that this is as true of democratic government as of any other kind. The purpose of democracy, after all, on which more in Book Five, is not to be democratic but to provide for good government.

Many of democracy's friendly critics think the problem is that the democracies are not democratic enough. But if we apply Machiavelli's teaching, we are likely to see it differently: the problem is that they aren't governed well enough.

Government

A government is a body of persons governing a state. This is the definition of the *Oxford English Dictionary*, in my opinion an excellent definition. It says what a government is—a few ministers—and what it does—governing a state.

Many political scientists would, I know, object to this as a narrow and formalistic definition. They would argue, for example, that civil servants not only execute orders but also influence the shaping of policies and that a realistic definition of *government* should acknowledge that it is made up of the entire machinery that generates governance.

I disagree. Such "realistic" definitions tend to become unwieldy so that we can never pin down this thing we call government, and without that clarity the analysis is all over the place. This definitional disagreement also reflects different ways of thinking about government and governing. My definition is personal. Ministers are leaders. They want to be of consequence. To that end they engage in battle with sundry others whom they want to make followers. The relationship between them and their civil servants, for example, is part of the mystery of rule, and I don't want to hide that away in a definition that says that they are one and the same. I want a definition that encourages me to ask how it comes about that servants do as their masters want, if that's what they do. The "realistic" approach is "structural" or in the nature of "systems analysis." Here, things are thought to work if the components of the system are streamlined and arranged in harmony with each other. Persons and the way they operate matter less than the shape of the systems they work within. For me, governance comes down to persons and how they engage on battlefields.

However, the "governing a state" part of the definition is iffy. Once we ask about effectiveness, we are asking whether governments in fact do govern, whether they move on from having power to using it to effect. I therefore make a small improvement on the OED's definition: a government is a body of persons governing or trying to govern a state.

Governments are made up of persons; let's call them governors or ministers. Their job is to govern; let's call that which they do and that comes out of it governance.

The English delusion

An influential idea in political thinking is that governments need to be strong in order to deliver. That idea is influential, probably, because it seems so obvious. How can a government get anything done if it is held back by all nature of constraints?

British political thinking, or English rather, as so often when something is said to be British, has been very much in that school. Governments must be strong and have autonomy of action. They must be in charge. It is strength that determines what they can get done.

Because of this view, Britain holds on to a perverse election system—first-past-the-post in single-representative constituencies—that is likely to preserve a near two-party system and produce a majority in Parliament behind one of the two major parties, although none of them are likely to obtain a majority of votes.* Smaller and aspiring parties call for a change in the election system toward proportional representation, but that is consistently blocked by agreement of the major parties. They obviously want to stick with the present because it is to their advantage, but they also can do that by referring to the theory that the English method comes with the benefit that it produces governments that are able to govern.

Furthermore, because of the same view, Parliament has been set up to work by rules that give the government control of its agenda. It may sound strange to non-Brits, but in a system dedicated to the sovereignty of Parliament, that sovereign Parliament is not in charge of its own work. The leader of the House of Commons, who manages logistics in that body, is a member of the prime minister's cabinet with the responsibility to arrange things in the Commons according to the expediency of the government. The House of Commons does not have a leader of its own choosing. It chooses a speaker, who presides over debates, but the speaker and deputy speakers are not in charge of the agenda and can only influence it marginally in exceptional circumstances. The defense of this odd arrangement is that the government must be free to get on with its business without having to deviate according to the whims of a Parliament that might decide on priorities of its own.

In fact, however, counterintuitive as it may seem, strength does not determine effectiveness. Rather, as a general rule, governments that operate with hands tied, constitutionally speaking, are more likely to be effective. If a government is able to ram its policies through a compliant legislature, it may look forceful. But if you wish policies to work and endure, you are better off having a legislature that will scrutinize and double-check what you propose and cut some of the sharp edges off it in a spirit of compromise so as to make it acceptable not only to your side but also to those who ideally would have wanted a different policy. We can see this in well-functioning democracies where things are arranged differently from the Westminster model. In many of them, coalition or minority governments are the norm, such as in the Scandinavian countries. Some, such as Germany, have constitutional designs of checks and balances that deny their governments the autonomy that in the English view is essential. If we look to the record of effectiveness in

*In Britain's 2019 general election, the Conservative Party won a solid majority in Parliament, 365 of 650 seats, with 43.6 percent of the vote. On a gain of one percentage point in the share of the vote, it gained forty-seven seats compared to the last election. The Liberal Democratic Party increased its share of the vote from 7.0 to 11.5 percent of the vote but still won only eleven seats, one fewer than in the last election. There were 336,000 votes for every Liberal Democratic seat, as compared to 38,000 for every Conservative seat.

MOTHER OF PARLIAMENTS?

Medieval Europe invented a theory of society. Everyone had a rightful station according to the "estate" he or she belonged to. There were three estates, sometimes four, but usually three: the nobility, the clergy, and the rest, the commoners. Each estate had its specific function. Society was in order when the estates provided according to their functions.

This was God's order. At the top of the pyramid was the king, who ruled by God's grace and whose responsibility it was to maintain God's order. However, kings, although answering to God, were also to some degree dependent on "the people." They needed their consent, most basically to raise taxes. For this purpose, they took to using meetings of estates, the forerunners of today's national assemblies. It was the king who convened and dissolved estate meetings. The estates assembled separately, and laws were made by being passed around until the estates agreed. The French *États généraux* were first convened in 1302 and finally in 1789, when the third estate delegates, the commoners, declared themselves to be the National Assembly and set in motion the events that became the French Revolution.

Gradually, Europe abandoned the theory of estates. Society came to be seen as made up of people, of persons, of citizens. Meetings of estates were abandoned as mechanisms of representation and replaced by modern national assemblies.

But not in Britain. Britain's Parliament is still a meeting of estates. It consists of nobles, clergy, and commoners. They meet separately, nobles and clergy in the House of Lords and commoners in the House of Commons. Law is made by being passed between the two houses until there is agreement. Parliament is convened and dissolved by the monarch, currently Queen Elizabeth II. Her government decides Parliament's agenda.

The mother of parliaments, it calls itself. The grandmother of parliaments, we should probably say.

different systems, it does not seem, to put it carefully, that Britain stands out in any advantageous way or that governments in muddled (through English eyes) systems do worse in delivery. Comparing, for example, the effectiveness of governance in Germany and Britain, it's clearly Germany One, Britain Nil.

But that does not sway the prevailing view in Britain that remains wedded to the theory that government delivery depends on government strength. This essay is an argument against that theory. I will suggest that what governments are able to deliver depends more on behavior than on strength. I will suggest that it depends only to a very small degree on the strength they have behind them and to a very large degree on how, once in position, governors are able to work on and with a range of actors in front of them. I will refer to that large and diverse constituency as their *others*.

Does that mean that I already now have to turn my back on Machiavelli? Did he not precisely argue that rulers who are to prevail must be strong, indeed ruthlessly and brutally strong? Possibly, but perhaps not. What he certainly suggested was that if you are an autocrat who is not trusted by the people, you have no other option than to resort to ruthlessness. That's your recipe for staying in charge. Was he also saying it is a recipe for effectiveness? Probably not.

Governing

There is a view that governments run things. In Great Britain, the prime minister, we say, runs the country, the secretary of health the health service, the transport secretary the highways, and so on. We take that seriously. Patients are left on beds in corridors in a hospital up north, and the health secretary has to answer for it in Parliament. Some highways are not deiced on a frosty night, and the transport secretary is held responsible. Leaders, too, take it seriously. At the opening of the final TV debate before the British 2010 elections, Gordon Brown, then prime minister, said, "There's a lot to this job and I don't get it all right. But I do know how to run the economy, in good times and in bad."*

There is also a view of how governments run things. They do that with the help of tools or instruments.[3] Governments, says Christopher Hood in *The Tools of Government*, detect problems and act on them with the help of the tools at their disposal. These include control over information and resources, authority in the form of legal powers, and the management of people, land, equipment, and so on.

Finally, what enables governments to put tools to use, it is thought, is that they have power. Politicians get into government by winning power, and power enables them to get things done.

But all that, I suggest, is wrong. It's just too orderly: get power, do. It's too systemic: get the machinery to churn, and things happen. I think governing is a puzzle and agree with Jeffrey Pressman and Aaron Wildavsky that "it's amazing that government programs work at all."[4]

On power, I've concluded that it's not all it has been cracked up to be. Power gives governors a certificate to direct things, but once there they must

---

*What was behind the "I don't get it all right" was that Brown had just made the blunder of getting caught on microphone deriding a critical interlocutor as "that woman" and "bigoted" and was still in the process of groveling for forgiveness. The corridors and highways examples are from recent debates in Britain's Parliament.

also have the ability. No more than a driver's license says how good a driver the holder is does power say how good a governor its winner will be. Governments do not work directly on society; they work on others. Whatever they want done, they depend on someone else to do it. Always, these someones stand between them and things happening out there in society.

As for tools, no government I've seen—and I've worked for quite a few—has had any toolbox at hand into which ministers could reach when they wanted to do some governing. The tools Christopher Hood refers to are not stored in government offices but spread around in a myriad of agencies of administration and beyond. Information, for example, one of his tools, is not under ministers' control but is filtered through to them by their officials who can, and often do, manipulate what they tell their bosses.

Which gets us back to Machiavelli's difficulty. If power does not do it and governments do not control tools, how do they get things done? To better understand that, I dig down below power and instruments and start from a question Richard Rose put to us years ago in an obscure essay: what, "in plain man's language," do governments *do*?[5]

Governments—those small bodies of persons—do one thing and one thing only: they give orders. There is no other direct output or product from a government's work. It's worth stressing the point. Governments *do* very little. That may be contrary to how we mostly think about governments at work. Often when we discuss problems in society, we think of the many ways our governments could rectify them. If it is poverty, they could, we say, transfer income. If it is inequality, they could tax the rich. If it is market distortion, they could regulate. But making up lists of things governments *could* do, is, in response to the simple question of what they do, wrong language. Governments do not actually do the kinds of things we are accustomed to saying that they do. They tell others to do it. They do not, for example, regulate. They may order officials to impose new regulations on, say, banks, but after that it is anyone's guess what actually materializes by way of new rules and how the banks respond. It is interesting to reflect on what governments could and should do, but first we need to be clear about what they actually *do*. They give orders. That's the full and unambiguous answer "in plain man's language" to the question of what governments do.

Since the only thing governments are themselves in control of is the giving of orders, and since orders do not follow through to things happening in society unless civil servants and citizens do as they are told, our governors need to get us to oblige them. Their problem is obedience. Leaders must be able to get orders obeyed. "If the state is to exist," said the ever-unsentimental Max Weber, "the dominated must obey the authority claimed by the powers that be."[6]

This is a game of adversaries up against each other. Governments cannot with effect ask more of others than they will accept and must do their asking in such a way that the asked are willing or forced to comply. Others start from a disinclination against obeying. Government orders come with burdens: do as I say, change your ways, do this job, make this effort, pay these taxes. Those on the receiving end must be brought over by persuasion or coercion.

It may not be pleasing for us citizens to think that our lot is to obey. Libertarians, anarchists and radicals on the barricades do not have obedience on their minds. But it is childish to think other than that governments must order and that many orders are disagreeable. Our lot is to grin and bear.

Government orders are of three kinds: commands, requests, and signals. Orders are commands when compliance is compulsory. A law is a command. A budgetary allocation is a command to get a job done. It is not at the discretion of civil servants to do or not as they are told, nor of taxpayers to hand over what the law prescribes. Requests go to superiors over whom the government does not have power of command, to the legislature, as when it requests a budget or laws to work with, and to the courts when it asks for a ruling in its favor. Signals are suggestions, encouragements, ideas, and nudgings.

Commands may be compulsory, but that is not to say that they will necessarily be complied with. Many other reactions are available to the reluctant recipient. He can refuse. That may get him into trouble, but if he refuses, he refuses, and the command does not get followed. Or he can maneuver around it to avoid its consequences. If it is for an extra tax, it becomes more tempting to hide away some of one's income or to pay contractors without bothering with the VAT. Or a command may just be ignored in the hope that no one cares or notices. Or it may be obeyed in appearance only: slowly, sloppily, with deliberate forgetfulness.

With requests and signals, compliance is not obligatory. But make no mistake about it: they are both orders. When the government requests a budget from the legislature, it is telling the lawmakers what to give it. Out there in the population, signals are the smart way of getting people to do what they should but may not want.

Requesting and commanding are the obvious means of governing, but effectiveness depends crucially on persuasion, hence on the subtle use of signals. This soft use of power is the least well-known skill of statecraft and therefore worth exploring in a bit of detail.

Once we start looking, we see signals everywhere. People are endlessly told by their governments how to behave and what to think. We are advised to eat healthy food, to not smoke, to not drink and drive, to save more and spend less, or the other way around if the economy is lax, to practice safe sex, to read worthy literature, to not litter the landscape, to buy homemade products, to pick up and dispose of dog droppings, to economize with water and electricity, to wash our hands before eating, to pay careful attention to consumer information on food products, to exercise. Parents are encouraged to read to their children. Prime Minister Mendès France encouraged the French to drink more milk and less wine (in vain).

Businesses are encouraged to pay workers a decent salary, or to not give excessive pay raises, depending on the state of the economy, to take measures for workplace safety, to offer employees help with childcare, to minimize noise and pollution, to invest in modern technology, to help workers improve their skills, to support neighborhood civic activities. Churches are encouraged to do charitable work among the poor, pharmacies to dispense free syringes to drug addicts, trade unions to explain to members the need to be responsible workers, lawyers to devote some of their time for legal assistance to those who cannot pay, doctors to be cautious with prescriptions. And so it goes on. Hardly anyone or any activity is free from advice about what to do or how to think. Campaigns for or against this, that, or the other are a constant feature of modern governing.

Silliness galore, of course—but far from only silliness. The best leadership may be in wise action, but speaking is still indispensable. Prime Minister Edward Heath's biographer, Philip Ziegler, tells a story of Cecil King trying to persuade Heath "to set up a propaganda department responsible for explaining his policies to the world. His job, replied Heath, was to govern, not to explain. That remark explains a lot of Ted's mistakes, commented King."[7] Governments need to inform, to sell their policies, to make themselves trusted or at least believed, to encourage, to persuade, and to manipulate when that is called for. A government must be seen and heard and make itself the center of attention, and it must outmaneuver those trying to outmaneuver it. It needs to control the issues that become salient in the press and public awareness and not let others take hold of the agenda. It needs to lead and to display leadership.

During the ten years of Tony Blair's premiership in Britain, the politics of signals fell into disrepute as "spin." He and his people just kept talking too much and exhausted their public. It's a fine balance, and poor old Blair was so eager to talk and to put a positive gloss on things that he kept chipping away at the authority he was trying to fortify. They did what any government of any caliber must do but messed up on getting the melody right.

Still, although spin might be thought of as annoying, it is worth driving home that there are very good reasons for governments to make use of signals, beyond the promotion of their own excellence.

- Signals are the government's inputs into the deliberation between itself and citizens, and within the citizenry, and deliberation is the fertilizer on which political culture can flourish.
- Citizens do not just *have* preferences: preferences are formed, and it is part of good leadership to contribute to infusing citizens with a will to reason and cooperation.
- There will not be effective governance unless governors follow through to motivating the dominated to obey their authority. There will not even be authority since the governor needs to present himself and his project to the governed in order to extract authority from them.
- Underlings must be persuaded that they ought to obey and then nudged to actually complying: without persuasion, no compliance.
- Governance depends on "vision," and there is no way of communicating a sense of purpose and direction other than to engage with the citizenry.
- If a government has an intention and can realize it through encouragement, it would be wrong to go about it in more complicated and possibly repressive ways.
- If wrong or inadequate information is the cause of damaging action, the government should obviously inform.
- Signals can be used when commands are impossible or unethical or when the control of compliance is not practicable. Preventive health care is a case in point. If we could improve diets, reduce the consumption of junk food, cut down on smoking, avoid the abuse of alcohol, and increase physical activity, there would be immeasurable gains to happiness and health, as well as to state budgets.
- Signals are cheap and may be an available policy when more costly measures are not affordable.
- They are not coercive.
- Even when more decisive action is necessary, for example, to command people to pay a bit more tax, commands need to be followed up by explanation and persuasion. A government may be in its full and undisputed right to command people to pay taxes, but it must nevertheless *beg* them to do so. It must respond to their tacit question about why they should give up more of their hard-earned cash and free the taxpayer from the temptation to persuade himself that he has just cause to resist.

In the experience of COVID management, we have seen the absolute centrality of signals to public administration. Governments have explained, guided, encouraged, discouraged, and nudged in an incessant flow of messaging, day in and day out. The demand for information from the public has been near insatiable. Clarity, consistency, and authority in information and guidelines became essential tests of leadership. The failure in America to control the epidemic was a result not of inadequate capacity but in large measure of inconsistent and hesitant messaging. That damage followed through to further confusion about vaccinations and the rollout of the vaccination program. If ever the folly of Heath's distinction between governing and explaining was to be proved, here it was in dramatic fashion.

There are also bad reasons, obviously, which may lead governments to the politics of signals. Among these is the often irresistible inclination to know-it-all-ism. Many of us no doubt have an urge to teach others about life; ministers for their sins are listened to and may find it difficult to keep quiet.

The simplest form of signal is pure information, for example, about the dangers of smoking or the wisdom of taking exercise, in the hope that people will behave sensibly when only they know the facts. Information campaigns may be followed by guidelines of behavior, for example, campaigns about healthy diets with rules of guidance (such as five to seven slices of bread a day, as recommended in a memorable campaign in Sweden in the mid-1980s, or five units a day of fruit and vegetables, as recommended by a British government committee on nutrition in the late 1990s, so successfully that "your five" has established itself in daily parlance). Recommendations may be followed by incentives—those who invest in pension plans are rewarded with tax reliefs—or by disincentives—those who continue to smoke in spite of good advice will have to pay an extra tax. Signals may be combined with commands, in which case the signals attach to the policy in question to encourage compliance.

Deciding and implementing

Governments give orders first to get decisions made and then to get decisions once made acted upon.

Decision-making is the easier part, not easy but easier compared to what follows. Obviously, all kinds of things may go wrong already at this stage. A government with a narrow majority in the legislature may be held for ransom by renegades in its own ranks. It is enough for anyone in Britain to remember the case of Prime Minister John Major up to his defeat in 1997 or Theresa May after her failed snap election in 2017, both held hostage by unforgiving Euroskeptic ideologists within their own party. Or governments may be in internal disarray and unable to agree within themselves, for example, in multiparty systems where governments are often coalitions, in particular if antagonistic parties have to team up.

The reason things are still comparatively simple at this stage is that those involved are few and close to each other—ministers and their near others. Any government in a normal democracy will ex officio be able to order its near officials to reasonably do the planning it has to get done and is likely to find them willing and sometimes eager. The government and legislature should usually know each other well enough that the government will only by rare accident make a proposal to the legislature that it does not pretty much know will be accepted.

But then decisions must be implemented. This is where things get serious. There are now many more others involved, and many who are distant others.

Second-round orders go first to the same officials in the same ministries who previously prepared the decision, but now as an order to put the decision into effect. That changes things dramatically. The government is dealing with the same people but in a different way. While it previously told its officials to prepare things on paper, it is now telling them to make things happen in life. As I know from my own experience as a government servant, planning is easy (and fun), implementation difficult (and frustrating). When it comes to implementation and to preventing initiatives from running out in the sand, ministers must follow through and follow up and follow up again, and again—and that is very, very, very hard going.

Orders now flow not only from ministers to servants but also from ministries to underlying agencies with mainly implementing duties. Say the government wants to increase the level of the income tax. The minister of finance gets her officials to draw up a proposal to the legislature with the necessary background material and does the political fine-tuning in a couple of rounds with her government colleagues and the relevant lawmakers. The minister puts the proposal to the parliament that puts the label of "law" on it—possibly with some modifications, since legislators like to feel useful—and turns around and tells the same officials in her ministry to get the law put into effect. Those officials then turn to the relevant underlying agency, call it the Directorate of Tax Collection, which redesigns its system for extracting income taxes according to the new law and mobilizes as best it can its innumerable local suboffices to do the job. The world of implementing agencies is much larger than that of the ministries. These agencies are more removed from the center of power and often spread out over the country, and, from a minister's outlook, more anonymous.

No minister can ever take it for granted that she can easily get her ministry to do as she wants. A new government may have won an election and taken up office, only to find that it has inherited a civil service that will not throw itself into active service for the new regime. When Aneruin Bevan became minister of health in the Labour government in Britain in 1945 and set about creating the National Health Service against the grain of planning during the war and under the preelection coalition, he had to outmaneuver the top mandarins in his ministry, who had been in charge of the planning he now rejected, and ally himself with younger officials whom he could count on to work for his policy.[8] A minister is obviously in a position to direct her officials to prepare the legislation she wants to push through, but no one can order officials to enthusiasm. Or for that matter to not make mistakes: In 2004, John Prescott, the British deputy prime minister, arranged a referendum in the North East on devolved power to regions. He put much work into the campaign and recorded a phone message saying, "This is John Prescott. I am ringing to urge you to vote in next week's referendum." It was to go out to households across the region in three bursts around teatime, but the technician programming the machinery got the timing wrong so that thousands of sleepy households answered the phone at four thirty, five, and five thirty in the morning.[9]

However, although all kinds of things may go wrong in the inner circle for all kinds of reasons—conflicts, quarrels, power struggle, paralysis, tugs-of-war over turf, mistakes and miscalculations, disobedience, backstabbing, mischievous leaks to the press, and what not—in the larger scheme of things this is manageable. A ministry can be reasonably handled by any minister who is not completely without charm and administrative skill. But when she turns her hand to implementation, she will find herself on more wobbly ground and dependent not only on officials in her own secretariat but also on those Michael Lipsky called "street-level bureaucrats." To get a ministry to cooperate may be a bit of a frustration; to get the whole apparatus of agencies on different levels of responsibility and their thousands of managers and clerks to cooperate, coordinate, and pull together is a nightmare.

Implementation is often local: services have to be delivered where people live and work. The trouble with implementation, therefore, is not only distance and that orders must travel down through multiple layers of administration, but also local interests and local government. Always, local people see things differently from how they are seen centrally. They think central authorities want to command them too much, do not understand local circumstances, and do not give them the resources they need to implement central commands. Local interests are always suspicious, and often contemptuous, of those people up there in the capital. Local governments always feel under siege and always want to protect, and if possible to extend, their domain of authority. Even local subagencies that are part of the central government's apparatus are often local in their identity and torn between their duty to execute orders from above and their inclination to see things from below.

Even that is not the end of it. The orders contained in political decisions also go out into the country to those who are really distant: to businesses, organizations, voluntary agencies, schools, families and to all the people who make them up as directors, workers, members, husbands, wives, teachers, pupils, and so on. This is where things start to get not only difficult for the government, but desperate. It may be hell to get administrators to cooperate and do as they are supposed to, but that is at least to deal with people whose job duty it is to obey orders from above. Once ministers are into telling ordinary people how to go about their life and business, they find themselves on very shaky ground indeed, considering that "people" include all sorts: capitalist tycoons, dysfunctional families, speeding motorists, teenage delinquents, underpaid teachers, tax cheaters, overzealous social workers, arrogant surgeons, businesspeople on the take, reactionary unions, publicists and influence hawkers, demoralized transport workers, know-it-all professors, irresponsible journalists, drug dealers and mobsters, manipulating advertisers, dumbing-down broadcasters, and libertarians who just want to be left alone. The line of command is now very long, for example, from the minister of agriculture in his office to the prairie farmer who is tilling his soil. Will the order be heard, understood, and respected? Those expected to obey and comply are numerous. How does a lonely commander get thousands and thousands of people to walk in tandem? What rights do ministers have to order? What duties do people have to let themselves be ordered, and how inclined are they to obey what they are told? It may be a duty for citizens to obey the laws, but that is not much for a minister to lean on if anonymous citizens strongly object to the laws imposed on them. Within ministries and agencies, ministers may hope to have support from a culture of administration; out there in the citizenry, the culture may be very different, such as entrenched skepticism of "big government."

Finally, and importantly, the government now meets interests, in everything from local governments via union captains to business leaders. No matter what a government decides and in whatever area of policy, there will be persons and groups and institutions who see the orders they are asked to comply with to be contrary to their interests. If the government decides, for example, to lower the speed limits on highways, it will find motorists to be against it, probably backed by mighty motoring organizations or a car industry in control of jobs. The government may want to impose its will on society, but society is a messy matter to deal with, made up of endlessly crisscrossing constellations that can and will counter, resist, or frustrate if they can.

Governments meet counter-interests and counterpowers already within its inner circle and in the civil service. But that is nothing compared to the resistance it meets when it tries to push its orders beyond the inner circle and into the population. All governments want to think that their policies are popular, and sometimes they are—for some. But they will not have been long in office before they discover that ingratitude is the normal thanks they get for all the good they do.

Others

A government's *others* are of four kinds: bosses, officials, mediators, and citizens. Its bosses are the lawmakers, those the government nominally works for. Officials work for the government. The mediators are the courts and their judges who work under the direct authority of the law. Citizens are their own women and men, on no government's beck and call.

The government wants its will to prevail but is dependent on all these others for that to happen and can take none of them for granted. It needs to make the legislature obey its requests, but no legislature will easily do that, in part because if it does, the government will ask too much. It needs to make officials obey its commands, but officials have interests of their own and often think of themselves as better qualified than their ministers. It needs to get citizens to comply, but citizens want to get on with their lives with as little interference as possible. It needs to get the courts to refrain from undue obstruction, but the courts are autonomous and under no government's command, and often hungry for influence of their own.

Governments are sometimes said to be in charge, but they are not. What the ladies and gentlemen of government have to do, day in and day out, is to engage in battle with those they depend on and bend them to their will. This is one reason why we are advised to start from the sharp and personal definition of *government* that I have suggested. Governance is not something that is churned out of an impersonal machinery. It is the outcome of battle between persons: governors, lawmakers, officials, citizens, and judges.

The first problem for any (democratic) government is to handle its own bosses, those who make up the legislature. This is relatively simple in a parliamentary system provided the government has a majority, in which case it can normally get pretty much what it wants. The lawmakers are likely to make a bit of fuss about it to enable themselves to feel that they matter, and twig what they concede, but that's just going through the motions.

It is more difficult in a system of shared power, such as in the American case, because the legislature is now more autonomous. In a parliamentary system, the government can threaten the legislature, ultimately with resigning or calling a new election. That threat puts fear into those who sit in the legislature, who might lose their seats. In shared power systems, legislatures cannot be threatened, and governments must live with the legislatures they have. We can therefore learn more about the difficulty of handling lawmakers by looking to America than to, for example, Britain.

America offers two recent contrasting case studies, the presidencies of Lyndon Johnson and Barack Obama. These were opposites in their relations with Congress. Johnson, until his demise, was a master of getting Congress to give him what he wanted. Obama was never able to get the collaboration he wanted from his Congresses. The settings were different, including majority and minority constellations in the respective Congresses. But in the American case, party majority does not matter all that much, certainly nothing like in parliamentary systems. When President Obama managed, in his greatest legislative achievement, in 2010, to get the Affordable Care Act passed, he had a solid Democratic majority in Congress but still obtained no more than the slimmest majorities because of resistance to parts of the bill on his own side. A British prime minister with a majority can, for the most part, assume an amenable Parliament. An American president, whether he has a majority or not, never can. He must get Congress to go along with him case by case and always fight down dangerous hostility.

President Johnson knew and understood the institution of Congress intimately, having been a US senator from Texas for a dozen years. From that knowledge he concluded, first, that he needed to stay close to Congress and keep its members close to the presidency. It was not a matter of being cuddly, which he certainly was not, but about never giving members of Congress reason to feel that they were not taken seriously. Second, he knew, irrespective of party constellations, that he would never have a majority he could just count on. In whatever he wanted, he knew that he would need to win over the necessary majority. And he knew, from his knowledge of how Congress works, that to win majorities, he would have to work from Machiavelli's book and deploy all available means and to do so with whatever ruthlessness was required. Hence, his modus operandi would include to flatter—as much as possible of that—and to threaten, bully, shame, and blackmail as required and possible. It was not pretty, but it was effective.

President Obama did not have Johnson's intimacy with Congress. He had three years of experience as a US senator (and before that as a state senator in Illinois) but no firsthand experience of the House and was not a man of Congress the way Johnson had been. He had a strongly hostile Congress against him, in particular when the Republicans won majorities and set themselves on a course of unprecedented noncollaboration with a president they had decided not to honor. Still, the stalemate between Obama and Congress was a result not only of Congress's approach to the president but also of the president's approach to Congress. While Johnson had worked from Machiavelli's book, Obama worked from the rule book. In his dealing with Congress, he was correct, something Johnson never was, but not close, something Johnson always was. Obama's Congresses were hostile and would have remained hostile no matter what he did, but also he facilitated their hostility. It is not enough for an American president to respect Congress; he must undermine the instinct in Congress that it is not being respected. He must win from members of Congress a *feeling* that they matter. Nor did Obama work on members of Congress in specific legislative matters the way Johnson had done. He worked on them by persuasion, and did so very hard, for example, in the pivotal case of the Affordable Care Act. But he did not have Johnson's ruthlessness in his dealings with members whom he needed to persuade. He did not have the inclination for raw politicking on that level. He had awful— there is no other word for it—Congresses to work with but was also himself less than effective in his dealings with them. Those Congresses were stubbornly set on noncollaboration, but part of the blame for gridlock in Washington during his tenure still lies with the president and his distant approach to Congress. Johnson's approach was akin to Teddy Roosevelt's recommendation in foreign affairs: speak softly and carry a big stick. Obama did not do enough soft talk and did not carry enough stick.

The two lessons for governments to get the backing they need from their legislatures, then, are, first, to keep them close and make them feel respected, and, second, to make sure, when it comes to the real test, that you have the means to put fear into their souls. In the latter, you should consult the power book before the rule book.

A cardinal feature of the polity, discovered S. E. Finer, in his magnificent *History of Government from the Earliest Times*, covering 5,500 years, is "baron-management." The king "could give effect to his orders only through them [the barons]. Therefore, they must be induced to give enthusiastic support (the best outcome) or acceptance (the next best) and discouraged from foot-dragging or, at the worst, open resistance."[10] In fact, all officials of all kinds of governments are barons, if of different dignity, and Finer's rules have universal validity. Governments need to both prevent and animate. They need to put their officials into straightjackets to make it difficult for them to do less or different things than they are told, and they need to lead them along so as to win their acceptance and sometimes possibly even some enthusiasm.

Modern governments have the service of a brilliant straitjacket into which they strap their officials. It's called bureaucracy, in the West an invention of the twentieth century.[11] A bureaucracy is a system of defined rules, duties, divisions of labor, and lines of command, and is a miracle for anyone who wants to rule. It makes it possible for governors to issue orders and be reasonably confident that they reach their destinations, and it makes it difficult for officials to disregard or disobey. With bureaucratic order, more or less, governors have a good chance of not having to suffer (too much) foot-dragging and of obtaining some degree of acceptance.

Not much is generally thought more uninspiring than public bureaucracy, but the magic of this invention for anyone who wants to govern cannot be overstated. When Dwight Eisenhower, who knew something about management, took up office in the White House in 1953, he had to design his own headquarters-style administration as a novelty in a previously disorganized office. His own view was that "organization cannot make a genius out of a dunce, but it can provide its head with the facts he needs, and help him to avoid misinformed mistakes."[12] That's one of the things bureaucracy can do for a leader, but the benefits go much further. Political decisions that are to be effective need to be prepared carefully before they are made and implemented with determination after they are made. This requires coordinated effort by usually hundreds or thousands of officials, and getting all these people to pull in tandem is a herculean task. When there is bureaucratic order, it just works. Ministers and others hardly even notice, but it's a miracle.

However, governments want more from their staffs than acceptance. They need them to engage with their policies in a spirit of wanting to make them work. Otherwise they will only do what they must, and governance will grind to a halt. I know from my own experience in government service that this is not abstract theorizing. Civil servants, even loyal and dutiful ones, work very differently for different kinds of political bosses and are, if made to feel uninspired, perfectly able to subvert.

It is a great difficulty in leadership to strike the spark of enthusiasm in the heart of officials. It may be within reach in the initial stage of decision-making but is at best elusive in the next stage of implementation. In the first stage, ministers are working with officials who are inside the enchanted world of power and who have the thrill of participating in the giving of orders. A touch of enthusiasm is not impossible. In the next stage of implementation, the officials that ministers now lean on are distant and outside of the inner circle and do not have the thrill of power to animate them. Orders are given by someone "up there" and get sent down to the implementers, who sit on the receiving end. Enthusiasm is now too much to hope for and even acceptance difficult to obtain.

Bureaucracy prevents disobedience, but it does not create willing obedience. On the contrary, bureaucratic order comes with the cost of discouraging the engagement that is needed for a policy to find a swift way through the administrative maze and into effect in society. I have observed elsewhere a remarkable story in Britain when Gordon Brown, as chancellor, poured new money into the National Health Service with next to no effect in better outcomes for patients.[13] Although he gave the people who worked in the service more money, a good deal of it as rewards to them personally, they reacted by slowing down on work and effort. While much was done to improve bureaucratic order, notably by organizing work around detailed target schemes and box-ticking work plans, nothing or not enough was done to prevent the stifling effect of bureaucratization on morale. The challenge for a minister is to both use the bureaucracy without which he can get nothing done, and at the same time to release those who work within it from its strictures and animate them to inventiveness and initiative.

The encouragement of public servants is more difficult than the designing of public systems. Bureaucracy is systemic, encouragement is personal. It is psychological, it depends on human knowledge, it rests predominantly on the subtle use of normative leadership, and it depends on getting the melody right in the specific context of culture, time, and place. Ministers, like political scientists, are perhaps inclined to think too much in terms of systems and to not quite remember that systems are made up of people and perform depending on how well the people who inhabit them work and collaborate. The answer to the problem of encouragement is for political bosses to be motivational leaders with the ability to spread motivation through huge and heavy bureaucracies. Crude leadership does not give much in return. The psychologist Frederick Herzberg called it "kick in the ass management," of which he said that it produces movement but not motivation. "If I kick my dog, he will move. But when I want him to move again, what must I do? I must kick him again."[14]

There is huge potential in motivational leadership for bosses to get the best out of their servants. People do respond to rewards and punishments, but what the author Daniel Pink calls "drive" comes from self-direction. And self-direction again comes from what he calls "the purpose motive," that workers are able to recognize purpose in their jobs and see progress toward it in their efforts.[15]

So leaders should be inspirational, but can they? It is much to ask. Who can hold up a project that inspires? Who can handle what President George Bush called "the vision thing"? Who has the gift of charisma? Who is a natural entrepreneur and leader? Some can and do—Franklin Roosevelt, Churchill, Reagan, Thatcher—but they are few and far between. It is not impossible, and leaders should aspire to be inspirational—but it is difficult.

The lesson here for effectiveness in government is the importance of the choice of leaders. Governments, parties, and organizations are in business to be effective. If systems are to work, they need good leadership. Good leadership again depends on good leaders, on the right people being put in charge. All this is to underline the importance in the choice of political leaders to consider not only their politics but equally their skills.

Courts have the power—some more, some less—to overturn a government's orders by declaring them unlawful or unconstitutional. That is a good side to democratic rule because it helps to hold the rulers under control and increases the likelihood that their orders, those that survive, are seen to be legitimate.

But for effective government, it's a problem. The best situation is one in which the courts serve as safety valves to prevent excess but exercise restraint with interfering in government business. That balance, however, is elusive. Courts, like others, when they get a taste of power, are inclined to like it and to scramble for more. In court autonomy, there is an inherent tendency to court activism.

The political role of courts depends on the constitutional setting and the political-legal culture. Where constitutions give the courts a central role in the political system, for example, where there are designated constitutional courts, such as in Germany, they will be important actors to which governments just have to accommodate themselves. Where there is a culture of litigation in which it is seen to be normal and acceptable for citizens, businesses, and organizations to appeal government decisions to the courts to prevent or to delay action, such as in America, government effectiveness will suffer. That is all the more so if the tendency to litigation is encouraged by a culture of court activism.

In the absence of cultures of restraint, the government side should seek to constrain court activism. That is more doable than is often thought. The extreme case is the United States, where the Supreme Court has taken on powers beyond what is prescribed in the Constitution, so much so as to have brought the powers in Washington out of balance with each other and undermined the intended delicate system of checks and balances. Americans obsess about conservative or liberal leanings in the court system. The fundamental problem, however, is court activism.

Many observers believe that the strictures of the American Constitution make serious constitutional reform prohibitively difficult. Even the eminent Robert Dahl, in *How Democratic Is the American Constitution?* and *On Political Equality* is radical in analysis but reluctant in prescribing reform. But this reticence is misplaced. It is true that it is difficult to change the Constitution, but the constitutional system works according to a range of conventions that are not prescribed in or protected in the constitutional text and that could be changed easily if there were a will to do so. Court activism is one such convention. The American Supreme Court is not as powerful as it has itself come to think and that many observers have come to believe. The Constitution that gives the Supreme Court the job of guarding the lawmakers does not leave the guardian unguarded. The trouble is a strange reluctance on the side of the legislature and executive to use their powers to rein in runaway courts, not the absence of such powers. There is nothing in the Constitution to prevent Congress from constraining a Supreme Court that is out of control. Rather, up against a Court that takes on powers it should not have, the Constitution gives Congress a duty to constrain it. The Court has appellate jurisdiction "with such Exceptions, and under such Regulations as the Congress shall make" (Article III, Section 2).

Supernational courts are a more recent innovation that present national governments with a potential problem. The extreme case is the European Union's Court of Justice. This court is tasked with interpreting European Union law and ensuring its equal implementation in member states. Other courts with supernational powers are, for example, the European Court of Human Rights and the International Tribunal for the Law of the Sea. These courts are vastly different in authority. The Law of the Sea Tribunal, for example, has the legal power to make rulings that are binding on nation-states (that are party to the United Nations Convention on the Law of the Sea) but no power of enforcement (as exemplified in its 2016 ruling against China in a dispute with the Philippines over rights in the South China Sea, which China just ignored). Like national courts, these courts serve to hold government action to the straight and narrow. In that, we should want them to be effective but not overwhelming. Unlike national courts, powerful supernational ones are subject to little or no counterpower in global governance. This is a case of unfinished constitutional work. Supernational courts are here to stay, but they should not be as free from controlling counterweight as they now are. The EU Court of Justice, for example, has become, as one would expect in

HOW TO TAME THE SUPREME COURT

If the American Congress were to pull itself together to restore balance in the relationship with the Supreme Court and punctuate its excessive activism, it would find that the Constitution gives it many instruments for so doing.

Congress could, first, preferably with the assistance of the president, put the court under the moral pressure of well-argued criticism. President Franklin Roosevelt and his allies did that when they came into office in 1933 and found the court dead set against their New Deal policies and dogmatically obstructive. In three years, by 1937, and before he was able to change its composition, Roosevelt had a compliant court.

Second, it could engage the court by overruling its decisions in new legislation. This was another Roosevelt technique and one that has been used by later Congresses. The Civil Rights Act of 1991, for example, overturned nine Supreme Court decisions that had narrowed interpretation in previous law. After the infamous *Citizens United* ruling, which swept away one hundred years of legal tradition to restrict corporate political funding, Congress should have restored relevant regulations in new legislation.

Third, Congress could increase the number of justices. The number of nine is not written in stone, and the Court has previously been both larger and smaller. The threat to "pack" the Court was yet another Roosevelt technique. There are strong arguments for enlarging the court. As it is now, too much power is vested in too few hands. That power should be diluted in a larger court to ensure more robust deliberation.

Fourth, Congress could use its power to introduce exceptions and regulations. It could, for example, appoint a tenth justice and impose a requirement of a majority of at least six for a ruling, thereby avoiding the embarrassment of five-to-four majority rulings in important matters. (In fact, a five-to-four ruling is a pretty sure sign that the court is political rather than judicial and is deciding on a matter that should have been left for normal political resolution.) It could impose a majority rule for an appeal to be accepted for court hearing (presently a minority of four is sufficient).

Finally, Congress could deny the Supreme Court a budget or cut its budget. It is obliged to provide that justices are paid but not to increase their compensation beyond where it stands, nor to pay justices a salary for life on retirement, or any other pension for that matter, nor to fund the court's lavish administration.

A full-blown confrontation in the United States between Congress and the Supreme Court is unlikely, but that is not because the Constitution ties Congress's hands and makes the court all-powerful. It is also unnecessary. If Congress would assert itself, it could easily put enough fear into the court to deflate its exaggerated view of itself and get it into line.

Court activism sits not only in the Supreme Court but in lower courts and the broader judicial system. A comprehensive reform is a tall order, but Supreme Court reform would still be useful. The Supreme Court sets the tone for the rest of the system.

the absence of balancing counterpowers, just too powerful for anyone's good. Even the benign European Court of Human Rights has step by step extended its authority beyond that intended when it was set up.[16]

Citizens, as seen from government offices, are friends or enemies. "We must suppose that, whatever the motive, most of the orders are more often obeyed than disobeyed by most of those affected." So says H. L. A. Hart, perhaps the most respected authority in modern jurisprudence.[17] If that is right, most citizens are normally friends, with the enemies making up a remaining minority.

But why should we suppose that most people obey? Hart put it down to "a general habit of obedience," but that is too optimistic. The iron law of governing is that, basically, people do not want to obey. For most people their most direct and necessary interaction with their government is that they pay taxes, and we can safely say that very few would pay what they are obligated unless they were forced to by refusal being difficult and dangerous. Most people do mostly pay up, but all tax collectors know that it is not out of mere habit.

If most citizens mostly obey, it is because they have reasons to do so. Such reasons are in the double influence of pull and push. If governance is attractive, citizens are pulled into obedience because they do not have reasons or excuses to disobey. But that's not enough: obedience depends also on citizens being pushed into line by controls and coercion. When pull and push stack up, citizens are offered a deal they cannot refuse and mostly go along, more or less, with what is expected of them. Things may then look and feel feather light as if by "habit," but that is only because the pressures that stack up upon citizens, which are many and heavy, are out of sight.

What pulls citizens into obedience is fair governance and good leadership. Governments distribute goods and burdens in the population. If they do that unfairly, citizens have the excuses they need to persuade themselves that they are in the right to disobey, ultimately to revolt. If governance is fair, they are denied those excuses. For example, tax compliance is dependent on taxation being perceived to be fair because perceived unfairness justifies evasion. It gives taxpayers the excuse they need to follow their inclination to not pay up on what they can hide away.

If leaders exercise good leadership, they are likely to be rewarded with obedience, partly because they attract obedience by their demeanor and partly because they, again, deny citizens excuses for disobeying. If citizens can persuade themselves that their leaders are fools, they can feel that they have no duty to heed them. Obedience from citizens to governments, then, depends on governors ahead of citizens. If governors govern in such a way that they deserve to be obeyed, they have a good chance of being obeyed.

What pushes citizens into obedience are rules and culture. The strongest rules are those that carry the name of "law." A law carries with it the authority that is contained in that label. There are two reasons why laws are or should be obeyed: first, that the label of "law" is a certificate that the order around which it is wrapped is legitimate, and, second, that obedience can be enforced with the threat of punishment.

The political culture is an amalgam of mindsets and conventions. A good culture sits on a sociological foundation of trust and we-feeling. Upon that foundation, there is hope for the relationship between the rulers and the ruled, that the rulers be committed to the public good and the ruled to consent and compliance.* It is the stuff of a virtuous circle of vibrant two-way deliberation that breeds trust and feeds back into its own foundations. A bad political culture is fractured from the foundations and up. Where cohesion is absent, deliberation is difficult, trust in short supply, and obedience beyond the enforced even more so. The shared identity among citizens and between them and their governors unravels, and political life disintegrates into a downward spiral of distrust. Governance falters, and dysfunction feeds back into the population as a confirmation that politicians are useless and government a mess of interference and inefficiency.

Hart may well have been right that most people can be expected to mostly obey. But not everyone, and his "general habit" is hardly an explanation.

Friends are of two kinds: insiders and outsiders. Insiders are the government's people who will tend to obey, mostly, because they see the government as being theirs. Outsiders are opposed to the government, but in an opposition that is based on loyalty to the state of which the government is the custodian.[18] (In Britain's Parliament, the opposition is "her Majesty's loyal opposition.") They too will tend to obey, mostly, if more grudgingly than insiders, because they, even if they dislike the government, see the state to be theirs.

The enemies are those who have abandoned loyalty and who see neither the state nor therefore the government to be theirs. Some people are just angry and hateful and turn their hatred on politicians, politics, and government. However, anger and hate are sentiments that on their own mostly generate resentment and from there follow through to political apathy, unpleasant but not dangerous. Others are animated by ideology, that toxic cocktail of

---

*The term *public good* is taken from George Washington. The man who created the American presidency started governing with an inaugural address, thereby establishing a convention that American presidents still abide by. In his first inaugural address, Washington defined the job of government as "the discerning and pursuit of the public good."

certainty and righteousness. It is ideology that makes for hot and dangerous enmity. That kind of enmity becomes a force when ideological movements are directed not simply against the government of the day but against the very idea of government, and when those movements gain control of real political resources. Those resources may be economic or mobilizational. Economic resources are money to work with. Mobilizational resources are generated from the whipping up of anger, such as racial hatred or prejudice against outsiders and immigrants, or in the form of contempt for "the politicians" collectively, and the turning of such sentiments into organization.

The regulating factor behind cohesion between rulers and the ruled, then, is loyalty. Not agreement but loyalty. Order, trust, and legitimacy, and indeed obedience, depend on an underlying sentiment of loyalty to the state, to the idea of government, to, in some general meaning, the system.

The origins of loyalty, in turn, are as elusive as is the secret of a democratic political culture. But much depends, again, on how governors govern. Citizens will be loyal if they are given reasons to be loyal. They have reason to be loyal if governors govern in such a way that citizens are led toward friendship and away from enmity.

Machiavelli again

Machiavelli's warning, that those who want to govern better be effective, is as pertinent as any could be for the state of modern democracy. We are in the middle of an economic revolution of globalization, information technology, and automation. We are in the aftermath of the most disruptive economic crisis since 1929. We are fighting a deadly pandemic. Democratic governments have not dealt well with these matters. Winners have got away with it, surfing the tide of rising inequality, leaving losers behind.

Governments have big things they want done, but all they can do is to give orders, and that to *others* who are reluctant to obey, sometimes strongly, sometimes with enmity. Somehow, a small group of ministers has to dominate a big population. They have to make their will reach over the canyon that separates their great ambitions from their little capacities. There has to be leadership by leaders who are skillful and have the grace of authority.

Governing is a people business. To get a grip on how it works, we need more language than the structural one of power, systems, bureaucracy, organization, instruments, and the like. We do need that language, but we need in addition the language of behavior. We need the language of governors and others, of leaders, followers, underlings, friends and enemies, and of bosses, officials, citizens and mediators, of entrepreneurs and enforcers. We need the language of orders, compliance, and resistance, of obedience and revolt, and of commands, requests, signals, nudgings, and askings. We need the language of skills, encouragement, persuasion, loyalty, subversion and hate, inspiration and motivation, of respect and contempt, of pull and push, and of coercion and enforcement. The language of Machiavelli.

Everyone knows that governance is difficult, but how difficult? I land on the side of very, very difficult. You have won power and think you are there; more likely you are in trouble. From now on, it's relentless and unforgiving hardship.

Everyone knows that effective public policy is a matter of making good decisions and then following through on their implementation, but what is the balance? I land on the side that getting decisions made is easy and that it's in implementation that things get seriously difficult. Decision-making is the fun part. Implementation is relentless, tedious, hard uphill work, against always resistance. It is in the hands of myriad distant others who often dislike what they are told to do and over whom ministers have little control.

Everyone knows that leadership is a matter of both commanding and persuading, but what matters the most? The relationship between commands and signals is that commands are useless unless backed up by signals, whereas signals are often used on their own, when commanding is not possible or productive. Surprisingly, it is the politics of signals and persuasion, rather than of command and force, that is the constant in government action. Signals, messages, projects—this is the stuff of successful government.

Everyone knows that effective governance springs from a combination of good structures and competent leaders, but how much from each? I land on the side that very much depends on persons, leadership, and skills. Some political scientists (in the "new governance" literature) believe that governance has become more complex than it was in simpler olden times and that governments are increasingly constrained in the options available to them.[19] But this is a case of the more things change, the more they are the same. Now, no less than previously, when governments get done what they set themselves to do, it is under good leadership. Power, too, of course, is necessary, but in the end governing remains what Machiavelli explained it to be: a craft.

BOOK THREE

The Problem of Freedom

"The reason for this [that people live contrary to their real interests] is a false conception of liberty . . . liberty is assumed to consist in 'doing what one likes.' The result of such a view is that . . . each individual lives as he likes—or, as Euripides says, For any end he chances to desire. This is a mean conception [of liberty]. To live by the rule of the constitution ought not to be regarded as slavery, but rather as salvation." So said Aristotle, nearly two and a half millennia ago, weighing into a debate that is still running.[1]

Aristotle the philosopher was a son of Athens the democracy (although not born in Athens and living elsewhere much of his life). He lived to the age of sixty-two, dying in 322 BC. Not a long life, yet he left monumental legacies across the whole spectrum of philosophy, ranging from epistemology, physics, biology, medicine, and psychology to ethics, rhetoric, poetry, politics, and more. He also followed the money, going into the service first of Hermias, the tyrant of Assos, and then taking up the invitation of Philip of Macedon to tutor the future Alexander the Great (although hardly for the money alone: he could not refuse the king of the Greeks—but he did decline to follow Alexander when he set off to conquer the world). Later in Athens, he set up his Lyceum, no doubt for paying pupils (but like present-day attention seekers also giving free public lectures), and was finally able to leave a hefty legacy of wealth. In political thinking, he stands as the founding philosopher of democracy, as his teacher, Plato (who also made philosophy a business), stands as the founding philosopher of autocracy.*

---

*Diogenes, in *Lives of the Eminent Philosophers*, says that Aristotle left nearly four hundred written works, which he lists over five pages of titles, and also reproduces his will, which takes a page and a half. Plato's will is half a page long.

Aristotle has been called "aristocratic" in his approach to freedom.[2] He was critical of mass democracy and warned of the "tyranny of the majority," as have later thinkers, such as Tocqueville, whom we will meet in Book Five. He thought that freedom depends on certain capacities in the person, in particular the capacity to deliberate, and that it was natural that not everyone could be free: not slaves, not women, not even "laborers and other such." (But Edith Hall, in *Aristotle's Way*, her love letter to the great man, thinks that if she could sit him down today, he would be persuaded to change his mind on the dignity of women.) We should continue to heed his warning against democratic perversion, but we have moved beyond his brand of aristocratic restrictions in freedom. In this, he was simply wrong, and although it is not long ago that he was generally held to be right, it is now no longer an accepted view that women and workers are naturally unfree. One reason is mass education. With compulsory education to a high standard, we can safely take it that everyone, and not only a minority of educated men, have Aristotle's capacity to deliberate.

Aristotle thought that we humans should live not on our own as individuals but with others in community, that it is only in togetherness with others that individuals can flourish. We each rely for prospering and happiness on the guidance of community, of the *polis* in his Greek. That community should deliver for you and me, but also do so in a way that you and I are not crushed. So there we have the problem of democracy in a nutshell: we need to be governed, and we want to be free. Plato thought the combination impossible and set the freedom part of it aside. That remains the view of present-day autocrats. The sophisticated ones, such as in China, promise the people order, but on the condition that they renounce freedom. What a mean promise, compared to the brazen democratic vision of having both!

Some modern-day libertarians, such as the followers of the philosopher Ayn Rand, who are plentiful in present-day America and elsewhere, also reject the combination. For them, community is tyranny, as is government beyond the bare necessity. That position is logical if you, contrary to Plato and followers, start from freedom as your supreme value but, contrary to Aristotle and followers, think of it as only a matter of doing as you like. Freedom is then what you have if anything that might stand in the way of doing your own thing is removed. You are free if obstacles are absent.

Not so, said Aristotle. His alternative was not to dismiss the value of freedom but to think of it as the presence of relevant conditions. He called it "the constitution," by which he meant, or so we may think, the guiding influence of togetherness.

Our question, then: is freedom what remains if obstacles are absent or what emerges if conditions are present?

Choice

Doing what one likes is a mean conception because it may be something one just happens to want. What we should live by is not likes or even interests, but interests that have more to them than just being wants. The way to do that is to obey the constitution. That sounds like a contradiction; it is as if freedom comes from obeying.

Some modern thinkers—I will call their thinking "choice theory"—have tried to avoid Aristotle's contradiction by sticking to the idea he dismissed, if with a twist. Freedom may not consist in doing what one likes but in *being able* to do what one likes. Isaiah Berlin, the most prominent modern theoretician in this school, on whom more below, said it's about there being no coercion. What one then does with one's liberty is another story, an important story but not an issue of liberty. "Everything is what it is: liberty is liberty, not equality or fairness or justice or culture, or human happiness or a quiet conscience."[3]

However, this just brings in another contradiction. If freedom is the freedom to do as one might wish, it would seem to be freedom for whatever one might wish. One writer who has taken choice theory in earnest and followed it to where it logically leads, to what he calls "real freedom," is Philippe Van Parijs.[4] If it's for whatever one might wish, that might include, for example, to live as a surfer on Malibu Beach. If we truly believe choice theory, we would believe that someone who has that wish has just as much a right to live in that way as someone who is happy to work for a living, and that there should be no obstacles on him in realizing that wish. From this Van Parijs has suggested that governments should give everyone a basic income so that all people are assured the means to actually do as they wish, including to live as a beach bum if that is what they want. But that's just bizarre. We all know that we may not be able to live as surfers on Malibu Beach and that there are many other things in life we cannot have or do, but we do not for that reason cry foul about having been deprived of liberty. Those of us who live under democratic rule, live with thousands of laws and government decrees that prescribe what we should do and cannot do, and handle that with little difficulty.

One reason to think there might be something wanting in choice theory is that most of its followers themselves have not been able to fully believe it. Van Parijs wanted to, but that led him, as happens to professors, to a theoretical proof of something that is obviously false.

Choice clearly has a part in any story of freedom, but most thinkers have found that if choice is a good thing, that is not for the goodness of choice itself. John Stuart Mill, in *On Liberty*, defined freedom as the right to make one's own choices: "Over himself, over his own body and mind, the individual is sovereign. . . . A person should be free to do as he likes in his own concerns. . . ."[5] But that was premised on a view of *why* we should be free to do as we like. For him as a utilitarian, it was because he thought we then have a good chance of finding happiness and because without freedom we are likely to be miserable. Free choice, then, is a means toward something else that is the higher good. And before Mill, Adam Smith, in *The Theory of Moral Sentiments*, the book he published before his more well-known *Wealth of Nations*, took the same view, arguing that what is "the most useful to the individual" is prudence and self-control. That's Aristotle again, just with a different wording. If you are not able to use your freedom of choice well, it will not be of much good to you. Later, Isaiah Berlin started out wanting to be as basic as possible on the meaning of freedom but nevertheless came down on Aristotle's view that freedom is not its own purpose. Already in 1951, in a long letter to a colleague, although offering no definition of freedom and going off in many directions, he observed that "this [when the desire for choice is broken] is the ultimate horror because in such a situation there are no worthwhile motives left: nothing is worth doing or avoiding, the reasons for existing are gone."[6] The horror here is being deprived of the ability to aspire to what is worthwhile. The blessing in being free is not to run around and make choices all the time but that you can relevantly ask yourself what to want.

Liberal thinkers who have moved on from choice theory have come to the same conclusion. One such is the American philosopher John Rawls, hugely respected for *A Theory of Justice*. A just society, he argued, is one in which everyone enjoys basic rights and commands basic goods. Applied to freedom (which was not the concept Rawls addressed himself to), we would say that to be free, a person needs to have the right to make her own choices, but in addition that she must also have the ability to make use of her rights. Another one is the Israeli-British legal philosopher Joseph Raz, whose (not always easily readable) works deserve more broad attention than they have received. He defined freedom as autonomy and autonomy as a matter of being able to exercise choice in so far as it is choice worth making.[7] A free person is not someone who just follows desires such as they are but someone who is "the author of his own life." The Indian economist Amartya Sen and the American philosopher Martha Nussbaum have broadened the grip on choice even more. Together, they have developed what they call the "capabilities approach," which they have applied to both the philosophy of well-being and the analysis of economic purpose. In this approach, freedom resides in "functionings," and functionings are understood to be valuable beings and doings, not any beings and doings one might wish for but beings and doings that make one's life good.[8]

A similar voice, coming from the entirely different experience than of free academic thinking, is that of the Chinese activist for human rights and democracy Liu Xiaobo. He died in prison on July 13, 2017, eight years into an eleven-year term, whereupon the dictators in Beijing set to make him forgotten in the world. In 2010 he was awarded the Nobel Peace Prize, which he was prevented from receiving in person and which earned him the reward at home of a life in confinement. When he died, his ashes were scattered at sea to prevent a grave from being established to which family, followers, and admirers could visit. He was also a formidable philosopher and ethicist. He knew more about freedom and its absence than most, and his fight was obviously for the end of coercion. But in his philosophy, freedom was never about that alone. What makes freedom valuable, he argued, echoing Berlin at his most reflective as well as the post–choice theory thinkers above, is that it enables the individual to aspire to that which has value, and that value in life is found in truth, civic responsibility, and human dignity. Remarkably, for a man rotting alone in a Chinese prison, he was able to think of liberty as a necessary condition for a decent life, but not more than that, not the be all and end all of the alternative system to the one that was oppressing him and others.[9]

Berlin's hypothesis

In the essay "Two Concepts of Liberty" (1958), Isaiah Berlin launched a grand project to salvage choice theory. The two concepts he identified were the "negative" and the "positive," freedom *from* and freedom *to*. In the negative concept, you are free if you are free from coercion. In the positive concept, there is more to it. Being able to do as you like is not the whole story. You are not free unless you are able to use your liberty well so as to make something meaningful of your life. Negative liberty is the understanding Aristotle had rejected but that Berlin set out to defend.

Berlin recommended the negative way of thinking about freedom because he thought it the safer idea politically. Positive liberty, he argued, was more susceptible to being perverted in the sense that it could enable a certain understanding of freedom to be used as an argument in support of nonliberal government. It was a dangerous idea to flirt with. His warning was pertinent. This was at a time when liberal and Marxist philosophies were strongly up against each other, as were democratic and Communist regimes of government, and when a Marxist-Communist theory of freedom that was not grounded in a notion of basic liberty had a strong standing. The logic was typically that what really matters for people, what gives them "real freedom," are social goods, such as guaranteed employment, health care, and free education, and that autocratic government is the price that is paid to give the political regime the power to deliver such goods. When I worked in the United Nations Department of Economic and Social Affairs in the early 1980s, and followed debates in the Economic and Social Council, this relativism of freedom was very much on display. Representatives of Europe's Communist governments would ridicule the "formalistic" freedom of democracy and insist that it was their people who enjoyed the freedom of social equality and safety. (They were wrong even on their own terms, as we now know, but their story then had considerable traction.) Today the Chinse leaders reject "western" notions of liberty, which they with Berlin's language brand as "negative," and insist that they have given the Chinese the positive freedom that comes from stability and from some 600 million of them having been lifted out of poverty.

Against this view, Berlin set out to defend the principle of freedom as not being prevented from making one's own choices, end of story. He worked away on the "Two Concepts" project for the rest of his life. The full flow of that project came to light only after his death when its many works, long dispersed here and there, were brought together in a single volume. We could then see that he started with the notion of freedom as the absence of coercion as his hypothesis, that he tried throughout to defend that hypothesis, but that as he worked on, this defense was gradually weakened.[10] In fact, it was doomed already ahead of the project's launch, as we have seen above in the 1951 letter.*

Even in "Two Concepts," in which negative liberty is defended as the bastion of freedom, positive liberty, although raged against, and in pretty intemperate language, is not thrown out. So certainly in the introduction to his *Four Essays on Liberty*, ten years later, in which he replied to critics. Negative and positive liberty are both attractive ideas. The primacy of one does not lead to the rejection of the other. They "start at no great logical distance [but] the fundamental sense of freedom is freedom from chains. . . . The rest is extension. . . ."[11]

Freedom is now complex—what is extension is not nothing—and it is not easily said just what it is. In a retrospective essay written in 1996, freedom has come to rest on negative and positive liberty in pretty equal measure, although still with the qualification that the danger of "frightful perversions" is greater in positive than in negative liberty.[12]

---

*It is, to be fair, not quite right to criticize Berlin's definition of freedom since the question he was addressing himself to was not really What is freedom? but How should we think about freedom? His difficulty was only that he was never able to fully reconcile his political position on how to think about freedom with a solid philosophical position on the meaning of freedom.

The story line in these works, as I think they should be read, is that the point in separating out negative liberty is that something in the broader complexity of freedom is *fundamental*. Negative liberty is not everything there is to freedom, but it is where freedom starts. The way to protect against "perversion" is to insist on the *primacy* of negative liberty as the first and most basic condition. That makes a lot of sense when we bear in mind how Fascist and Communist rulers have wanted to persuade their people that they have "real freedom" without basic human rights. This clear sense of where things start and what comes first—the "fundamental sense"—is what should be taken as the lasting and important result of Berlin's project.

For the rest, a fair reading of his work is that he started with strict choice theory as his hypothesis but that in the course of his project the hypothesis falls. He left us with an unfinished project.

Aristotle, then, survived the most sophisticated attempt to prove him wrong. Well and good, but there is still that circle to square that Aristotle left us to sort out, that freedom comes from obeying.

Boudon's reason

Choice theory is a branch of a more comprehensive theory of the human condition. This is the view that human beings are by nature rational in the meaning that they know their own good and for the most part are able to manage their affairs as well as is possible in their own interest.

If that is your outlook, choice theory is the way you would be likely to think about freedom. If we humans are by instinct rational, there is no reason for others to be concerned with what any individual might aspire to. He or she is himself or herself the competent judge of that. What we should worry about is whether he or she has the space to follow his or her aspirations, whatever they might be. If people can make their own choices, they will make good choices. As long as they can do as they like, they are fine. It is if something stands in the way of their free choice that they are in trouble.

But if that is not where you start, if you do not think rationality is instinctive and that therefore choice may well go wrong for you, then choice theory would not be your thing. Choice theory just collapses into nothing without the assumption of instinctive rationality.

It is no wonder that Aristotle did not take to this way of thinking. He started from a different view of human nature. It is not by the absence of influence from others that we are best positioned to live sensibly, but by deliberation with others to reach a sound understanding of our own good and a safe maneuvering through the inevitably complicated maze of choice and decision-making.

The anti-Aristotelian view of human rationality has won a broad following in social philosophy and in the social sciences, under the brand of "rational choice." Fortunately, that is not the only way to think about rationality, and also not the best way. When I arrived in Paris in 1996 to start a year of research there, I was invited by the sociologist Raymond Boudon to a seminar on the for me then astonishing theme of *la rationalité des valeurs*.[13] That was the beginning of a long friendship with Boudon, and also my introduction to a theory that says that a rational person is someone who makes life choices, large and small, according to good sense. He sets himself goals that he sees to be sensible and uses the means that are available to him wisely. The problem of rationality, then, goes to the choice of goals as well as the use of means. In rational choice, goals (or preferences, as these people like to say) are given; they are, in the theoretical language, "exogenous." What we make choices about that are subject to rationality is only the use of means for, in the language of the theory, the maximization of utility. Not so, argued Boudon; there is no rationality without rationality in ends as well as in means.

Over many years and in innumerable books and articles, Boudon, associating himself with a long tradition going back to Aristotle, with later highlights in the works of, for example, René Descartes, Immanuel Kant, and Max Weber, elaborated on *la raison*. The key words in this oeuvre are "reasons" and "good reasons," and eventually also "common sense."[14]

Not many thinkers who are serious about the human condition would probably have much time for rational choice in its expansive understanding. Who in their right mind would think that human rationality is *really* no more than a matter of instrumental effectiveness? Nor does that view have much support in the history of philosophy. Descartes, in *Discours de la méthode*, started his whole exercise from the view that it is "good sense," and not, for example, smartness or singlemindedness, that is "the one thing in the world best shared." Max Weber included *Wert* (value) on a par with *Zweck* (instrumentality) in his conception of rationality, the duality Boudon elaborated on by including in his notion of reason decisions about intentions as well as actions.

Recently, rational choice thinking has been given a much welcome, and belatedly Aristotelian, body blow by the psychologists Daniel Kahneman and Amos Tversky, who have shown that the rational *homo economicus* is an entirely fictional character.[15] We humans are prone to making mistakes about what is in our best interest because of confusion and because mechanisms of bias are at work in our minds. We lie and cheat, and we cheat on ourselves. The preferences we go by are often the ones that win out in competition with others not because they are superior but because they are familiar, easy, or convenient. And because we are prone to misunderstanding ourselves, we are also prone to being manipulated by others. It is just wishful thinking that we, if left to our own instincts, will make good choices.

From this has followed a turn in economics, and perhaps in other social sciences, toward "behavioral" theory, which we may well see as a return to Aristotelian wisdom. I might like to think of myself as a capable person who is able to sort out my own ways by my own good sense, and probably so would you. But we would both be wrong. If I appeal only to myself, I am at risk of falling into one of two traps. The first one is haste. I would be in danger of deciding too quickly and of not thinking ahead as carefully as I should. The second trap is the temptation of convenience. I let myself be persuaded by what I am hoping for and fail to consider counterarguments I should have considered. The remedy is to trust not only yourself but also to consult and listen to others: family, friends, peers. That slows things down and makes it more likely that you consider all relevant arguments and listen also to the unwelcome ones. This form of togetherness, the habit of discussing with and consulting others, is the essence of what I throughout refer to as *deliberation*.

Obviously, we do not want to give up on the aspiration to human rationality—and we should not even give up on rational choice, properly managed. But if people do not make good choices just by being left to themselves, how do they do it? With the help of guidance, said Aristotle, "the rule of the constitution." That's where *la raison* Boudon style takes us.

The Boudon view and rational choice have something in common that informs the way all rationalists see the world: an inclination to think of people as autonomous actors in life with the gift of sound judgment. But this is also as far as the common ground reaches. So different are these approaches that it is not fruitful to see them to be competing theories at all. Neither is true or false or right or wrong compared to the other; they are not comparable in that way.

Rational choice has much going for it, but as a methodological tool rather than a theory in any proper meaning. It is not a proposition about human nature except for the entirely obvious, such as that most people out shopping want value for money. It is rather a device to peel away the complexities of human agency to enable the modeling of behavior on the simplest possible assumptions, such as that values and preferences are taken as given and to be all of equal dignity. Since our job in the social sciences is to make sense of the world by portraying it as simpler than it is—everyone knows that the world is complex, and no one needs a social scientist to tell him that—we often work from simplifying assumptions. Rational choice is an admirably logical system that does a job, but that is also all it does. As a tool, it has proved its usefulness, as is in evidence in the best of economic science. Gary Becker, for example, pioneered the use of economic analysis in areas of study that were mostly thought of as being outside of economics, such as family life, and demonstrated its usefulness there too.[16] For example, one reason birth rates are now very low in many affluent populations is that the opportunity cost of children has gone up.[17] That's an observation rational choice makes sense of. But it is also because many parents have fewer children than they want to have and aim to have. That is not explicable by rational choice. Rational choice theorizing, then, can tell us something about some of the ways people are likely to make choices, but not how life works, all things considered. Imposing simplifying assumptions on, for example, the observation of family life is helpful for teasing out that something, and that's the job those assumptions do.

A good theorist will work from simplifying assumptions without investing moral meaning into them. It may be fruitful to assume preferences to be given, but using that tool of analysis does not oblige any thinking man or woman to embrace the belief that all preferences *really* are equal. The confusion comes in when theorists take their admiration for the elegant simplicity of rational choice to extremes and start to think of simplifying assumptions as pronouncements on the human condition.

Boudon's approach is something else. It is a proposition about the nature of rationality. The question that follows from rational choice, properly applied, is this: if we assume carefully calculating, perfectly informed, self-serving makers of choice, what would they do in this or that situation? The question thinkers in the line from Aristotle to Boudon ask is this: what does it take for people to live sensibly? In rational choice, rationality is a given. For Aristotelians, it is the mystery.

It is useful to think about human action in terms of goals and means. We set ourselves goals and use available means to advance them. Boudon's *raison* is built on a set of ideas about how this may be done sensibly.

The choice of goals is often thought to be of a different kind than the choice of means: we apply values to the choice of goals and calculus to the choice of means. But that's a false division. Values obviously come into the choice of goals, but not only values. We also calculate. If you live on a working man's salary, you do not set yourself the goal of acquiring a villa in St. James's in London. Calculus obviously comes into the choice of means, but not calculus only. No sensible person believes that ends justify means.

So when we go through life making choices, we make choices about goals as well as about means. There is nothing "exogenous" about preferences in real life. In both cases, we go about it in much the same way by applying a mixture of normative and instrumental considerations (plus, probably, a good deal of instinct, intuition, and guesswork). My ideal as a rationalist is that people should mostly be able to do that with good sense, but I do not take it as a given that they do. I think instead that it is a pretty difficult matter, to put it carefully, to sort out one's aims in life. There are unreflective lives, shortsighted lives, silly lives, greedy lives, ruthless lives, mean lives, evil lives, destructive lives, self-destructive lives, criminal lives, futile lives, selfish lives, and so on. People sometimes live in ways they want to avoid. How might they be able to do that? Other people, maybe most of us most of the time, live pretty sensibly. If so, how do we do that? People who live reflectively, prudently, and productively are reasonably in control of their lives and pretty likely to be sensible on their own terms. How do they manage to be in control?

Good choice would seem to depend on finding sensible answers to three questions. First, a question of *worthiness*. What is it worth aspiring to, investing resources in, and doing? Second, a question of *propriety*. What is it acceptable and right to aim for and to do, and what is within the bounds of decency? And third, a question of *effectiveness*. What works and what is productive?

Worthiness goes primarily to the choice of goals, but not only. We sometimes attach autonomous value to the way things are done, as in the saying, "If it's worth doing, it is worth doing well." Propriety goes primarily to means, to what it is proper or not to do, but again not only. It is not immoral to aspire to be a great tenor on the world stage, but if you have no singing voice, it's not a sensible ambition. Effectiveness also goes primarily to means, but there are also more or less effective or ineffective goals. It is ineffective to set yourself goals that are either too modest or too ambitious to be useful.

Reason is a competence: you see it in people who make life choices that are worthy, proper, and effective, and who balance these concerns in a sensible way. "We must reason about the true goal and about all the evidence to which we refer our opinion (said the Greek philosopher Epicurus); for otherwise everything will be full of confusion and disorder."[18]

If we take it that it is difficult both to decide what is good and what is effective, how do people go about living lives of reason? In rational choice, what people are thought to have in mind is to maximize their utility. But if it is more complicated, if they balance the maximization of utility against the demands of worthiness and propriety, how do they do it? How are things arranged in their minds?

It is not that reasonable people are not self-serving; it is that they are not *only* self-serving. The way to think about reason is not to dismiss self-interest but to not stop with it. Self-interested effectiveness is obviously essential and entirely relevant to someone who sets out to live sensibly—but not sufficient. Reason goes beyond instinct and includes also the ability to temper self-interest in the choice of ends, say, to avoid blind egoism, and to temper effectiveness in the choice of means, say, to avoid unbridled ruthlessness.

Reason, then, is grounded in restrained self-interest—in Adam Smith's prudence and self-control again.

Restrained self-interest rests on various subabilities. It is still, again, self-interest. One component therefore is the ability to calculate and make good guesses about effectiveness. In the insistence that there is more to it, we should not skip first base and get so fancy as to overlook that whatever a reasonable life is, it is also an effective life.

But that's not yet to live sensibly. If all you were capable of were calculus and effectiveness, you would be, in the words of Amartya Sen, "a rational fool." There is the second ability of restraint. That rests on a sensitivity that some ambitions are better than others and some means right and others wrong, and from a willingness to abide by such sentiments. When we act out of restraint, we are paying attention, for example, to the long-term good, to others, to future generations or to the environment, or to decency, altruism, or charity. That's not something we can just assume comes with human nature. It is something each of us must master. It is after all about the individual holding back on what might be to her benefit.

There is no mystery to the pursuit of self-interest, but restraint is not obvious. The sensitivities that enable self-control sit, in Boudon's language, as *beliefs* in the individual's mind. Beliefs are reasons for thinking and doing. If I believe that I should always do what adds to my own utility, I have given myself a reason for never doing anything that does not come with some benefit to myself.

The ability to restraint is grounded in a specific class of beliefs that are commonly called values and norms. These are maxims of a higher order that make themselves felt from the back of our awareness and enable the individual to discriminate in more practical matters. Boudon calls them "axiological" beliefs. Values are beliefs that help us to distinguish between good and bad. Norms are beliefs that help us to distinguish between right and wrong.

What makes a belief a reason for the individual to be swayed in practical concerns is that it is a belief he has faith in, a belief he believes in, so to speak. That's what lets him be guided by it without necessarily doing so for only reasons of calculus or for fear that others will sanction him. With values and norms comes an awareness of difference between good and bad and right and wrong and a disposition to reflect on worthiness and propriety in one's decision-making. With faith in one's particular values and norms comes the inclination to follow up on that awareness in thought and action. The goodness of equality becomes a value for me if I make the belief that equality is a good thing *my* belief. The beliefs that I make mine are those that have some power for me, those I have faith in.

I call this *faith* because in the end there is something intangible about beliefs and their force. When a belief is established in the mind of a person, it has some force for her that cannot be fully pinned down. She *knows* it to express what is good, right, or true. She *knows* she should live by it. She *knows* that others, too, ought to share it and live by it.

Faith, then, first, separates those values and norms that you make yours from those you discard. In various ways—from parents, from teachers, from priests, from scientists, from celebrities, from politicians, from conventions, from laws—society offers you a menu of beliefs to consider. Some recommend the belief that equality is a good thing, others that it's each man for himself. Even values and norms are things we do not just have but must choose. The values and norms you make yours are those you attach faith to.

In addition, faith enables you to actually live by those values and norms you make yours. It is what enables you to do in fact as your axiological beliefs recommend in theory, including when that costs something. For example, a speed limit of 70 miles per hour on highways tells you how to drive, but it still takes something more than knowing the rule to actually do as it says when on the road, or to overspeed only moderately. It takes the backing of a principle that you accept as authoritative, such as "It is wrong to not obey the law."

The inner competence to reason, then, rests ultimately in this elusive faculty, which I call faith, a faculty that enables the person to actually believe in her beliefs and make them signposts for her opinions and actions. We need something to resort to in order to find the strength of conviction to *really* accept principles of right and wrong and get beyond only paying lip service to laudable ideas. If you have faith in a belief, that belief presents itself to you as a reason by which you make decisions. Values and norms that you have faith in are reasons behind your decisions about what to aspire to and how to go about it. You are now not deciding hither and dither in the dark just because you have the right to do as you like, but going about your business in ways informed by guiding reasons. You are on the way to a life of reason.

However, you are not quite there. A person who is in control of his own life is doing not simply what he has reasons to do, but what he has *good* reasons to do. If faith makes of a belief a reason for choice, how can one know that what faith puts to one as a reason is a good reason? Blind faith is clearly not the stuff of reason.

The alternative to blind faith is evidence-based faith. You may be so fortunate as to possess the ability to take your own beliefs about right and wrong seriously and to more or less live as you learn, but as a rational person you still want to discriminate in your use of that ability. You want your faith to be invested in such beliefs that there are *good* reasons to have faith in. Resort to evidence is the rational way to decide which, in the larger menu of potential beliefs, to make *your* beliefs. Which leads us to a final question: where does good evidence come from? We need evidence, said Epicurus, but we must also reason about the evidence to which we refer our opinions.

The tyranny of wants

What you obey when you make a choice could be a coercive force that dictates to you what to do and not do. If so, obviously—and this is Berlin's "fundamental sense"—you are not free. But even in the absence of coercion, your choices are still in obedience to something, at the very least to your wants (or aims or goals or intentions or preferences). If your wants are not your own and you still obey them, you are also not free.

The problem with speaking about freedom and reason in the same breath is that things may start to sound restrictive and moralistic, as if to suggest that freedom conforms to some specific and narrow morality. But the meaning of Boudon's *raison* is that the choices you make are, first, your own choices and, second, choices you make for good reasons. Reason is not defined by a certain content of choice. It rests on the capacity for choice, and that capacity includes freedom from being pushed around by wants that have fallen down upon you from you know not where. It is not that reason lies in a tight space of petty bourgeois limitations but that your choices, whatever they are, are grounded in a sound understanding in yourself and of your own good. You want to be the master, but you are only your own master if, in addition to not someone else being master, you are yourself in charge of your thinking as well as your doing. Making choices that are worthy, proper, and effective does not make them any less your choices. It is not for the privilege of living a shallow life that we want freedom, that we fight for freedom, that people die for freedom.

It must be correct to treat the inability to be in control of intentions as a form of unfreedom. A political dictatorship denies you the ability to act freely. A psychological dictatorship denies you the ability to decide why to act. There are dangers to one's freedom in one's inner self. Any psychologist will be aware of that. The classical philosophers, from Plato on down, generally thought psychological freedom a necessary (although mostly not sufficient) condition of personal freedom. The Stoic tradition is directed to the wisdom of liberating oneself from one's wants, rather than indulging them. So is Buddhist thinking. In the Lord's Prayer, millions of Christians day in and day out beg not to be led into temptation and to be delivered from evil. Ever since the sociologist Émile Durkheim more than a century ago mapped the social correlates of suicide, sociologists have known that the individual who lives in a state of unrestrained liberty lives in mortal danger. This person, far from being the master of his destiny, is likely to be lost in an overwhelming world he cannot comprehend, without the anchorage he needs for purpose, reflectiveness, and power of action. "Even though the idea of freedom is sometimes formulated independently of values, preferences and reasons, freedom cannot be fully appraised without some idea of what a person prefers and has reason to prefer. . . . Rationality as the use of reasoned scrutiny cannot but be central to the idea and assessment of freedom. . . . To deny that accommodation . . . would involve, in effect, a basic denial of freedom of thought [and have] the effect of arbitrarily narrowing permissible 'reasons for choice,' and this certainly can be the source of a substantial 'unfreedom.' . . . The 'rational fool' is, in this sense, also a victim of repression."[19]

There are many ways beliefs may be irrational in the sense of not being your own and still operating in your mind as wants. You may be addicted or compulsive. The alcoholic who knows he should resist booze but is unable to because he wants a drink is not free. The compulsive shopper who buys things for the sake of buying is not free. I knew a compulsive shopper. Her small home was crammed with detergents, shampoos, toiletries, paper towels, and other stuff that she would buy whenever on offer and pile up at home so that there was hardly space left to live. This is not a trivial predicament. She was under no coercion, far from it: the supermarkets offered no end of choice; there were no restrictions of rationing; she had money to spend. But she was self-destroying. Some thinkers, the economic historian Avner Offer for one, who are pessimistic about modern consumerism, warn that there is an effect of increasing abundance, once it gets beyond a level of reasonable material comfort, to cause people to lose control and become slaves of excessive passions.[20]

Even if your wants are not pathological, they may still be irrational. You may be the victim of intelligent advertisement, propaganda, or manipulation. If so, wants are planted in your mind by others for their own purpose. No one who lives under advanced capitalism can be blind to the power of advertisement. No one who knows anything about Fascist or Communist totalitarianism should have any illusions about the power of propaganda. Germans who screamed in adulation of Hitler may have though they loved him, but they were not free agents. Nor are the Chinese who, with the machinations of censorship and propaganda, go jingoistic under the influence of Xi Jinping's "China Dream" of "national rejuvenation." No one who observes the collusion of money and social media in contemporary democracies can have any doubt that there are forces of manipulation at work. The voter at the ballot box may not know it but could well be nudged to voting as someone else has schemed.

Absence of coercion is a condition of freedom, the first condition. But not a sufficient condition. Once you can make your own choices, you are still only free if the choices you make really *are* your own choices: if you are not a puppet of demons in your soul or of manipulations, open or hidden, by others who are able to plant beliefs in your mind.

That, then, is the link between freedom and reason. You are not an autonomous person in charge of yourself unless you are in charge of the whys of your life. And you are not in charge of those whys unless you can apply reason to your decisions about them.

The free citizen

What might Aristotle really have had in mind when he spoke about the blessing of living by the constitution in the context of freedom? It would seem that he was thinking of freedom as a way of living, as something one *does*. That's different from the freedom of choice theory. Here, freedom is something one *has*; it comes from having rights, while what one does with one's rights is something else, outside of the meaning of freedom.

The freedom of choice theory is the freedom of the consumer, the individual, on her own, concerned with her own utility, in demand of the right to do as she wishes for her own good, unrestrained. In Aristotle's universe, as well as that of, for example, Raz, Sen, and Nussbaum, and Liu Xiaobo, freedom is in the life of the citizen. For Aristotle, living by the rule of the constitution is to be a citizen, a free citizen immersed in his society and in the *polis* that enables him to live his own life.[21]

The free citizen possesses the freedom of the consumer, the right to do as he likes. That, however, is a very peculiar kind of freedom. If you don't have it, if you live under coercion, your life is stunted. But once you have it, it is in itself pretty trivial. He who builds for himself no more than a life of living as he likes for his own utility makes for himself a life without more meaning than the satisfaction of possibly unreflected wants.

Having the right to do something is not a reason to do it. The citizen in a democracy has the right to not vote (except in a few countries where voting is obligatory), but that is not a reason to not bother. Living in a society of free speech, I have the right to say almost anything to almost anyone. But that is not a reason for me to go around offending people. If you are an obnoxious person who offends others willy-nilly, it is not much of a defense to stamp your feet and shout back that I do it because I have the right to.

The consumer takes charge of her rights and does with them what happens to be her pleasure. The citizen takes charge of her rights and uses them for purposes she has good reasons to pursue. Of these two, it is the citizen who is master and the consumer who is slave.

What is unfreedom?

History has been on Berlin's side in that obtaining freedom has often been seen as a matter of sweeping away coercion. That's the freedom people over the ages have been willing to give their lives for and that they in many countries continue to take to the streets for. I have said it is fundamental but not everything, which is not to belittle what is fundamental.

Coercion and its absence have historically been linked to the national condition. In the great national movements in nineteenth-century Europe, the battle for freedom was the battle for national autonomy.[22] In the twentieth century, decolonization was a movement for freedom under national independence. In China, in 1949, the nation was liberated from "the century of humiliation" under foreign domination and occupation. The Cuban revolution of 1957 was fought in the name of liberty from American domination. In Europe, after the fall of the Berlin Wall in 1989, the central nations won freedom with the liberation from Soviet overrule. In the Middle East, the Palestinian and Kurdish nations are fighting for freedom in the form of national autonomy.

The idea that a people cannot have freedom unless they live in a national home of their own makes sense. Domination is coercion. Take control nationally, and the coercion of foreign domination is no more.

The freedom for which Machiavelli's life was a quest, in the subtitle of Erica Benner's fine biography—*Be Like the Fox: Machiavelli's Lifelong Quest for Freedom*—was from internal coercion, the freedom of the republic, as opposed to the coercion of monarchy. In a republic, he and others at the time thought, people can live in freedom under their own state.

The French Revolution, until it went bad, had as its aim a constitutional monarchy, which is a system of divided powers at the top to abolish the autocratic power of the monarch. That would enable the people, it was thought, to live in freedom as envisaged in the Declaration of the Rights of Man and of the Citizen (1789), which again became the freedom of Mill and Berlin: the right to do what does not harm others. Freedom in this meaning would also have been an inspiration of the February Revolution in Russia in 1917, which not only tamed but abolished the monarchy (but which was overtaken by a second revolution later in the year to restore tyranny, if in a different guise). Toward the end of the twentieth century, freedom came to one country after another in Latin America as military dictatorships were overturned in favor of democracy.

People do fight for national freedom, but that, regrettably, does not ensure personal liberty. In the Italian city-states, republican rule may have offered citizens more freedom than under monarchy, but freedom in any modern sense would still be in short supply, or in supply for only a minority of the population. Cuba did free itself from American domination, but the people of Cuba did not attain freedom, nor did the Chinese just because Chinese rulers took control. Whether national autonomy for Palestine or Kurdistan is likely to come with freedom for the respective peoples is perhaps less than obvious.

Today, in a globalized world, we can probably not even take national autonomy to be a condition of freedom. The structures that may or may not be coercive, notably economic ones, are increasingly supernational, and nation-states may have less capacity to being the protectors of their citizens' liberty.

The absence of internal political coercion brings us nearer to personal liberty. Where there is well-functioning democracy, people have political freedom, and the "fundamental sense" will, ideally, have been secured. But does democracy carry us all the way to Aristotelian freedom?

Boudon was optimistic about history as a march of progress. He thought, in a Darwinian manner, that beliefs over time are tested through social experience and that the more solid ones survive as shared beliefs in the form of common sense. One of his final works was, in its subtitle, a "eulogy" to common sense.[23]

But that must be too optimistic. Reason is not, as assumed in choice theory, instinctive, but nor is it, as Boudon seems to have hoped, something that is just perfected over time as humanity moves on. It is something that we must work on and create and re-create in our own lives.

What, then, is it that is missing if you are not free? First, again, and obviously, personal sovereignty in the meaning of being free from coercion. But what more?

In my study of the Chinese political economy, I've had opportunity to reflect on this. I have concluded that the People's Republic remains a hard dictatorship and that the people who live under its rule are not free. That is not entirely obvious when we look at the way many Chinese people now live and is rejected, obviously, by the regime and the people who speak for it. They argue that Chinese people, or many of them, in the reformed and growing economy, do have pretty free lives and are succeeding in getting that boast believed. *The Economist* put it this way: "After the 1989 protests in Tiananmen Square, and their subsequent bloody put-down, the deal China's leaders offered the country changed: stay out of politics and you can do almost anything else you want."[24]

If we follow choice theory, *The Economist* has it right. Even I concede that: "Many Chinese, notably in the urban population and its middle and upper strata, can live distinctly modern lives. Many people have regulated work and leisure and some or much discretionary income. They have property and are home owners and consumers. They have household appliances and flat-screen TVs. They have smartphones, computers and internet access with a great deal of content. They can dress as they want and enjoy international music and entertainment. They have holidays. They travel the country and the world. They go to other cities on fast trains. Those lower on the ladder can aspire to move up."

However, that's still not freedom. The people I describe in that paragraph can, in practical daily affairs, pretty much do as they wish. But they do not live in freedom. "They, or many of them, may have joined the world of modern consumerism but not that of modern autonomy."[25] They have a good deal of choice, but there is still the matter of human dignity that Liu Xiaobo was so careful to add to his reflections on liberty.

A small group of friends gather for an evening of togetherness and discussion. They are six or seven, men as it happens, and they gather from time to time to talk about world affairs, cultural trends, governance in their little municipality, and other matters that take their fancy. They enjoy each other's company. They discuss well, and eat and drink well. Nothing unusual about this, but there is still drama at play. Their evenings are serious and jolly, the discussions robust and opinions sometimes harsh. The local mayor is a fool, and a story is told about him to rapturous glee. The prime minister, on her recent visit to Beijing, brought humiliation on the country and betrayed its reputation of standing up for human rights. They are not unreasonable men and recognize both difficulties and successes in governance, but also voice their criticisms freely of anyone they think deserves it. They listen to each other, correct each other on facts, and fault each other on opinions. They *deliberate*. The ancient Greeks called such gatherings *symposia* (although the orator Demosthenes said that Greek symposia were largely exercises in revelry, sex, and drinking).

Gatherings such as this, and larger events and meetings, or shorter encounters in other settings and circumstances, again and again, continuously, are the guts of free lives. The men around the table that evening do not think of it in that way; they are just having a good time and enjoying each other's curiosity about their world. Still, what they are doing is the doing of freedom. It's not mysterious, it's not abstract: freedom is a quality in daily and ordinary life. These men need not reflect on it being possible that they get together and exchange news and opinions freely. They are under no threat of coercion. It is obvious to them that they can criticize the vanity of the mayor, the prime minister, world leaders, and make fun of them as they will; that they can question their doings and policies, even their sanity; and that there is no risk to them in so doing. They do not need to be secretive or to hush up or disguise their opinions. The meetings I describe here, which are real, happen to take place in a small town in Norway. There, obviously, friends can get together for discussions without fear or worry. And they do; they make use of their liberty.

But say you are Chinese and live in an ordinary Chinese town. You are perhaps no less curious than the Norwegians about your world, near and far. You may have friends who are equally engaged. You want to understand the economic policy of the national government, the land management of the town government, and how far you can trust the news on state television. You and your friends may well gather for evenings of discussion and enjoy robust exchange and the making fun of pompous leaders, and you may well encounter no trouble for so doing.

But there is a difference. Gathering for an evening of discussion is not obvious and not something you can do without fear or worry. There is threat hanging in the air. You must count on the local security services being aware of it. They may not be, but you must expect that they might be. If you make it a regular habit of gathering, you can be pretty sure that "they" know and that what you are doing will start to look like organized subversion. It is likely that someone will invite you for a cup of tea and ask what you are up to, and correct your ways if they think you are on the wrong path. You may well discuss government policy and, like your Norwegian counterparts, criticize national or local bigwigs, but you can't do it without risk. You may be with good friends, but you cannot escape the suspicion that one or two of you might be informers. So even if you can gather and discuss, which is not obvious, you cannot exchange information freely. There are limits: questions that cannot be asked and sayings that cannot be said.

And there is another difference. If the Norwegian friends come up against something they don't know, they might bring out a computer or smartphone and look it up on the internet. So could the Chinese friends, but the internet they can look into is one of censorship and propaganda. The Norwegians' internet is imperfect, but the Chinese's version in addition is systematically biased. How, for example, can ordinary Chinese form a proper opinion about their government when they do not know, as most do not, that this government is maintaining a police state of extreme stricture in the western province of Xinjiang? Again, it is not abstract or mysterious. Unfreedom, like freedom, is in daily and ordinary life.

What friends are doing when they meet and discuss is to collaborate in seeking knowledge and understanding. Liberty is not just something to indulge in as a commodity of consumption; it is a tool for the arduous job of cultivating reason. That starts from an awareness, unspoken, no doubt, of one's own shortcomings, the awareness that Kahneman, Tversky, and others have turned into theory; the awareness that if you are to know your world, you cannot trust yourself only, you need to test your understandings against those of others. They are Aristotelians; they know that collective wisdom is superior to individual wisdom. That's why they get together and don't just sit each on their own and figure things out. In their discussions, they are working, in my language, on problems of worthiness, propriety, and effectiveness, seeking to articulate values and norms, and looking for evidence that can be used to back up faith. Obviously, they don't think of their evenings in these terms, but this is what they are up to. They are there, together, in a quest for the good sense that Descartes praised.

In free countries, people do this freely, and they express themselves freely. They can do that because of the absence of coercion. When they get together, that is in circumstances in which they have a fair chance of advancing their understanding of their world. The absence of coercion enables that but is not the end of it. It is the condition for their exchange to work as a method of cultivating understanding.

In the Chinese setting, this is again different. Because coercion is not absent but a part of the friends' reality, there is less availability to the seeking of knowledge and understanding. Not only is it more difficult to get together, not only is information less freely available, it is also more difficult, even if they can get together and when they can seek information, to use togetherness and information effectively. Discussions and information seeking therefore work less ruthlessly in the churning of opinions, knowledge, values, norms, evidence, and faith. What coercion denies them, then, is not just free speech, although that too, but also the access to understanding.

And there is yet another difference. When the Norwegian friends get together, they do that within, obviously, their own *polis*, within their particular political community. For them, that happens to be a culture of citizenship. It is a culture in which citizens see each other and think of each other as equals, pretty much, one in which they are used to relatively good governance and where there are traditions of transparency and freedom of information. It is a culture in which the stories people tell each other is that they matter, that it matters that they participate, that it matters and is worth their while to make themselves informed, that it matters that they express their opinions. It is a culture in which deliberation is ingrained in the way of life. That culture sits in the woodworks as an ether that works its way by osmosis into the minds of individuals and tells them, for example, that voting in elections is the thing to do, that making one's opinions known is the thing to do, that debating public affairs is the thing to do, that making oneself informed about the world, the large one out there and the small one nearby, is the thing to do. These men benefit from the influence of a democratic culture.

The absence of coercion makes it possible for people to get together in ways that enable them to improve their understandings of their world. A democratic culture encourages them to make use of that possibility. What grows in this meeting ground of Berlin's fundamental sense and Aristotle's living by the constitution is the freedom of citizenship. The ancients, including Aristotle, did not have much faith in ordinary people. Socrates argued that "the many" have no capacity for understanding justice, beauty, and truth. But we can now be more hopeful. Alfred Marshall, the father of modern economics, thought, as we will see in Book Four, that it was not ability but poverty that in his time denied the "lower classes" any share of a "refined and cultured life." I am arguing that we should think the common man or woman, on the one hand free from coercion and on the other with the support of a culture of deliberation, as capable of aspiring to the life the Athenians thought available only to a few.

Although far from mysterious and abstract, we do have theoretical language to resort to for explaining what it is that is available to the Norwegian friends and not, or less so, to the Chinese ones. The German philosopher Jürgen Habermas calls it "communicative rationality." He has built a vast philosophical-political edifice around a basic idea of deliberation (sometimes called discourse). Knowledge and understanding—reason—depend on deliberation. It is in human nature that we need to work things over in interaction with others. Consensus, cooperation, and social order depend on discourse.

THE WAY OF LIFE AMONG THE FOLKS IN THE VALLEY

When I joined Lillehammer University College as an adjunct professor in 2009, I gave an inaugural lecture under the title above, in Norwegian *Levemåten hos døla-folket før og nå*. The valley in question is Gudbrandsdalen, which cuts north from the town of Lillehammer through the country's rural heartland. I was exploring some of the region's cultural habits and beliefs.

My reference was the works of the great sociologist and ethnographer Eilert Sundt, who observed life in this region, and elsewhere in Norway, in the 1850s and 1860s. The people then lived in dire poverty but, found Sundt, sensibly. He observed what he called *skikker*, the habits and conventions people refer to for organizing their lives, and saw that they maintained *skikker* that helped them to make sense of their conditions, such as they were.

My reference was further two powerful but opposite predictions from two eminent thinkers. Karl Marx predicted that under advanced capitalism, surplus would flow to capital and workers would be relegated to impoverishment. John Maynard Keynes predicted that ordinary earners would escape the tyranny of material needs and use this freedom to enrich their lives culturally.

The Harvard economist Benjamin Friedman has suggested that life for ordinary Americans has turned out in support of Marx's prediction. Surplus has flowed to the rich and super-rich, while ordinary people's living standards have stagnated and their lives become dominated by "socially induced consumption preferences."

My question was whether Marx's prediction holds if you look to a very different place. I was observing life locally and in a polity where modern capitalism has a different footprint. In this valley, people have the kind of surplus Keynes predicted. Do they then, as he also predicted, turn to cultural enrichment? Or do they, as Friedman observes in America, stay hooked on consumption preferences that run ahead of them?

Conditions in the European periphery I was looking into differ from Friedman's America in many ways. It has become a pretty classless society (not the case in Sundt's time). There is equality: the rich are not really rich and the poor not really poor. Government has a strong and near presence through small municipalities with big powers. Most people, at least most men, will hold some kind of municipal office during their lifetime, if not on the council, then on some of the numerous municipal committees, in a democracy that, although not direct, is Athenian in participation. They will have, as Aristotle recommended, the experience, in some measure, not only of being ruled but also of ruling.

Life in the communities up and down the valley is, as in Sundt's time, arranged by *skikker*. And the contemporary *skikker* are in support of Keynes more than of Marx. The folks live well, have good houses, drive fine cars, holiday abroad, and enjoy it all. But it is not consumption that defines their quality of life. They turn their surplus into activity and participation. There is vibrant voluntarism in clubs, associations, and charity. People join up to arrange a myriad of cultural events, such as evenings of song and music, of readings, of drama, of discussions. There are excursions, art exhibitions, local opera, festivals of culture. And where some get out to arrange, the *skikk* is for others to get out to attend. These people enjoy their affluence, manage it well, and use it to partake (in a term we will meet in Book Four) of "a refined and cultured life." If we were to say with two words what defines their way of life, it would not be "having things" but "getting together."

I was engaging in a piece of social archaeology. As it is enough for the archaeologist to find a chip of pottery to disprove a theory that there was no population in an area in a certain time, it is enough to observe a cultured way of life in a small locality to disprove Marx's theory that advanced capitalism necessarily results in proletarianization. A single observation does not prove Keynes's opposite theory, but it does prove (and I suspect there are many similar local observations to be made, including in Friedman's America) that his prediction is not impossible.

Social stability does not just happen; it must be created and re-created, and a condition is that members of society engage in discourse with each other about societal concerns. It is on a foundation of continuous deliberation that good laws can be shaped and law accepted as legitimate, because it is then not just imposed but has grown out of participatory involvement. The meaning of communicative rationality, as I understand it, is that deliberation is the safe way for the rational citizen to seek out the evidence he can rely on in deciding how to live in his world. Solid understanding is that which is tested in deliberation with others. This method is not foolproof; you may still get it wrong. But evidence that has survived the test of deliberation is as reliable as we can get it. The Norwegian friends, when they go home after an evening of robust exchange, have reason to think that they know more about things than they would have without that evening together.

Aristotle again

It's just too romantic: do as you like, put flowers in your hair, dance in the sun, be happy. More likely, you put flowers in your hair, take to drugs, and life is a misery. Aristotle's language was direct, but he was right. To live immersed in the *polis* and by the rule that follows is indeed salvation.

Aristotle argued that freedom results when certain conditions are *present*. Berlin set out to argue that freedom results when certain obstacles are *absent*. His essay on the two concepts triggered decades of philosophical debate in which the contestants by and large took positions in one or the other camp, the positive or the negative.[26] Now in hindsight we can see that this should not have been so. "The distinction between 'freedom from' and 'freedom to' is needless."[27] It turned out in Berlin's project that he should not have contrasted the two positions as sharply as he first did (and he should certainly not have called his good freedom "negative"). The rest of us should have seen that his two concepts are not mutually exclusive and that their conciliation is surprisingly easy. Freedom depends, as the basic condition, on the absence of coercion. But there are also other necessary conditions, not instead of the absence of coercion but in addition to.

Berlin's negative liberty, more generally the freedom of choice theory, rests on the view that human beings possess instinctive rationality. We can then take it they will live in accordance with their real interests if only given the chance, and we can leave the rest of the equation to itself. If we instead, with Aristotle, go by the view that human beings are fallible political animals, we cannot take rationality as a given. If so, we must ask, as part of the meaning of freedom, what the conditions are of rationality and how it may come about that people, free from coercion, exercise liberty for their own "salvation."

According to Boudon, rationality, or reason, as he preferred it, depends on people being able to make decisions in life according to good reasons. The reasons I go by in deciding to do A rather than B are good reasons if they rest on faith that is backed up by tested evidence. I do A rather than B if I have faith in the reasons that favor A. I have good reasons for doing that if I have explored the evidence that gives clout to the reasons that favor A. The way to find robust evidence is to distrust yourself and to enter into the togetherness of deliberation with others.

It turns out that free choice in itself is vacuous; what gives it meaning is that you put purpose into it. Liu Xiaobo's experience was that liberty is for the purpose of truth and dignity. Adam Smith praised the virtue of prudence. Berlin tried to resist bringing more into it than absence of coercion but gave up. Boudon found that reason is a matter of living by the guidance of good reasons. Kahneman and Tversky taught that our brains play tricks on us, Sen that he who does not respect this is a fool, and Habermas that rationality is deliberative. To all of which Aristotle would have been entitled to say, "I told you so."

There can no doubt be too much togetherness, but it is the absence of togetherness that is paralyzing. Some people, exceptionally, thrive if freed from bonds. But for most of us it is in the community of deliberation that we can hope to flourish. Everything is what it is: togetherness is togetherness, not slavery, not coercion, not tyranny, not unfreedom.

BOOK FOUR

The Problem of Poverty

Alfred Marshall was the patrician professor of political economy at the University of Cambridge from 1885 until he retired in 1908. In 1890 he published his great *Principles of Economics*, finally. It had long been anticipated, but the author had procrastinated, filing away pedantically at his manuscript. His friends urged him to get it out. It was to set economics right. It was as monumental as expected, laying the foundations of economics as a science. It went through eight revisions and remains much read and much appreciated, if not always well understood.

The book speaks to us in the voice of an English Victorian gentleman: "It may make little difference to the fullness of life of a family whether its yearly income is £1000 or £5000; but it makes a very great difference whether the income is £30 or £150: for with £150 the family has, with £30 it has not, the material conditions of a complete life. . . . But the conditions which surround extreme poverty tend to deaden the higher faculties. Those who have been called the Residuum of our large towns have little opportunity for friendship; they know nothing of the decencies and the quiet, and very little even of the unity of family life; and religion often fails to reach them. No doubt their physical, mental and moral ill-health is partly due to other causes than poverty: but this is the chief cause. . . . Overworked and undertaught, weary and careworn, without quiet and without leisure, they have no chance of making the best of their mental faculties. . . . Now at last we are setting ourselves seriously to inquire whether it is necessary that there should be any so-called 'lower classes' at all: that is whether there need be large numbers of people doomed from their birth to hard work in order to provide for others the requisites of a refined and cultured life; while they themselves are prevented by their poverty and toil from having any share or part in that life."

Principles of Economics is a celebration of free enterprise, but with the provision that enterprise should be tempered by social responsibility. Remarkably, considering what neoclassical economics was to come to, this founding text starts from the problem of poverty. At the core is an intense sense of purpose, of moral purpose. Poverty is the ultimate degradation. The imperative, indeed the point of it all, both in the practice and the study of economics, is to overcome the evil of poverty. That defines the job of the academic economist: "the study of the causes of poverty is the study of the causes of the degradation of a large part of humanity." It is also why Marshall celebrated free enterprise, because he saw in its productivity the capacity to make poverty redundant. Embrace enterprise, and we can have the means to do good in the world. The ambition should be radical, not just to control or modify poverty but to *eradicate* it. Therefore, politics also should be radical. It will take productivity and abundance but also the generous sharing of income and wealth.

The question

The question that still inspires the study of poverty is exactly the one Alfred Marshall posed: whether it is necessary at all that the scourge of poverty shall exist. He was also right that this question was one that it had "at last" become meaningful to pose. Until the industrial breakthrough, poverty was the natural state of affairs for most people, and it would have been meaningless to suggest its abolition. Only with industrial growth and the economic and political restructurings that followed were the means created and within reach to imagine a state of material comfort for everyone. Marshall was looking forward to a political economy with that quality, and the realization of that vision was the task he set for the study of economics.

His immediate followers tried to hold their discipline to his standards. In 1920, the same year that the eighth and final edition of *Principles* appeared, Arthur Pigou, Marshall's successor at Cambridge, published another grand text, *The Economics of Welfare*. That book offered a proof, grounded in utilitarian philosophy, the bedrock of neoclassical economics, of the social benefit of redistributing income.

An optimistic view on poverty eradication is that abundance is sufficient, that if there is enough income all around, enough will trickle down to those at the bottom of the ladder. But that was not Marshall's view. He was optimistic about free enterprise for its capacity of accumulation but then thought, in a distinctly modern understanding, that redistribution was necessary to spread the benefits. "The system of economic freedom is probably the best from both a moral and material point of view for those who are in fairly good health of mind and body. But the Residuum cannot turn it to good account: and if they are allowed to bring up children in their own patterns, then Anglo-Saxon freedom must work badly through them on the coming generation."[1]

Toward the end of his book, he discussed political remedies. "The evil to be dealt with is so urgent that strong measures against it are eagerly to be desired. . . . To this end public money must flow freely. . . . Thus the State seems to be required to contribute generously and even lavishly to that side of the wellbeing of the poorer working class which they cannot easily provide for themselves." He recommends "prompt action" on universal social insurance—"something like that which prevails in Germany"—a minimum wage, adjusted to family needs and not just to the individual, protective regulations against "misuses of the Factory system," shorter working hours, that education "be made more thorough . . . with abundant leisure for school and for such kinds of play as strengthen and develop the character," compulsory standards for size and sanitation in housing, "this combined with a regulation that no row of high buildings be erected without adequate free space in front and behind," and so on in the spirit of a modern welfare state. All this is to be possible by redistribution from the rich to the poor, a shifting of wealth that is socially beneficent. "In many other ways evil may be lessened by a wider understanding of the social possibilities of economic chivalry. A devotion to public wellbeing on the part of the rich may do much, as enlightenment spreads, to help the tax-gatherer in turning the resources of the rich to high account in the service of the poor, and may remove the worst evils of poverty from the land."[2]

It was this spirit of moral responsibility that Pigou set out to salvage by encouraging economics to resist its temptation to think that it's all about abundance. He argued that if, say, £10 is shifted from a rich man to one who is poor, the sum total of utility in society increases. This is according to the law of diminishing marginal utility. As income increases, an additional increment yields steadily less additional happiness. Therefore, the poor man benefits more from the £10 than the rich man sacrifices, and not only the poor man but all of society is better off for the transaction.

Regrettably, this proof was not accepted in what became the mainstream. In 1932 Lionel Robbins, professor of economics at the London School of Economics, published a book on "the nature and significance of economic science." Here, he rejected Pigou's proof because of, as he argued, the impossibility of interpersonal comparison of welfare. Although for any person, the law of diminishing marginal utility applies, it cannot be applied to comparisons between persons. The rich man and the poor may have different preferences, and we therefore cannot know if one derives more or less happiness from the £10 than the other. Theoretically, preferences might differ in such a way that the £10 actually matters more to the rich man than to the poor. On this, we just cannot say for sure. Therefore, there is no basis in utilitarian science for any position one way or the other on the redistribution of income.

That was unfortunate. It is entirely obvious to any thinking person that an additional £10 matters more to a poor man than to one who already has enough money, and you have to be a pretty blinkered economist to think otherwise. But Robbins' scholasticism, which represented a total perversion of Marshall's plea for morality in economics, let the economists off the hook and allowed them to regress to the view that the study of economics is the study of accumulation and in that meaning "efficiency." That caused at least two lost generations when mainstream economics relegated issues of poverty, inequality, and distribution, and of social policy, to the margins of their profession.

It was not inevitable. The utilitarian principle is "the greatest happiness for the greatest number." As Joan Robinson, one of the few women in the profession, argued, the economists just chose to go with "the greatest happiness" and disregard "the greatest number," and in the process threw out any notion of moral purpose.[3]

This paralysis lasted until the end of the twentieth century. What then happened was, first, a significant scientific breakthrough. It turned out that welfare in the utilitarian meaning was indeed measurable and comparable—and then obviously that Pigou had been right all along. This breakthrough came with the use of survey methodology in the emerging field of happiness research.[4] That did away with the impossibility of interpersonal comparison and the excuse of utilitarian economics for not concerning itself with issues of distribution, and restored economics to where it should have been all the time, to a doctrine of justice. Second, a shift occurred in economic thinking to lift distributional issues out of obscurity. That was brought about by new theoretical ideas, such as "the capabilities approach" spearheaded in economics by Amartya Sen, by dogged persistence by a handful of economists who had always flown the flag of distribution, such as Tony Atkinson, and by methodological advances in the empirical study of income and wealth coinciding with the explosion of inequality in advanced capitalism.[5] In *The End of Poverty*, published in 2005, Jeffrey Sachs revived Marshall's imperative of a century earlier that it should not be necessary for *anyone* in a rich world to have their lives destroyed by poverty.

What it takes

There is no mystery in eradicating poverty. Marshall got it one hundred percent right, and that was before the later avalanche of (sociologically inspired) poverty research.

It first takes abundance. There must be enough income. If a family does not have enough income, the parents cannot, however much they will it, protect their children from want.

The power of accumulation, in the meaning economic growth, to push back poverty is strong. I have seen that in my study of contemporary China. There, severe poverty has been cut back from being the condition of the majority of the population to afflicting only a minority in the course of not much more than a generation. This has been achieved by economic growth alone and with next to no contribution from redistribution.[6]

But accumulation, although necessary, is not enough, and the power of redistribution is equally strong. In a typical family of four or five persons, two, three, or four probably have little or no income of their own. The reason they can still live well is that the income of the breadwinner(s) is shared between all family members. An increase in the income of the breadwinner does nothing for other family members until it is shared. In a family in which the breadwinner has ample income, other family members can still be in poverty if the earner squanders his income on, say, drink or gambling.

The importance of sharing, or the lack thereof, is also in evidence in the Chinese case. While the general standard of living has increased, "lifting" millions out of poverty, inequality has widened. The downward statistical trend in the number of people in severe poverty comes from people being "lifted" above the income poverty threshold. But not all those movements are as impressive as the raw statistics might suggest. Those who most easily move above the line are those who start just below it. They are then out of poverty according to the technical measure but may in real terms not have moved much and may be about as poor as they were. Their income position has improved but not necessarily their standard of living, at least not much. In spite of significant achievements in statistical poverty reduction, it is also correct to still describe China as a country of massive and oppressive poverty.[7]

We can thereby say, categorically, that the two necessary conditions for the eradication of poverty—the way it is eradicated in the typical family—are abundance and redistribution. There must be enough income to go around, and that income must be shared with those who themselves have inadequate earnings. Poverty can be *reduced* by abundance alone, but it cannot be eradicated without there also being sharing.

One result of the unfortunate turn mainstream economics took in most of the twentieth century was an absence of concern within that science with the mechanisms of redistribution. Marshall had looked forward to a different development: "A remedy is not easy, but this is one of those matters in which the rapidly increasing force of economic studies may be expected to render great service to the world."[8]

It was not to be. The one question of redistribution that excited post-Robbins mainstream economists was that of "disincentives." If your imperative is "efficiency," any "distortion" in what is thought to be the productive distribution of resources is to be avoided. Economists came to invest enormous efforts of research into the "disincentive costs" of, say, poor relief or unemployment compensation. This research, however, not only failed to yield results in any way commensurate with the investment of effort, it also distracted minds from straight thinking.[9] Of course there are costs; nothing good in life is free. The problem for mainstream economics was an indifference to the benefit, the reduction of poverty, and therefore a panic about costs.

The mindset Marshall had encouraged, but in which he was not followed, was different. On the minimum wage, for example: "If it could be made effective, its benefits would be so great that it might be gladly accepted, in spite of the fear that it would lead to malingering and some other abuses; and that it would be used as a leverage for pressing for a rigid artificial standard of wages, in cases in which there was no exceptional justification for it."[10] The obvious solution was to get the details of the scheme right in the trade-off between benefits and costs. Since the benefit was great—"the evil to be dealt with is urgent"—a bit of cost, although a pertinent matter in the design of redistributive schemes, was nothing to panic about.

What is it?

Ahead of Marshall, it was Thomas Paine in Britain and the Marquis de Condorcet in France, both pioneering advocates of liberty in the aftermath of the French and American revolutions, who invented the idea of societies without poverty. They imagined that no one would be condemned to living in ways that were below the acceptable.[11] They built on Adam Smith who, in *The Wealth of Nations*, had identified poverty as that which would cause shame and exclusion. Marshall himself, as we have seen, explained it as that which prevents people from having a share in the requisites of a refined and cultured life. This is the understanding of the problem that has carried through in more recent research, as a lack of "resources to obtain the types of diet, participate in the activities and have the living conditions and amenities which are customary, or are at least widely encouraged or approved, in the societies to which they belong."[12] Poverty is a demanding concept. It resides in deprivation, not just any deprivation, but that which is severe. That's why we call it poverty and not just deprivation. What makes deprivation severe is that it is unacceptable. To establish the thing poverty, then, we need more than statistics. It is finally a matter of moral judgment.

The pioneering work in the effort to turn this understanding of the problem into scientific measurement was that of Benjamin Seebohm Rowntree, a contemporary of Marshall's. A member of a Quaker family of industrialists in York, Rowntree was one of the great English academic amateurs of the Victorian age. Britain was at the height of its imperial power and the world's leading economy. The British, or at least the English, had grown rich on trade and industry. It was widely thought, in establishment circles, the nation's leading economist notwithstanding, that the problem of poverty had been overcome more or less or at least marginalized. Rowntree did not agree. It did not square with what he saw in the industrial areas. He saw that poverty continued to exist on a large scale, including in the working population.

Being another enlightened Victorian, he shared Marshall's view that it was a duty of a rich society to end degrading deprivation. But for that to happen, society needed to be educated about the facts of the matter and shaken out of its complacency. And it needed to be educated and informed in such a way as to be persuaded that there was a problem that needed to be confronted and dealt with. A society that was too content with itself for its own good needed to be guided to the right moral judgment about a shortcoming it was reluctant to acknowledge.

Rowntree's solution was to devise a measure that could not be sensibly dismissed as depicting anything but that which is unacceptable. He set himself to demonstrate that a significant part of the population in a rich society dominated by elite contentment continued to live in a way that no decent person should hold to be acceptable.

Later poverty research was critical of Rowntree for his "absolute" definition of poverty and recommended instead a "relative" definition. But that was a distraction. Not only is the distinction between "absolute" and "relative" a red herring: there is no understanding of poverty, and that includes Rowntree's as well as Adam Smith's, that is not relative to time and place.[13] But also Rowntree's approach had an integrity that later critics failed to credit. It had theoretical integrity in handling poverty as a demanding concept. It had strategic integrity in that the task of those who want to educate their society about the existence of the unacceptable is to guide, or if you will, force, that society, including its privileged elites, to the moral judgment that it is treating some of its people in a way that represents "the degradation of a large part of humanity" and that is therefore unacceptable.

His logic was to specify a basic consumption consisting of life's "necessities" for "physical efficiency" and to estimate the earnings that a family would need to cover the cost of necessary nutrition, shelter, and clothing. It would seem that no one could object to the logic that everyone should have at least that which is necessary for being "efficient."

He mobilized a team of assistants to undertake a survey of the living standards of the population of York. The survey covered 46,000 people, recording their precise earnings and consumption. The findings were published in 1901 in *Poverty: A Study of Town Life*. It revealed that about one in four of those surveyed lived on lower earnings than required to cover the budget of necessities (and that about another one in five lived in "secondary poverty," meaning that although earnings were adequate, they were used in such a way that some family members were still in want). The study thus confirmed Rowntree's hypothesis that the problem of poverty remained widespread, in Marshall's words that "the evil to be dealt with is urgent," and that its resolution depended on a combination of abundance and sharing. Industrial England was rich, but richness itself did not spare a "residuum" from poverty.

How to recognize it?

Marshall was optimistic about his society's ability to combat the evil of poverty. He thought that "as enlightenment spreads," there will be more "devotion" on the part of the rich to public well-being. He put his trust in in evolutionary progress, much as was Raymond Boudon's inclination about the march of reason in his eulogy to common sense, as we have seen in Book Three.

But, again, that is more optimism than warranted. Devotion, no more to the good than to reason, does not just emerge.

One way to create the necessary devotion is with the help of scientific research. That was Rowntree's thinking. If poverty could be measured scientifically and it then turned out that it remained widespread in spite of economic advancement, would not hard facts speak loudly enough for the devotion to deal with the problem to follow? Marshall thought, in the same way, that "the rapidly increasing force of economic studies" would uncover the details of how to go about combating poverty and that society could not fail to act once it was known how it could be done.

We now have a proliferation of research and statistics on poverty devoted both, following Rowntree, to establishing the facts and, following Marshall, to explaining the remedies. Strangely enough, the descriptive task of getting the facts right has proved more elusive than the explanatory task of elucidating the means. We now know how to do it, on which more below, but we are on less firm ground about the magnitude of the problem.

In many parts of the world, we know, because it is obvious, that poverty is deep and widespread, and no research is necessary to establish the urgency of the problem. In seriously poor countries, many people are forced by circumstances to live in poverty. In the world's many refugee populations, there is obvious poverty. But elsewhere, in affluent countries, the facts of the matter are not as straightforward. To some degree, we have regressed to the state of thinking that Rowntree confronted, a complacency that accumulation has done enough work on lifting people out of poverty so that the wholescale attack on the problem that Marshall recommended is not necessary.

Rowntree invented the methodology for the measurement of poverty that is still the most commonly used. The first step is to establish an income threshold—the poverty line—at the point at which those who live on less are said to be in poverty. The next step is to collect the data on how the population distributes above and below the line. Those below the line can then be counted. The extent of poverty in a population is given by the proportion below the poverty line.

Getting the count right, however, is not as simple as it might seem. As always in research, there is uncertainty. Have we been able to count everyone? Are the data good enough, and have they been processed in the right way?

Uncertainty is unavoidable, and that represents a big difficulty for research of this kind. The purpose is to persuade and to animate action. But society, or many in it, will be reluctant to be persuaded because in most cases the acknowledgment that there is a problem is painful. It is to acknowledge that our society has an ugliness to it and that we have been failing in decency—and that an obligation will follow to spend money on alleviating the problem. We may prefer not to know.

The final grandeur of Rowntree's study was in how he dealt with uncertainty. He wanted to persuade, but he knew that statistics do not speak with objective force and that the inevitable uncertainty that clings to statistical facts makes it possible for anyone who is so inclined to refuse to acknowledge them. He therefore devised his measure so that uncertainty would pull systematically in a single direction. He specified "necessities" so basically that it could not be said that his measure exaggerated the problem. It could well be that it undermeasured it, but it could not be an overstatement. He thereby turned uncertainty into a tool of persuasion.

Later research has been less prudent in its dealing with uncertainty. In a new generation of poverty research that emerged from the 1960s, notably in America and Britain following what was dubbed the "rediscovery" of poverty among affluence, the argument was precisely that Rowntree's method understated the problem.[14] This research, therefore, specified the threshold differently, essentially on a more generous understanding of necessity than Rowntree's.[15] There were good theoretical reasons behind this rethinking, but when translated into statistical methodology, it came with the cost to persuasiveness that uncertainty would now pull in both directions. Those reluctant to accept the statistical facts that now emerged could argue that the problem was being overmeasured.

What followed was a free-for-all in how and where to set the threshold, resulting in wildly different measures of what is theoretically the same thing. The World Bank in their global statistics now sets the threshold at US$1.90 per person per day (having lifted it from US$1 a day when they started this measurement to keep up with inflation) and with that standard finds that 9 percent of the world's population live in poverty (in 2017, the most recent global estimate) and that poverty thus defined is near extinguished in Western Europe, North America, and Oceania. But in the United States, the Census Bureau in its official poverty index sets the threshold at the estimated cost of a basket of necessities and classifies 10.5 percent of the population as poor (in 2019). In Britain the Institute for Fiscal Studies is the custodian of what has become semiofficial poverty statistics. Here, the threshold is set at a fraction of median household income, 60 percent, whereby the poverty rate in the most recent estimates (2018–19) is 22 percent of the population. In other research, the threshold can be set differently, for example, at a lower income fraction, such as 40 percent of median income, or at the income at which respondents in surveys report that they feel the crunch of poverty. In San Francisco, a family of four with an income of $117,000 is deemed to have insufficient means to make ends meet and is eligible for government housing assistance (in 2018).

If Rowntree's vision had been a single, definite, and irrefutable measure of the extent of poverty in a population, it is now clear that this is something we will never get. In terms of measurement, we are now doing it as well as can be expected. We know a great deal about the nature and extent of poverty in different societies from research and statistics of high quality, and the knowledge we can extract from this work is useful both for self-understanding and for the formulation of public policy.

But statistics are never going to tell us, except suggestively, how serious the problem is. A wide range of approaches has been established, and there is anyway that inevitable uncertainty that now cannot be harnessed in the way Rowntree hoped. More basically, the question we are asking is one that is not finally answerable in statistics. Poverty is what is *unacceptable*, and what that is can only be resolved by moral judgment. Statistics can help but not resolve.

The question of whether there is a problem of poverty in our society that we need to deal with in public policy must be answered by us citizens in some reasonable understanding of what we are to consider unacceptable in our particular society and in our time. We start from ample knowledge of the facts, and from there we must work our way through to a reasonably shared understanding of what those facts mean.

It might be, in some societies, that the good interpretation is that there is no problem of poverty and that no new effort is needed in public policy. If that, however, is not the good interpretation, we should expect of ourselves that we be persuaded by the facts so that we acknowledge that there are people out there who live in conditions that are unacceptable, and that this acknowledgment follows through to a "devotion" to public policies to assist those who live as no one should.

The road to persuasiveness and devotion goes through deliberation. Facts do not speak directly. They speak through interpretation. The problem of poverty is not what the statistics say but what robust deliberation concludes. It may be in my selfish interest to dismiss unwanted facts because I do not want the commitment to additional taxation that comes from an obligation to step up with new public policies. But if I have to defend that position up against others who read the facts differently, I may find it difficult to stand by my instinctive lack of generosity toward people who are clearly in want. On the other hand, if I am on a political mission beyond poverty relief, say in favor of a socialist economy—and there has been a good deal of zeal of this kind from the poverty lobby—and inclined to use selective statistics as a lever in that mission, I may find myself brought down to earth in having to deliberate on the matter with more sober fellow citizens. If we are able to deliberate effectively, we can sensibly hope that a reasonable shared understanding will emerge about the true nature of poverty in our society and a reasonably shared devotion to a program of public policy to deal with it.

Democracy is the best political arrangement for deliberation. In a well-functioning democracy, citizens and policy makers engage in continuous and never-ending conversation, and everyone, rich and poor, have a say, ideally an equal say, in the process. This is why it is likely that a society under democratic rule will come both to a reasonably good understanding of the problems that afflict it and to a reasonably good response in public policy to those problems. It is not guaranteed. Not all democracies are well functioning, and

even democracies that are not deficient do not always generate rational policies. But it is likely, at least more likely than under authoritarian rule.

What to do?

I agree with the historian Tony Judt, and others, that the building, in advanced western democracies during the twentieth century, and in particular
its second half, of modern welfare states has been a civilizing achievement
of monumental proportions.[16] It may not always be seen in this way now,
which is to be regretted, but powerful structures of social protection have
been put in place and endure, to the benefit of the people of these countries. It
is a project in the spirit of the founder of neoclassical economics, who urged
moral compassion for those afflicted by or in danger of poverty and argued
that the state in that interest should take action and contribute generously
with public money.

Behind this project of political engineering was the kind of consensus that
it is possible to create through democratic deliberation. It was because there
was a collective determination to deal with the problem of poverty with the
kind of wholescale approach that Marshall had recommended that Britain
could enact rapid education, social protection, and health care reforms in
the years from 1944 to 1949, that similar reforms could roll out elsewhere in
Europe, if usually on a slower schedule, and that an ambitious "war on poverty" could be launched in America in President Lyndon Johnson's State of
the Union address in January 1964. What resulted from these initiatives were
public policies of astonishingly generous sharing. There was never universal
agreement on the politics of the welfare state, far from it, but enough agreement emerged from the democratic tug-of-war that there were living conditions out there that were unacceptable, that people living in rich economies
were at risk of falling into poverty, and that society, "we," should provide for
state-organized protections against these miseries.

The grand welfare state reforms proved effective. Across Europe, North
America, and Oceania, because of protective policies, people are much less in
risk of poverty than they would otherwise have been. This is not always appreciated. Indeed, policies of social protection are nowadays often dismissed,
with a broad brush, as excessively expensive for little benefit. No doubt, social
policies may sometimes be poorly designed and may come with unintended
costs and negative side effects, but the tendency now to give the welfare state
project as such a thumbs down is ill informed. It is to some degree an influence from an economic science that made itself disinterested in social questions and their ethics and obsessed with esoterically defined issues of cost.

THE WELFARE STATE AND DIVERSITY

The welfare state rests on a broadly shared determination to distribute protection to all in need. That has proved possible to a remarkable degree, not only in, for example, the Scandinavian countries, where the welfare state footprint is clear to see, but also in, for example, the United States, which is sometimes thought of as being outside of the family of welfare state nations. Social protection there superficially may not look welfare state–like but in fact includes all major components: social security, health care according to need, family support, and poor relief.

It is sometimes argued that the welfare state has had its time and is not sustainable in increasingly complex societies. One such complexity is ethnic diversity. The experience so far is that welfare state arrangements, although of different designs, have proved possible across vastly different kinds of countries: large and small, more or less affluent, even countries as diverse as the United States. Ethnic diversity does not diminish the need for protection. Even though exclusion is not exclusively material, there is usually a material dimension, typically in such exclusion as is often the experience of ethnic minorities. Marshall again: "No doubt physical, mental and moral ill-health is partly due to other causes than poverty: but this is the chief cause." The welfare state, we can say, is a necessary condition of inclusiveness, even if not always, or ever, a sufficient condition. If anything, ethnic diversity reinforces the need for social protection as part of the foundation of democratically inclusive societies.

What may be more difficult in ethnically diverse populations is the finding of the consensus that is necessary for determined sharing, including a willingness to share beyond the circle of "our own." This, however, is not really a strain on the welfare state but on the ability to inclusive deliberation.

For the state of understanding and experience about the eradication of poverty, I go to Britain and Scandinavia. Britain, during and in the years following the Second World War, was the factory of ideas, not alone, of course, but leading.

Scandinavia is where the welfare state has been implemented at its most effective. These countries have been, on the one hand, the most successful of any capitalist democracies in economic prosperity, raising average standards of living to their highest level anywhere in the world, and, on the other hand, the most successful again in reducing poverty. The Scandinavian story, then, stands in evidential dismissal of the view that redistribution of income on a scale to be effective is too costly to be practicable. It also stands as evidence of the possibility of not only modifying but of eliminating poverty. Of course, if you are a social scientist worth your salt, you can devise some statistics to show that many people in these societies live below some theoretically specified poverty line, but the Scandinavians have in truth come as close as it is likely that anyone will to wiping the scourge of poverty off the social slate. This experience is one reason why we know as much as we do about what it takes not only to reduce poverty but also to overcome it. And the remarkable thing is that what we now know about what is necessary and effective is just what Marshall prescribed 130 years ago. He was not heeded then, but what he recommended was put in place sixty years later when the necessary deliberative consensus emerged after the Second World War.

The story of this combination of knowledge and deliberative consensus starts in wartime Britain in 1942, with a report commissioned by the government entitled *Social Insurance and Allied Services*. It was written by William Beveridge and became renowned as the Beveridge Report. He was tasked by the government to recommend an improved system of social insurance to be implemented once the war was won. It was not considered to be a very important assignment. In fact, it was a way of putting a piece of technical work into Beveridge's hands in the hope that he, a difficult but influential man, would then not interfere in more important war matters. Beveridge, however, to great surprise, turned a technical study of social insurance into a rallying cry for what the war was fought for, essentially to defeat Fascism for the purpose of creating in Britain and elsewhere societies with the dignity that they were free from poverty.

He had been asked to make recommendations for social insurance, and so he did. But he also found that it was not possible to deal meaningfully with social insurance in isolation from other social policies. His area of study did not include the other policies, but he got around that difficulty by writing a preface to his report in which he introduced assumptions about health care, family policy, and employment as necessary conditions for his social insurance blueprint to be workable. In effect, he proposed a design for a complete welfare state. That design was for a system of insurance against the "contingencies" that could plunge people into poverty—old age, illness and disability, unemployment, and a general discrepancy between needs and earnings—on a foundation of full employment, free health care, and support for families in the raising of children.

This ambitious design came into place in the British postwar reforms, although not exactly as Beveridge had recommended. For example, he had proposed that state old age social security should be in the form of a flat rate basic pension, whereas what came into place in the National Insurance Act of 1946 was a comprehensive state-run pension system covering both a universal basic pension and earnings-related supplementary pensions for wage earners. (Later, under Margaret Thatcher's government, the earnings-related supplementary pension was effectively, although not totally, privatized, bringing the pension system back closer to what Beveridge had recommended.)

In the Scandinavian countries, reforms similar to those in Britain came into being more gradually. "People's Pensions," comprehensive state systems similar to that in Britain, came into effect in Sweden in 1959 and in Norway in 1967, while Denmark and Finland introduced arrangements more in line with Beveridge's insurance proposals. Drawing on these understandings and experiences, we can now list what it takes, once there is abundance enough, for a society to rid itself of poverty.

But first, what can be done ahead of abundance, in economies that are not yet affluent? The good news is that a great deal can be done under those conditions as well.

At the turn of the century, the United Nations adopted a set of Millennium Development Goals (MDGs), one of which was to eradicate extreme poverty, the first step being to reduce by 2015 the proportion of people in the world living in extreme poverty to half of what it had been in 1990. When the development goals were adopted, this was widely seen to be hot air from the United Nations of little real-world significance. In fact, however, the MDG framework turned out to be a powerful inducement to coordinated action on a global scale. Confounding expectations, the goals of 2000 have by and large been achieved (although not in all countries). The reduction of extreme poverty (as measured within the MDG framework) to half was reached ahead of schedule in 2008. That must count as an encouraging success, although the achievement is somewhat tempered by the global result hinging to a considerable degree on developments in two large countries, China and India, and there on economic growth more than on sharing.

Accumulation hence does its work before it reaches a level of abundance. China is not yet an economy in which average standards of living are more than on a middle level globally, but the rate of extreme poverty, as measured by the World Bank standard, has been brought down from about 65 percent of the population three decades ago to below 10 percent today. In the World Bank's global statistics (which use a slightly more generous poverty threshold than the MDG framework), the rate of extreme poverty in the world is down from 35 percent in 1990 to just below 10 percent today, and the Bank's development experts are hopeful that poverty thus defined will be eradicated by at the latest 2030.*

---

*That projection is, however, in some doubt as a result of the COVID pandemic. The Bank estimates that the pandemic by 2021 had added about 150 million people in extreme poverty compared to the expected number of ca. 590 million had the pandemic not occurred.

But also, even in economies that are not affluent, much can be done by sharing. When Britain introduced the great social reforms at the end of the Second World War, that was in a ravished economy. It was recognized that no reform could rid the country of poverty overnight, but it was hoped that once the structures of sharing were in place, they would contribute to a gradual leveling in the distribution of income and a reduction in poverty. That indeed happened. In the period from 1945 to 1975, the distribution of income in Britain was steadily equalized.[17] We know the same from cases of progressive governance in the developing world today, such as in Kerala in India or Botswana in Africa. What was once the conventional view in economics that sharing must wait until it becomes affordable by abundance has now been forcefully dismissed in more up-to-date development economics, such as by Professor Partha Dasgupta, a contemporary Cambridge economist, in his *An Inquiry into Well-being and Destitution*. The constraint on sharing in many countries that are not affluent is more in governance than in affordability.

Back, then, to sharing under the assumption that there is enough abundance. What does it take?

First, it takes jobs and employment. There must be jobs so that people can generally work and provide for themselves and their families. This is the main way that abundance works through to a lessening of poverty. Although it is often said, such as in contemporary China, that people are "lifted" out of poverty, in actual fact it is those people themselves who do the lifting by working and earning.

Full employment was one of Beveridge's assumptions. The reason this assumption is basic is that without full employment, too much will be asked of sharing for it to be politically viable. In full employment, all who can are seen to contribute, and social protection is seen to be fair since it goes to those who cannot. If social security is seen to be dished out to people who should be able to fend for themselves, it will be difficult to maintain the consensus to uphold a system of generous sharing.

Furthermore, employment must pay adequately. This was Marshall's argument in favor of a regulated minimum wage. Minimum wage regulations are now in effect in many countries, including Britain and the United States. In Britain there has recently been an important movement forward in minimum wage thinking, in that it has become accepted, at least in language, that the minimum should be set, as Marshall recommended, at a "living wage" level.

However, minimum wage regulation has in practice not proved as effective as Marshall envisaged in eliminating low pay. The reason is that even where a minimum wage is enforced, labor markets have a way of finding mechanisms to escape the regulation, such as moving workers from being salaried employees to contractually self-employed. In America and Britain, for example, in spite of strict minimum wage regulations, a layer of very low paid work persists.

The Scandinavian experience has been different. Here, the problem of low pay has been dealt with primarily through wage negotiations between unions and employers, assisted by state mediation. This has been possible thanks to a system of strong and centralized unions, whereby wage negotiations are national and comprising the entire economy, and by an agreement between unions, employers, and governments that negotiated settlements should usually have what is called a "low-pay profile," by which is meant more of a pay lift at the bottom of the pay scale than higher up. It would seem that this has been a more effective way of eliminating low pay. The Scandinavian economies are different from the American and British ones in that they do not have a similar layer of very low paid work. Visitors meet the consequences in the form of high prices for the things tourists buy, such as hotel accommodation and food and drinks in restaurants. Those kinds of commodities are more expensive than in some other countries because of (in part) higher wage costs. The natives are generally, and surprisingly perhaps, more relaxed about these consequences than are sometimes visitors.

The ability of labor markets to work through to a lessening of poverty depends, finally, in addition to the availability of jobs, on a culture of work. Those who can must be prepared to take jobs and work. There is such a thing as cultures of poverty in which people, often for complicated reasons, not always of their own doing, are stuck in cycles of unemployment and dependency, sometimes over generations. Marshall recognized that a side effect of generous sharing is likely to be "some malingering and other abuses." That may be unavoidable, but it is strongly desirable, perhaps necessary, that the influence of culture pulls toward a minimization of abuse rather than to its encouragement. The reason is, again, political. If abuse is seen to be widespread, there is unlikely to be a consensus of generosity. One way in which Beveridge made what might have been a dry and technical report lively and influential was in the use of colorful language. The job, he said, was to slay the Five Giants of want, disease, ignorance, squalor, and idleness. Yes, idleness. There must be things for hands to do but also willing hands to do it.

Will there be jobs enough, and will they pay enough? The economic crash of 2008 first followed through to rising unemployment, but employment was, at least in many countries, relatively soon back to precrash levels. The COVID recession has again pushed up unemployment, but there is reason to expect that this recession, as well, will be overcome and that recession-induced unemployment will again be temporary. More generally, there is now some fear that globalization, automation, and artificial intelligence are eroding the demand for workers, in particular the kinds of low-qualification jobs that are the buffer against poverty for those most at risk. There is some reason for that concern. New technology does kill old jobs and causes pain to those depending on them. But it also creates new jobs. So far, the experience is that the creation of new jobs has kept up with the killing of old ones. Ahead of the COVID recession, unemployment was at a forty- or fifty-year low in the United States and Britain. To be sure, unemployment is high in some areas in Europe and elsewhere. But not universally so and therefore not a necessary affliction in modern capitalism. Similarly with low pay, a persistent problem in some, perhaps many, economies, but not universally so. Now as previously, neither full employment nor adequate pay is impossible, but both depend on public policies and labor market regulations.

Second, it takes insurance arrangements against the potential loss of income as a result of the normal contingencies of old age, illness, injury, disability, and unemployment. These are now standard provisions in most countries with more or less advanced economies. They are arranged differently, one difference being in the level of generosity in how much of the income loss is replaced. From the point of view of protection against poverty, the replacement level needs to be adequate but not necessarily high. There may be other reasons why it should be higher than necessary for pure poverty protection, for example, reasons of fairness, but the job under consideration here is done if the replacement income is at or above the poverty threshold.

Beveridge's proposal was for a relatively low level of replacement. He thought state social protection should provide for security against poverty and therefore be on a flat rate for everyone, irrespective of previous income, but no more. It would then be for those who want additional security, for example, a higher old age pension than on a poverty prevention level, to make additional arrangements on their own. His argument was that state social protection should be on a cautious level so as to discourage dependency and encourage work ethics. He was concerned, in other words, with avoiding as far as possible the "malingering and other abuses" that Marshall had been aware of. In the interest of protection against poverty, what matters more in insurance arrangements is that they are comprehensive, that no one in need falls through cracks in the system, than that they are generous.

Third, it takes an additional last resort protection beyond insurances against the standard contingencies. The building toward today's welfare state started, in earnest, in Germany in the 1880s, with the introduction of comprehensive, obligatory, and state-regulated social insurance against the loss of income because of industrial accident, illness, unemployment, and old age. These progressive reforms were, surprisingly, the work of the autocratic and arch-reactionary Otto von Bismarck, the German chancellor from 1871 to 1890. That this breakthrough came in Germany rather than in the industrially and economically more advanced Britain, and under such unlikely political leadership, is an intriguing story, which we, however, do not need to dwell on here.[18] The similar breakthrough in Britain, the "something like that which prevails in Germany" that was a part of Marshall's recommendations, came with the National Insurance Act of 1911.

Among the many motivations behind these and later social reforms was an ambition to break free from dependency on poor relief. Prior to social insurance, poverty was alleviated with relief, but relief was never adequate and always detested. It was generally mean, imposing burdens and humiliation on recipients for minimal benefits. The thinking was that social insurance would make poor relief obsolete. That, however, never happened. In Britain, in spite of the 1911 act, poor relief persisted. This was one of the reasons why social security was modernized further after the Second World War. The reforms now included not only better social insurance but also a new form of income support to replace poor relief. In the National Assistance Act 1948, the opening paragraph states that "the existing poor law shall cease to have effect." What came in its place was income support designed so that whoever was below a specified threshold of income would receive support to bring their income up to the threshold level. This was thought to be the final protection against poverty that would capture those, the few it was envisaged, who fell through the net of the other social insurances.

The characteristics of traditional poor relief were that the level of support was minimal, that it was locally administered, that support was calibrated to local standards, and that it was discretionary in the sense that who should receive what support and on what conditions was at the discretion of some local authority, usually a poor relief committee. All that was modernized away in Britain in the new income support. This was introduced as a national system under state authority, with a universal level of support throughout the country, establishing support as an objective right independent on any local discretion.

The Scandinavian countries took a different route. Rather than modernizing away poor relief, they retained it, although in a much improved form. Hence, strangely enough, the most advanced welfare states have retained the archaic form in last resort protection. Their social assistance, as opposed to British-style income support, remains locally administered, calibrated to local standards, and discretionary, to some degree, in the nature and level of support. What has been left behind is meanness. Scandinavian social assistance, although local and discretionary, is now generous. Similar anachronistic forms of social assistance have been retained in other European countries as well, such as Austria and Switzerland.

There are various reasons why anachronism has survived in some countries. One reason, certainly in Scandinavia, is that the local government lobby has been able to block attempts by the state to usurp this important element of local authority. But there have also been social policy arguments. The purpose of social assistance is to be the final safety net to catch those who fall through the cracks in the prior system of insurance. These people, it has been thought, are the ultimate residuum. They do not make up a homogeneous group with easily defined needs. In British-style income support, their needs are thought to be straightforwardly financial. But for many of these people, so the thinking is behind social assistance, their needs are not only or even primarily financial. Many may need service support ahead of financial support, and some may not be able to put financial support to good use. An effective form of support at this level should therefore be flexible, grounded in an understanding of local circumstances, and with discretion for providers of the support to design the right package of financial and service support for each client. In the British case, where last resort financial support is from a state system and last resort service support from local social services, the coordination is difficult and often elusive, to the detriment of some of the most helpless people in need of care.

From my own observations of how discretionary social assistance has been working in the Norwegian case, I have come to the conclusion that the success of the welfare state in that country toward the elimination of poverty owes more than is usually recognized to the luck the country has had in retaining its last resort support in archaic forms.[19] Locally based and discretionary but generous, social assistance does provide for effective financial support, but it is also combined with service support as necessary by the circumstances of each case. And it really has been a matter of luck. The state has consistently tried to centralize this authority out of local hands, and has gradually chipped away at local authority and discretion with ever more guidelines. Social policy experts in academia have mostly pushed for a modernized rights-based system on British lines. But luck has prevailed.

Fourth, it takes family support. It has long been observed that there is a life course pattern in the risk of poverty. The risk is high in old age, but also in the phase in which parents are raising children. This is because children come into the picture relatively early in the parents' life, when some may be less than safely established in work and also be working for comparatively low wages, and because, obviously, children have needs that present themselves as financial obligations on parents. Financial support to families with young children is therefore standard in the modern welfare state package.

Family support was central to the British reforms after the Second World War and remains a component of British social protection today. But this form of support has over the years been cut back in relatively significant ways and also redesigned. The universal child allowance that is paid to all parents irrespective of income has not been maintained in value and has to some degree been replaced by means-tested allowances to low-income families. The advantage of the universal allowance is that when it is paid to all parents, it will be received by all needy parents. That, however, is expensive, which accounts for the move to means-tested allowances. But the problem with means testing is that it is very difficult to get right. There are likely to be both false negatives, that some in need will not get the intended support, and false positives, that some who do not qualify are nevertheless able to claim. That arrangement, although possibly less expensive, is therefore likely to be less effective in poverty protection, and also exposed to a loss of legitimacy. Arrangements that work ineffectively for those in need and that are open to abuse represent a risk to the consensus that is necessary for the maintenance of the larger package of social protection.

Here again, the Scandinavian experience is different. Family support, as in Britain, was established as a universal child allowance, but, contrary to in Britain, it has been maintained in value and structure. The Scandinavian welfare state from the start has very much been built as a family welfare state. This is a legacy of concerns prior to the Second World War over "the population question," the ability of the population to reproduce itself and to provide adequately for the raising of children.[20] Some of those concerns faded with the baby boom after the war, but the family orientation of social policy survived. One of the distinctive characteristics of the Scandinavian welfare state is its broad, universal, and generous family support.

The benefit of active family support goes beyond protection against poverty narrowly understood. Families bring up children and are central to the preparation and education of the next generation. Assisting parents in this job, which is demanding and costly, is an investment into the next generation of human capital, as well as into the cultural foundation of democracy.

Fifth, it takes provisions of care in addition to financial security. In illness, injury, and disability, and in childhood and old age, many people need not only compensation for inadequate income but also care, particularly care that is affordable. Families remain the main providers of care, but they cannot meet all needs. If good quality care is not available, or not affordably available, many will incur costs that may reduce them to poverty.

The good organization of care is notoriously difficult. In Britain, health care is provided in the National Health Service as a universal right and free of charge at the point of use. That is a service of excellence and much appreciated by the population. Social care, on the other hand, as opposed to health care, is disorganized and inadequately provided for. That is to the detriment of many people in need and also heaps burdens on the NHS, which has to pick up the pieces from unmet social care, a job it is not designed to do. This mismatch between excellent health care and inadequate social care has resulted in a chaotic nonsystem that is currently lurching from one crisis to the next, a crisis that became critically visible in the management of the COVID epidemic. Needs are not met, costs are out of control, and the NHS, the most appreciated service in the British welfare state, has come under unsustainable stress.

This chaos is a result of policy neglect. The inadequacies of social care, including up against the process of demographic aging, has been recognized for decades, but successive Parliaments and governments have been unable to take the action they have known to be required. Others have been less paralyzed. In Germany, for example, the early introduction, in 1995, of a separate long-term care insurance (as a fifth pillar of social insurance after health, industrial injuries, pensions, and unemployment) preempted the chaos that has not been avoided in Britain. (So much, again, for the English Delusion that strong government means effective government.)

This failure in the British welfare state puts in question the survival of the consensus that emerged during and after the Second World War that society, that "we," should provide for protections against acknowledged and unacceptable miseries. It is also a case study in the wisdom of Beveridge's insight that a functioning welfare state consists of a range of provisions that together do the job by working in a reasonably coordinated way with each other.

Sixth, it takes the acceptance of cost. It will cost, and money must flow. Taxes must be paid. If there is to be sharing, those who have something to share must share.

Will there also be a cost to the economy in a lower capacity than otherwise for accumulation and abundance? There are no doubt disincentive costs in sharing, and some of those will be unavoidable, as Marshall was aware of. These costs can be reduced by careful policy design but hardly eliminated.

However, there are also economic benefits. It works like this. If, for example, unemployment compensation on a poverty-protection level is available, it is to be expected that some workers will opt for unemployment rather than work and withdraw their labor, or some of it, from the economy. Why would someone whose prospect is low pay in a bad job not think that paid unemployment might be a preferable alternative? On the other hand, the availability of an unemployment safety net might help other workers to make the most out of their abilities, for example, make it easier to leave a bad job in search of a better one or to accept risk in entrepreneurship. Taxes work likewise. If the tax on income is increased, some workers might work less because work pays less, but other workers might work more because they need to make up for the loss of cash in hand. Economists call this, respectively, "substitution effect" (choosing leisure rather than work) and "income effect" (choosing more or better work rather than less or worse). The best that can be said from masses of research on behavioral responses to taxes and transfers is that substitution and income effects by and large balance each other out. That explains the Scandinavian experience of high-performing economies in which people live productively without destructive "disincentive costs" resulting from generous transfers.

In this catalog of what it takes, drawing on the British and Scandinavian cases, there is much similarity of experience. We know what the necessary components are of a welfare state that can slay Beveridge's Five Giants.

But there are also two notable differences. One is in the organization of last resort protection and one in family policy. These are sometimes thought of as second-order social policies compared to the heavy components of social insurance, but that is to underestimate their significance. Social protection overall depends heavily on protections of last resort. The Scandinavians have been more successful that the British in the eradication of poverty. In my analysis, that is in large measure thanks to the way they have dealt with social assistance and family policy. They have had the good fortune of resisting the lure of "modernization" in last resort support and of retaining social assistance in archaic form. And they have had the good fortune of persisting with universal and generous family support.

Marshall again

There is a difference between reducing and eliminating poverty. The first is easy and not politically demanding. If there is economic growth, it must be an economy of extremely bad luck if there is no improvement in standards at the bottom of the distribution.

But if poverty is to be eradicated, there must also be sharing, and that must be on a grand scale. The experience is that it takes a complete welfare state with many components, and that these arrangements must be well designed to work effectively together. This is extremely demanding, both technically and politically. It is no small thing for a population to agree to sustain those in need and to accept high taxes. It is no small thing to coordinate the many components of a welfare state into a harmonious system.

It has been suggested that the technical problem could be overcome by rolling all forms of income support into a single universal payment to everyone that is sufficient to prevent anyone from falling into poverty, no matter the circumstances. This is the "basic income" proposal that I have visited in Book Three.[21] But that is the social policy equivalent of selling snake oil. A basic income on a level to prevent poverty and paid to everyone would be so expensive that there is no way it could be politically acceptable, all the more because most of it would be paid to people who do not need it. A basic income on a level that might be politically acceptable would be inadequate to protect against poverty and would therefore not eliminate the need for conventional welfare state provisions. It's common sense: if something looks too good to be true, it probably is too good to be true. Eliminating poverty is possible but difficult. There is no easy way and no single fix. We need to do the job.

Alfred Marshall started from the position that poverty is morally unacceptable. He explained what it would take to overcome it. It would take "the State," and it would take "public money flowing freely, generously and even lavishly," what we today know as the welfare state.

He could also explain that this coming about would depend on a "wider understanding of the social possibilities of economic chivalry," on a "devotion to public wellbeing," and on advancements in "enlightenment." But what he could not explain was where that understanding, devotion, and enlightenment would come from. Indeed, all that initially failed to emerge as he thought it would, certainly from his own domain of "the rapidly increasing force" of economic science.

When it did emerge, it presented itself as a new political consensus, or enough of a consensus, after the shock of the Second World War. No one in their right mind would celebrate that war, but it is a sad paradox that without the shock of war, it is unlikely that the "will and the resources" would have materialized.[22]

What we see, then, is that the main impediment to the elimination of poverty is not technical and not economic, but political. We know what must be done. Since it has been done, we know that it is workable and affordable. But doing what must be done depends on Marshall's "devotion," on consensus. We must agree that poverty is unacceptable and, since we have the technical and economic capacity, that we have a responsibility to do away with it. The best hope we have for reaching and maintaining such consensus is robust deliberation within a democratic political order. That is our best hope partly because in that political order even the poor have power and voice, and partly because that political order is conducive to reasoned agreement.

BOOK FIVE

The Problem of Democracy

A dashing young French nobleman, a junior judge in his home country, Alexis de Tocqueville traveled through America for nine months in 1831 to observe democracy in action. He and his colleague and friend Gustave de Beaumont had obtained a commission from the French government to study the American prison system for the purpose of informing prison reform in France and duly did report on that matter. But Tocqueville's interest was more ambitious. He wanted to explore how a system of political equality worked and to let the French know that democracy was possible, practicable, and safe. He thought France was stuck in a sclerotic social and political organization of aristocratic inequality that stood in the way of progress and was in need of an injection of modernity.

He was, as he no doubt expected, impressed with what he saw. The Constitution was only forty years old and had been framed as a master class in ambiguity by men who did not much esteem common folks and did not think of themselves as democrats. One of the Founding Fathers, John Adams, thought they were laying the foundations of a "natural aristocracy." But under its first presidents, Thomas Jefferson in particular, it was edged away from its tendency toward electoral oligarchy (although the direct election of senators was mandated only in the Seventeenth Amendment to the Constitution in 1912). By the time of Tocqueville's visit, government had been put on a steady, if troubled, democratic footing, with representative government at its core. Under this order, and in the absence of aristocracy, citizens were equal and saw each other as equals. There was a relationship of harmony (of sorts) between government and people that made for stability (of sorts) of governance from above and trust (of sorts) in governance from below.

The America through which Tocqueville traveled was a society with extremes of inequality. It was an economy of chattel slavery, the most brutal form of disempowerment ever invented. The frontier territories were law-less, the native populations being driven out of their ancestral lands and deci-mated and their civilizations left in ruin, much encouraged by the govern-ment of the time under President Andrew Jackson. Women were excluded from democratic participation. Tocqueville was aware of this, if sometimes in ambiguous ways, but he also saw an absence of hierarchy among those who were included in the polity. That was the equality he reported on in two vol-umes of *De la démocratie en Amérique*, published in 1835 and 1840, still today one of the most authoritative works in the library of democracy.

Tocqueville was admiring of American democracy, sometimes cringingly so, but also critical, sometimes darkly so. He saw, on the one hand, that de-mocracy was real and was being made to work for the Americans. It was be-ing made to work not so much because it was laid out under an orderly con-stitution but rather because that constitution rested on a democratic culture; the system worked because people believed in it. Absent were the aristocrats who would stand above the people and look down upon them. Present, in-stead, were associations. This was a culture of local communities and church and affiliated religious groupings. There were associations everywhere, he would write, "not only commercial and manufacturing companies, in which all take part, but associations of a thousand other kinds, religious, moral, se-rious, futile, general or restricted, enormous or diminutive. Wherever at the head of some undertaking you see the government in France, or a man of rank in England, in the United States you will be sure to find an association." Citizens were not loners; they had belonging. They were not on their own up against the might of the state but had the support of intermediate structures that cushioned what might otherwise have been confrontational state-society relations. They were not at the mercy of the state, which therefore was felt to be not overwhelming.

By the time he made it to the writing of his second volume, and with more distance, he was more critical. Not only were rafts of citizens excluded from the polity, but also there was an undercurrent of dysfunction within the polity itself. The balance in state-society relations was delicate and subject to disintegrating, even to what he called *le despotisme doux*, soft despotism. There could be an erosion of freedom within a shell of democratic formality, which citizens might allow to fester out of indifference, gradually and unper-ceptively. Democracy had it in it to go bad.

There is a direct line from these observations by Tocqueville during the infancy of American democracy to the works of its most eminent recent stu-dent, Robert Dahl. He was the Sterling Professor of Political Science at Yale University through the second half of the twentieth century and continued to work there until well into his nineties. (He died in 2014, ninety-eight years old.) In a string of learned works he was at one and the same time a firm defender of America's democracy, including in the awful period when it was under disdain by analysts of Marxist inspiration, and a sharp critic of short-comings in that same democracy, setting a standard we, his followers, should aim to honor. Toward the end of his life he pulled together what he had learned about democracy in general and democracy in America in particular in three brief and beautiful books, *On Democracy* (1998), *How Democratic Is the American Constitution?* (2001), and *On Political Equality* (2006).

In *On Democracy*, he follows Tocqueville on the importance of culture. No democracy can work well with the help of only a constitution, however carefully designed. It depends on support from below, from ways of thinking, from beliefs, from the way people see each other, think of each other, and deal with each other, from habits of trust and confidence. It depends on being *wanted*, and being wanted depends on it being understood. "The prospects for stable democracy in a country are improved if its citizens and leaders strongly support democratic ideas, values and practices. The most reliable support comes when these beliefs and predispositions are embedded in the country's culture and transmitted, in large part, from one generation to the next. In other words, the country possesses a democratic political culture."[1]

He also follows Tocqueville in finding fault in the democracy he admires. In *How Democratic Is the American Constitution?*, his despondent answer is, "Not very." He is critical of a poorly representative Congress, in particular the Senate. He is critical of the power that the Supreme Court has come to hold, which he describes as "an aberration." He is critical of the convoluted way the president is elected, which on numerous occasions has caused a candidate to win the presidency without a majority of the popular vote (as happened for Donald Trump in 2016).

More generally, he thought the American Constitution too rigid and re-sistant to reform and improvement. It invites Americans to think that their democracy was created once and for all in a superlaw that contains in its paragraphs the secret of how it should be done—then, now, and forever. "My aim in this brief book is not to propose changes in the American Constitution but to suggest changes in the way we *think* about our constitution."[2] With the view having taken hold that the Constitution is holy, Americans are discour-aged from recognizing imperfections in their democracy and from the aware-ness that any democracy, their own included, needs constant renewal.

American democracy has paid a price for the rigidity of constitution and mindsets. In *On Political Equality*, his final book, Dahl thinks that a failure to stand guard over democracy in action, rather than over the wording of a document framed more than two hundred years ago and for an entirely different society, has allowed the hollowing out of the reality of political equality. The main culprit is the easy access to political influence of economic inequality. "Because of a decline of the direct influence of citizens over crucial governmental decisions, and also in the influence of their elected representatives, political inequality might reach levels at which the American political system dropped well below the threshold for democracy broadly accepted at the opening of the twenty-first century."[3] He brings us back again to the cultural underpinnings of rule that is safely democratic, to equality, to beliefs, to mindsets. It is as if he were seeing in the twenty-first century the creeping erosion of freedom within a shell of democratic formality that Tocqueville had warned of almost two hundred years earlier.

There are lessons to be drawn. The first one is about the primacy of culture. We need to stand guard over democracy; it can easily fail. The ability to guard over it comes from the way we *think* about democratic governance and ourselves. We can put it as strongly as this: If the political culture itself is democratic in prevailing beliefs and habits, almost any minimally democratic constitution will do. And if the culture is not democratic, no constitution can save the day.

A second lesson is about the imperative of reform. All democracies are imperfect. They are living things. They need to be maintained. Democracy is a process of trial and error. We must be sensitive to failures and mistakes and seek better ways. Circumstances change, in domestic economies or world affairs, and democratic governance must adjust. For confidence in the political system, citizens need to see that leaders are attuned to shortcomings and willing and able to work for improvements. Continuous and never-ending reform is part and parcel of the democratic enterprise. If leaders and citizens think their democracy has found the Holy Grail, it is doomed.

What is democracy?

Robert Dahl defined democracy as mostly practiced today by listing the arrangements that, at a minimum, are necessary for modern representative government. He called it "polyarchy," rule of the many. These conditions are that top officials are elected by citizens, that there are free, fair, and frequent elections, that there is freedom of expression and association, that citizens have access to alternative sources of information, and that citizenship is inclusive.

These are, of course, relevant and recognizable conditions, and this is very much the accepted way of defining democracy. On reflection, however, there are a number of difficulties with this way of approaching it. There is a logical difficulty. Identifying the conditions of a thing is not to identify the thing. If these are the necessary conditions, what are they conditions for? What is it that follows if these conditions are present? What is it, for example, that is being secured by free and fair elections? It cannot be that we value democracy for the purpose of having free and fair elections. Free and fair elections are a way of doing democracy, but what is it that then gets done? To get inside the meaning of democracy, we need more sense of purpose than is contained in the Dahl type of definition.

There is an empirical difficulty. The minimal conditions are intuitively attractive, but once we look out into the world of democratic variations, and we will explore this below, we see many well-functioning democracies in which some of these conditions are not present. Democracies are vastly different in how they have developed, and by what experiences and traditions, and in the way they operate. Dahl's definition is open to many such variations in that it lists only basic conditions, but it still is not open enough to match the facts of the world.

And there is a problem of consistency. More than most other theoreticians, Dahl has insisted on the importance of culture. When he reasons over what it takes for democracies to operate in a robust matter, he includes the underpinning of a democratic culture. But when he gets to the definition, culture is no longer there, not even as a condition along with other conditions. In his theoretical and empirical exercises, culture is always included, but in his definition, he includes only constitutional arrangements.

In trying to get beneath the conditions of democracy to the thing itself, I have fastened on three components, the three C's of culture, conversation, and contract.

1. Democracy is a *culture*, not just a constitution but a constitution that is embedded in a culture. No constitution can deliver without the underpinning of a democratic culture. Why? Because life under democracy comes not only with benefits but also with burdens and is therefore demanding on citizens, because democracy must therefore be wanted, because that again depends on democratic values being entrenched in mindsets and habits.

2. Democracy is a *conversation* between citizens and between citizens and leaders about the rights and duties of governments and of citizens respectively. Why? Because the habit of deliberation is the lifeblood of a living democratic culture.

3. Democracy is a *contract* between the state and citizens in which the state makes *two* commitments—it promises citizens order, and it promises to protect their liberty—and in which citizens wield the power over the state that obliges it to deliver for them and they, in return, to offer it loyalty.

The purpose of democracy is not to be democratic

Democracy's purpose is to provide for safe and effective rule. Rule is effective to the degree that it delivers order and safe to the degree that it does so without undermining liberty. The basic arguments for democratic rule are two: that it being under popular control is likely to be safe and that it being by popular consent is likely to be effective.

The ways democracies operate are all over the place. It is done in one way in America, in a different way in Britain, and differently yet again in South Korea or Germany or Costa Rica, and differently from all of these in Switzerland. And so it must be. Since historical experiences and traditions differ, the same arrangements could not fit everywhere. No one would design a democracy in the way it is arranged in Britain, but Britain's Parliament has a history that goes back almost 800 years, and it just would not work to impose a democracy that is theoretically ideal but removed from that long tradition.

What democracies have in common is a *purpose*; how they are arranged differs vastly.[4] One way is not necessarily more or less democratic than another. In fact, we have no metric for the degree of democracy. Democratic regimes can be better or worse, of higher or lower quality, or more or less effective—but about "more democratic" we do not know much. Switzerland has a democracy that works differently from most others. Is it more democratic? Who knows? We know what is democratic and what is not. But be skeptical when someone wants it done in this or that way on the argument that their way is more democratic. More likely than not, they have fastened on an opinion that they want to push on to you.

So there is no single right form of democracy. There is no way of doing democracy that is *the* right way. Participatory democracy is not necessarily better than—than what? More democracy is not necessarily better than less—whatever that might mean. It is possible to rank democracies by quality, but that is not the same as democraticness.[5] The fact that a decision is made democratically does not make it right. The point of democracy is not to make policies democratically but to make good policies. If we make a mistake democratically—and that happens often enough—it having been made democratically is not a reason to stick with the mistake. Democratic assemblies scrap or change democratically made policies all the time.

Democracy is *not* its own purpose. We are, or should be, in favor of democracy because we have good reasons to believe that democratically underpinned government is more likely than any alternative that we are aware of and have experience with to deliver reasonably safe and effective rule.

Minimal conditions

Robert Dahl specified the minimal conditions of democracy in our contemporary understanding. These should then presumably apply across the broad range of ways in which democracies are made up. But when we look to democracies in action here and there, we find that they have surprisingly little in common.

Is it necessary that top officials are elected by citizens? Not so. Dahl's criterion is hardly that *all* top officials be elected, but when we look out over the landscape of real existing democracy, what is striking is how many are not. Cabinet ministers are usually appointed, either by the chief executive, for example the American president (with the approval of the Senate), or by the national assembly of elected representatives. Britain is unusual in that only members of Parliament can hold ministerial post, but that still includes members of the House of Lords, who are not elected. Anyone can be picked out of the populace and made a minister by being made a member of the House of Lords, and all British governments have ministers of this kind. In the American case, the president is not elected by citizens but by an Electoral College consisting of delegates who are themselves not elected but appointed. That may not be ideal, but it is not undemocratic. In many democracies, presidents are not elected by citizens but by the national assembly. In constitutional monarchies, the monarch, head of state, is neither elected nor appointed but comes to office by inheritance. Some of the best functioning democracies, such as in Scandinavia, are hereditary monarchies in which monarchs play more significant roles than just being ceremonial.

Some officials who are very top indeed are as a matter of principle not elected. That applies to most judges, including judges of the highest courts. In Britain, judges in primary courts are magistrates. They are not professional lawyers but lay judges chosen from among citizens, but not by elections.

If not all top officials need to be elected, is it necessary that some are, for example, those that make up the national assembly? Only up to a point. Not all national assemblies are made up fully of elected representatives. In Britain's Parliament, the upper house, the House of Lords, is made up of appointed, hereditary and ex officio peers, and other democratic national assemblies have second chambers made up partially of appointed members. Many people want such archaic arrangements abolished, for which there are good arguments, but Britain's strange upper house does not make Britain a nondemocracy. It might be thought more democratic if the upper house were elected, but no one would say that Britain is not a democracy as things are.

Still, it would be difficult with today's understanding of democracy to con-
ceive of an arrangement in which at least the deciding core of the national
assembly were not made up of representatives elected by citizens. Why? Because the contract between citizens and the state depends on citizens holding
controlling power over the custodians of the state. Citizens cannot trust the
holders of state power to respect them unless they, the citizens, have power
over them. When citizens elect representatives, they can choose people they
trust. That is why elections must be free and fair; otherwise citizens cannot
control who their representatives will be. Equally importantly, they can dismiss representatives who have proved themselves not up to it. In electoral
democracy, the obligation of representatives to present themselves for reelection is crucial. It is reelection, more than election, that gives citizens power
over their representatives. It must therefore be correct, as Dahl says, that elections should be not only free and fair but also frequent.

Above, I have not included elections in my definition of democracy. That,
however, does not mean that I dismiss elections from the practice of democracy; far from it. I will offer a robust defense of the election method, but we
should not think that this is the meaning of democracy. It's only that we (so
far) have found no better way.

Is inclusive citizenship necessary? It should be but is not. Inclusive citizenship has not been and still is not the state of affairs. The reason citizenship
should be inclusive is that if some sections of the population are denied citizenship rights, they will not have the power to compel representatives to respect
their interests. The state can then not be trusted to treat and protect all citizens
fairly. That was the lot of women before they obtained the vote and of many
African Americans in the United States before the Voting Rights Act of 1965.

However, there was democracy before there was inclusive citizenship.
Athenian democracy was brutally exclusive: slaves, peasants, women, and
foreigners, probably 70 percent of the adult population, were not citizens. The
political system Tocqueville admired in America in the 1830s was exclusive on
the same lines but was still a democracy. There was democracy before women
obtained the vote, although democracy of exclusive citizenship.

Still today, democracy functions without fully inclusive citizenship. One
big section of the population remains excluded: children. We may not usually
think of that as exclusion from citizenship, and we may think that parents
and other adults look after the interests of children. But exclusion it is, and
it is likely that both society and children suffer from it. In social policy, the
pensions of retired people have stronger protections in public policy than do
provisions for children and families with children. In Britain, as we have seen

CHILDREN AND VOTING RIGHTS

There is a small lobby in democratic countries in favor of a children's vote. I first lent my voice to this following in an article in the then *International Herald Tribune* on December 14, 1996, under the heading "In a Democracy, Children Should Get the Vote."

It is mostly thought obvious that children should not have the vote because they cannot vote, but that is sloppy thinking. The principle of universal suffrage is that all citizens have an equal interest in government matters and that therefore all citizens should have an equal say. That must mean that children should have the vote. If a practical way could be found, there is no issue of principle standing in the way.

In recent years, great advances have been made in the recognition of children's rights. Children cannot manage property, for example, but that does not mean that they cannot have property. The solution is that someone is appointed to be the custodian of the property on behalf of the child until he or she is old enough to take care of it. The custodian has a duty to manage the property in the best interest of the young owner.

The similar logic in respect to the vote would be that all children have the right to vote but that this right is managed on behalf of the child by a custodian until the child comes of age. That's a practical solution that solves the *could* question. Since there is no independent *should* question standing in the way, the matter is resolved.

The solution I have advocated is that the children's vote is managed on their behalf by (normally) the mother, so that she acts as the custodian of a second children's vote in addition to her own. There is every reason to trust that mothers would manage the second vote on behalf of their children, as we trust custodians to manage children's property. Voting by proxy is an established routine in many democracies, including Britain and the United States. Since there is a way that concurs with current legal thinking and established conventions to put voting power behind the interests of children, there should be no reason to deny children this right, as they are now not denied other rights just because they for a while need help to manage them.

in Book Four, 22 percent of the population are classified as poor. The proportions for children and pensioners are 30 and 16 percent, respectively. That is explicable by the voting power of pensioners up against the absence of voting power for children. There is not adequate voting power behind the citizens whose interests are the most long term, which may help to explain the often short-termism of public policy. In the last few years, schoolchildren across Europe and beyond have taken to the streets (and boycotted schooling) in manifestations to demand effective action from their governments to counter the threat of environmental decay. It has been heartwarming to see children in mature engagement. They are protesting against what they see as a lack of adequate concern on the part of older generations for long-term problems that threaten their future. The mindset that children's interests are looked after by parents and adults, and that it is therefore not necessary that children have full citizenship rights, is the same as an earlier erroneous mindset that it was not necessary for women to have full citizenship rights.

Are the freedoms of information, expression, and association necessary? Here, the answer must be in the affirmative. These rights may not be completely without qualifications—some forms of hate speech are sometimes banned, and some democracies ban the formation of certain nondemocratic parties—but barring aberrations, these are unquestionably necessary freedoms. They are necessary for citizens to inform and educate themselves and therefore for being citizens. They are the building blocks of a culture of deliberation.

In my definition of democracy, I include a continuous conversation between citizens and between citizens and leaders as a part of democracy itself; in other words, not only that there is freedom of information, expression, and association but that there is a habit of citizens making use of these freedoms. It is dire for democracy if honest disagreement deteriorates into shouting matches of distrust. In Dahl's minimal conditions, it is enough that these freedoms exist, and it is not a requirement that they are made use of. I here go further than Dahl because I start from a different definition.

I find that it is the conditions that pertain to the democratic culture, those of information, association, and deliberation, that are absolute, while those that pertain to constitutions, such as how top officials are selected, are less set in stone.

Why democracy?

Does it matter if we are governed democratically? It is not obvious that it does. The democratic way of working is often seen to be convoluted and indecisive and democratic governance to be ineffective. Support for democracy in democratic countries may be less than decisive, with, for example, participation in elections on a downward slide and young people opting out of politics in the traditional understanding. Add to that the assertiveness of leaders in autocratic systems and their boast that they are presiding over models of government that are superior to those of democracy in delivery and problem solving, and we who want to be democracy's defenders have a real challenge on our hands that we must respond to.

Since democracy needs to be wanted, we need to reflect on why we should want it. It is being asked *why* it matters, and we must answer. We are being told by leaders in successful autocracies that it doesn't. It is easy for people to accommodate to autocracy and be happy to accommodate. In China, there is much support in the population for Xi Jinping's regime, in spite of its systematic tightening of dictatorship.[6] A democratic culture needs the confidence that democracy holds the moral high ground over the alternatives. We need to justify democracy with some force and in some detail.

Again, I start from Robert Dahl. In *On Democracy*, he lists the "desirable consequences" that democracy is likely to produce. He is careful to remind us that real democracies have many defects, that no democracy is as good as the ideal democracy, and that some fall way short. The desirable consequences he suggests are probabilities, not certainties. Not even the disadvantages of autocracy are absolutes; they are likelihoods and risks. Still, the likely benefits of democracy are such that "democracy is, for most of us, a far better gamble than any attainable alternative to it."[7]

Below, I produce my own list of advantages, twelve in all. We should hold on to democracy because, for all its faults, it comes with surprisingly many and big advantages in governance and quality of life above any known alternative form of government.

Methodologically, I am following the guidance of Max Weber, to whom I've otherwise paid tribute in Book One. A productive way of understanding a thing, he suggested, is to describe it as an "ideal type," that is, to describe it as it could be but does not necessarily conform to in all respects in real life, as that to which real-life manifestations might aspire. All things of human making are quirky. Peel away the quirks, and we see the essence of the thing, in a crystallized, thought experiment kind of way.

First advantage: avoidance of tyranny. The understanding that the flip side of democracy is likely to be tyranny is as ancient as democracy itself, as is in evidence in the Athenian stele of democracy, which is on the cover of this book. Writes Robert Dahl (in *On Democracy*): "Perhaps the most fundamental and persistent problem in politics is to avoid autocratic rule." That tyranny is an endemic danger in government is abundantly clear from history, including the history of the twentieth century, and clear enough today when we look to, for example, China or Russia or Saudi Arabia. In all autocratic systems—absolutist monarchies, aristocracies, oligarchies, outright dictatorships—there is an overwhelming risk of tyranny. In democracies, the combination of government above and safety below is possible. It's ingenious: we get both protection and protection from the protectors. We can allow our governors to hold power and be leaders because we are not at their mercy.

Second advantage: rights. What enables the people to control the government is that they have rights. Under democratic constitutions, citizens have the right to life, the right to speak, the right of assembly, the right to discuss, the right to information, the right to criticize, the right to worship (or not to worship), the right to publish, the right to property, the right to fair trial, the right to vote. Furthermore, democratic constitutions impose on the state a duty to respect the rights of citizens and to maintain institutions dedicated to their protection, such as an independent judiciary. If a constitution does not enshrine basic rights and ensure institutions for their maintenance, it is not democratic. Under autocracy, governments have rights, not people, or at least power from above trumps rights from below.

Third advantage: autonomy. Democracy is premised on liberty. Autocratic regimes may allow people a good deal of choice in their daily lives (as we have seen in Book Three in the case of China's autocracy), but they cannot allow them the autonomy of political liberty, basic human rights, free access to information, and the freedom of assembly. Autocracy denies people these freedoms because—and I here refer to the experience of China again—they may use them to form networks or associations that may enable them to stand up to the dictators. What democracy allows is finally the social existence of the autonomous citizen—the life of truth, responsibility, and dignity that Liu Xiaobo thought of as the rewards of liberty.

Fourth advantage: rule of law. In democracies, the law prevails. Governments cannot do what is not authorized in law. Retribution cannot be brought down upon citizens that is not sanctioned in known law and managed through due process. People do not live in fear that someone will come knocking in the night and take them away. Property has legal protection and cannot be expropriated except by due process and with compensation. Contract is regulated by law. Public policy, policing, surveillance, land management, punishment— none of these are at the discretion of the governors. Citizens have protection and predictability in life and business. In short, there is rule of law.[8]

Autocratic governance can be regulated by law. In China, that most sophisticated of autocracies, both public policy and civil life have in recent years been increasingly regulated by law. That is an improvement for citizens in that there is less unpredictability. But in this and other autocratic systems, what results is at best rule *by* law, not rule *of* law. Under autocracy the rulers are above the law, not the law above the rulers. One reason a regime needs to be autocratic is that it cannot prevail with rule of law.

Rule of law is not impossible in political systems that are not democratic, or very imperfectly democratic. Hong Kong until recently, although not governed democratically, or fully democratically, benefited from a rule of law regime, including with an independent judiciary and freedoms of speech, information, and assembly. However, while rule of law without democracy is not impossible, it is very unlikely. Hong Kong is perhaps the only known case, and at the time of writing that privilege is being crushed for being intolerable to the overlords in Beijing. Democracy without rule of law, on the other hand, is not possible.

Fifth advantage: equality. At the ballot box, every citizen is equal: rich and poor, capitalist and worker, Black and white, man and woman. Each has a vote and no more influence than resides in the vote, and all votes count the same. Then and there, for a moment, power is equalized. The logic of equality is commanding. To the degree that there is political equality, the agenda of public policy is likely to reflect the balance of opinion and of interests in citizenry. To the degree there is political inequality, special interests will be able to distort the agenda of public policy.

But there is an uneasy coexistence of political equality and economic inequality. Nearly a century ago, Justice Louis Brandeis of the United States Supreme Court warned dramatically: "We may have democracy, or we may have wealth concentrated in the hands of a few, but we can't have both." That was at a time of economic crisis combined with extremes of inequality in wealth, much as our own time. But it turned out he was wrong. Democracy in America survived, thanks to political responses in the policies of the New Deal to excesses of economic inequality. Economic inequality is a strong force in society, but so is political equality.

Could economic inequality reduce political equality to irrelevance? It would seem that the answer in the first instance is no. Where democracy is established and has taken hold, the fact of economic inequality does not in itself turn political equality into an empty shell of formality. There are still equal rights and equality before the law. However, it would also seem that economic inequality combined with other conditions could make political equality (partly) redundant. In an elegant book on economics and politics titled *Equality and Efficiency: The Big Tradeoff*, published in 1975, the economist Arthur Okun gave the relevant condition the name of "transgression." Economic inequality is not necessarily a threat to political equality by its mere existence, but it becomes a threat if economic power is allowed to transgress from markets into politics.

The crude mechanism of transgression is corruption. If money is allowed to buy policies, political equality is reduced to a pretense. A contributing cause to democracy not taking hold in Russia after the fall of the Soviet Union has been entrenched corruption.[9] The sophisticated mechanism of transgression, however, is to use economic power to usurp political power in ways that may not be technically corrupt or illegal but which nevertheless destroy the impact of political equality. The increasing sway of private money in American politics, which we have visited in Books One and Two, and on which more below, is of this kind.

Sixth advantage: citizenship. With rights come responsibilities, such as the duty to respect the rights of others. There is no freedom for me that does not acknowledge your freedom. Your right to promote your interests is tempered by your duty to accept that I have equally valid interests. Democratic citizens have a duty to contribute some participation to the polity, to make themselves informed, and to make their views and interests known. They are expected to participate in elections (although in most democracies this duty is moral rather than legal) and obliged to (reasonably) oblige their governments. In democracy, duties are the flip side of rights. In autocracy, there is the servitude of duties without rights. It is the dialectic of rights and duties that makes for grown-up citizenship.

Seventh advantage: effectiveness. Strangely enough, and sometimes contrary to appearances, democratic government is generally the more effective government. One might think autocratic governments have the advantage that they can just get on with things without having to face dissatisfied NIMBY (not in my backyard) citizens or succumb to the short-termism of the next election. The rapid delivery of, for example, high-speed rail and new airports and city subway networks in China in recent years is sometimes taken as evidence of that advantage. But democratic governments have effectiveness advantages of their own. They have an interest in delivery since citizens hold power over them. Autocratic governments may be able to get on with it, but that assumes that they are intent to deliver for citizens in the first place. Why should we assume that they are when they are not under the pressure of people power? Democratic ones have it going for them of ruling by consent. That is helpful for them to get their policies accepted, since they are policies agreed upon through due process.[10] And they have it going for them that they are meritocratic. Position is attained through competition. Political competition works out so that less motivated and qualified candidates do not prevail. Citizens can thereby have some confidence in their representatives and the policies they enact. To be sure, it does not always work out in real competitions that that the most qualified candidates win. Sometimes, far from it, often because the competition has been corrupted. But often, elected representatives are probably better at their jobs than critical citizens are prone to acknowledging. In autocratic systems, political position is attained by selection from above. Here, the most important qualification is usually obedience upward and trustworthiness in the maintenance of autocracy.

The best available evidence on effectiveness in government is in the World Bank's Worldwide Governance Indicators. The highest scores are for the countries of North America, Western Europe, and Oceania, all democracies. There are no nondemocracies in the top range of this indicator (with the exception of the city-state of Singapore). In East Asia, the high-scoring countries are Japan, South Korea, and Taiwan, while China, the darling of democracy's detractors, is in the middle range, in a group of countries that includes, for example, India, Kazakhstan, South Africa, Argentina, and Mexico. The other indicators in the World Bank's analysis are "voice and accountability, political stability and absence of violence, regulatory quality, rule of law, control of corruption." There is a high level of correlation between these indicators and government effectiveness, suggesting that it is the institutional solidity that is a feature of democratic systems that gives these systems the edge not only in fairness but also in effectiveness.

Did the democracies fail the test of COVID management? Some did, others not. In Asia, both democracies and autocracies performed well. In Europe, some democracies performed comparatively well, others less well. In the Americas, both the United States and Brazil failed to provide their populations a level of protection that should have been expected. In this matter, it would seem that democracy or not is not the explanation of differences in performance. The United States probably had a good infrastructure of epidemic preparedness but saw that advantage squandered by poor political leadership.

Eighth advantage: prosperity. Democracies are prosperous countries, and prosperous countries are democracies. In Europe, the progress in prosperity under democratic stewardship after the Second World War was simply monumental and beyond anything anyone could have imagined at the beginning of the period.[11] No similar progress occurred for any population on the other side of the Iron Curtain. More recently, democratization has been followed by increasing prosperity in Spain, Portugal, Greece, and the countries of Central Europe. In Latin America, the democratic exceptions (until recently) of Costa Rica and Uruguay have also been the region's more prosperous countries (although even Uruguay succumbed to military dictatorship from 1973 to 1985). In Africa, Botswana is the most successful country both democratically and economically.

There are exceptions. One is Singapore, an affluent nondemocracy. Another, the other way around, is the great democracy of India. Although economic growth has in recent years been strong, India should have done better in terms of prosperity. But within India, the rule still applies. Kerala is the leading state in both democracy and prosperity.

CHINA'S PERFORMANCE

China's official GDP statistics are broadly accepted to be unreliable. The most so-phisticated work (that I am aware of and have reviewed in *The Perfect Dictator-ship*) to correct the official statistics is that of the economist Harry Wu at The Conference Board, an international consultancy. That has resulted in an adjust-ment downward in the official growth rates, to the effect that actual annual growth in years with official rates of about 10 percent turns out to have been about 7.0 to 7.5 percent. That's still very strong but not the double-digit growth the regime has tended to boast. Taking the best growth periods for China and other East Asian countries, and using statistics of comparable specification, this work finds about the same best performance growth in Japan, South Korea, Taiwan, and China, albeit with China's best performance growth slightly behind that in the three other countries. These four countries all started their contemporary modernization shortly after the Second World War. Today, Japan, South Korea, and Taiwan share three qualities: they are high-income countries, they maintain reasonably effective systems of social protection, and they are democracies. China is a middle-income country, one of the most unequal countries in the world in the distribution of income and wealth, more backward in social protections than economic resources should allow, and a dictatorship.

China is sometimes thought of as the great economic success story of our time. But that is a myth that needs to be exposed. China's economy is very big, and China therefore has much clout, but that bigness is blinding and tends to be confused for performance. China's economic growth has been typical and not exceptional by the standards of East Asia, and its modernization has fallen way short of that of neighboring Japan, South Korea, and Taiwan.

Are democratic countries prosperous because of democracy? We cannot say for certain, but there are good reasons to think that democracy is con-ducive to prosperity. In some cases, the time sequence is in favor of this hy-pothesis. The new democracies in Europe have grown to prosperity after they became democracies. South Korea and Taiwan took off in development un-der autocratic regimes but went on to grow economically to the level of high income after having transformed politically to democracy, possibly avoiding "the middle-income trap" thanks to the good luck of modernizing politically in time.[12] That is a strong hypothesis because democracy makes for a society of open information and exchange, which, again, is the fuel of entrepreneur-ship and productivity.

Some of the reasons we should expect democracy to encourage prosperity are the following: Citizens are more likely to feel secure under regimes of protection and predictability and therefore more confident in enterprise. They have freedom of movement and can follow the productivity in labor markets, and free access to information and deliberation. They are more likely to have the protection of safety nets to fall back on and therefore more able to take on economic risk. There is rule of law, including property and employment law, and therefore more security in job and enterprise and less susceptibility to corruption and gangster rule. Governance is more likely to be effective and therefore more likely to deliver infrastructural and other forms of support. Democratic polities coexist with market economies, and market economies have proved to be more efficient than command or monopolistic economies.

Ninth advantage: poverty. In a democratic system, there is less risk than otherwise of citizens being left behind in poverty. There are two reasons. First, the country is more likely to be prosperous, and with more prosperity there is likely to be less poverty. Second, it is more likely that there are antipoverty policies in place. The reason for that is that even the poor have a share of political power. Competing political parties and elites need the votes of the poor, as they need other votes, and must therefore to some degree satisfy the interests and demands of the poor and those at risk of becoming impoverished. If you have the vote, someone in government is likely to take an interest in you. If you have the right to stand up for your interests, you are less at risk of your interests being disregarded.

Tenth advantage: peace. Democratic countries do not fight wars against each other. This is true today, was true in all of the twentieth century, and was true in the nineteenth century in that countries with then democracy-like institutions did not fight each other. A more democratic world would promise to be also a more peaceful world.

The observation that countries in which governments are under some form of popular check are less likely to be warring was first made by the German philosopher Immanuel Kant in a publication of 1795 entitled *Zum ewigen Frieden* (Perpetual Peace). Here he not only proposed the equivalent of a UN Charter in which countries commit themselves to peaceful coexistence. He also recommended that countries should adopt republican constitutions since that would make them less prone to war.

The peaceful inclination in democratic governments is due partly to the distribution of power in the population. Since the glories of war accrue mainly to elites, and the costs of war fall disproportionately on the populace, elites may incline more to war where they are not answerable to the populace and be more restrained from war where they are under popular control. Other reasons may be that democratic leaders and citizens learn the art of compromise, that they see people in other democratic countries as similar to themselves, and that their communality encourages a habit of peaceful nego-tiations and treaties.

Democratic countries have not in the same way been able or willing to avoid war with nondemocratic countries. They have fought wars of more or less defense against nondemocratic aggressors, as in the Second World War. But they have also fought wars of aggression in self-interest, as, for example, the many and violent colonial wars that Britain and France engaged in during the nineteenth and twentieth centuries, including Britain's atrocious Opium Wars of state-sponsored drug running against China.

Eleventh advantage: management of disagreement. Democracy is, among other things, a way of managing disagreement without repression and of forg-ing cooperation out of conflict. In autocratic systems, the social good is de-fined from above, and a duty of obedience is imposed downward. Autocratic governance depends on a pretense of agreement and therefore the repres-sion of disagreement. Democratic governance is grounded in an acceptance of disagreement and an ideal of cooperation without repression. To get on in society, we need agreed upon (more or less) goals and procedures on many matters, some of which are controversial. There is no such thing as a public policy that is the preferred policy of everyone, and there is no such thing as a public policy that does not come with costs to someone. In a democracy, ideally, everyone is entitled to state their views and fight for their interests. At some point, however, a shared position needs to be found somewhere in the landscape of disagreement. That can be done democratically, for example, by voting in a national assembly, or in a general election or a referendum. Some citizens will unavoidably be disappointed in what becomes the shared posi-tion, since it will not be their preferred position. The ingenuity of democracy is that since everyone has had a say in the process leading up to joint deci-sions, or the opportunity thereto, there is a good chance that everyone should be able to, even if grudgingly, accept the outcome, even when it is not their preferred outcome.

Some thinkers have taken the impossibility of agreement to be an argu-ment against democracy—how can public policies reflect the will of citizens if citizens cannot agree?—but that is logic turned upside down.[13] It is *because* of the impossibility of agreement that we need democratic ways to find acceptable policies. If we could just add what each of us prefer into a single best choice, we could leave public policy to computer programmers. But, as the political theo-rist Albert Weale has shown, there is no such thing as "the will of the people."[14] We will different things, and the quest for *the* true will is futile. The political tug-of-war is not to find out what *the* people want, but to find a reasonable balance of opinion in the many things people want. In democracies we do not agree; we muddle through with the help of acceptable compromises.

Twelfth advantage: tolerance of imperfection. The case for democracy is not perfection. It is more modest: democracy is likely to be the better form of rule for most people. To be democratic is to accept the imperfect. It is because we humans and our communities are messy that we need the cumbersome democratic way of managing our affairs. The tolerance of imperfection is an extension of people's tolerance of each other. Democracy is never finished but always in the making, and will so forever remain. The vibrant democracy is not the finished one, but the one in which shortcomings are acknowledged and the imperative of continuous reform recognized. Only dictatorships can aspire to perfection. The philosopher Karl Popper, in *The Open Society and Its Enemies*, argued that it is the idea of perfection that causes ideologically determined regimes to go tyrannical, since the next logical step after certainty is that ends justify means. Democracy is built on tolerance, on the recognition, in the words of Immanuel Kant as paraphrased by Isaiah Berlin, that "out of the crooked timber of humanity no straight thing was ever made."[15] That which gives the spirit of democracy its majesty is tolerance of the imperfect in the human condition.

These are my twelve advantages of democracy compared to the alternative of autocracy. They are the reasons why we should defend democracy. They make sense of the preference of people anywhere in the world, when given the choice, for democratic government. People fight in the streets, and put their lives at risk, because of these advantages.

In identifying advantages that flow from democracy, I am suggesting that good consequences follow because of democracy. In methodological language, I am speaking not only of correlations but of causations. I am arguing that good things happen to people *because* they live under democratic rule. That gets me on to what is often difficult terrain for a social scientist: the ascertaining of causality and the direction of causality. Often, social science research is inconclusive on causality, and you will find social scientists in honest disagreement, for example by referring to different bodies of empirical evidence.

The difficulty is not as serious as it may look. Some of these advantages are aspects of democracy itself more than consequences that follow from democracy. Rights, autonomy, rule of law, political equality, safety from tyranny— these are monumental benefits that come as part of the democratic package, not things that may or may not materialize later after democracy has been introduced. Respect of disagreement, the ability to compromise, and tolerance are building blocks inside a democratic culture.

Still, can we take it to be established fact that democracy does deliver these benefits? For example, it would seem obvious that there cannot be tyranny where there is democracy, but that is still not to say that the absence of democracy necessarily results in tyranny. It could be benevolent autocracy. The city-state of Singapore is probably an autocracy that leans to being benevolent. But since there is more experience of tyrannical than of benevolent autocracy in the world, we are still on safe ground to say that autocracy comes with a risk of tyranny. That is now in evidence in Hong Kong. Rule of law there is being discontinued, because, as might have been expected, it turned out to be intolerable to the autocrats in Beijing.

Do democratic countries tend to be affluent because they are democratic, or are they democratic because they are affluent? Competent social scientists will answer that question differently. For my part, I am persuaded by both logic and experience that democracy is conducive to affluence, but it would be dogmatic to claim that democracy always and necessarily follows through to affluence. That, however, is not the kind of claim that is being made here. In the identification of democratic advantages and autocratic disadvantages, we are not in the land of absolutes and indisputable causalities but of probabilities. We are saying that on the balance of probability, there are advantages to democracy that present themselves as real and substantive. Where there is democracy, there is not tyranny; there will be rule of law; people will enjoy rights, autonomy, political equality, and citizenship; they are likely to have prosperity and protection against poverty; governance is likely to be effective and peaceful; and there will be tolerance of the inevitability of disagreement and imperfection. Under democratic governance, life for most people is likely to be safer and better than it might otherwise have been. That is not abstract theory. It is practical reality corresponding to practical experience.

There are weak links in my chain of advantages. One such is in the claim to equality. It is very difficult to maintain the reality of political equality in the context of rampant economic inequality. It is not impossible: at the ballot box all voters *are* equal. Democracy can live with a range of social inequalities, for example, in prestige, in fame, in ability to make one's voice heard. But economic inequality is something else. It concentrates heavy power into a few hands and with so weighty interest at play that the power in question will unavoidably want to put itself to work politically.

The problem is, first, inequality itself. When there are wide differences in affluence, the rich and the poor become different populations who inhabit different worlds in lifestyles and mindsets. They come to not know each other, not respect each other, and not care about each other. Economic tribalism spills into political tribalism to destroy familiarity, trust, and we-feeling, and drives wedges into the cultural foundations of democracy. When democracy came to an end in Athens, a contributing cause was that the rich grew indifferent to community and turned their backs on social collaboration. We are seeing the same today with many of the superrich opting out of any notion of common cause, buying themselves free from the world of public services on which most people rely, and going to extremes to avoid any fairness of taxation.[16]

The problem is, second, if the pressure of transgression cannot be held back, that inequality in the economy works through to destroying competition in the polity. If money is able to control nominations and elections and if public policy is dictated by economic power, then the equality of the ballot box becomes irrelevant. If I, as an ordinary citizen and voter, do not count, why should I care? This was Dahl's warning of the way the American system might "drop below the threshold of democracy."

The erosive effect of economic inequality on democracy is at its most conspicuous in America: the plague of mega-expensive politics, the organized force of monied and corporate interests, the culture of polarization and distrust. The nonaristocratic equality that Tocqueville saw and admired in the young republic is no more. The superrich are a modern-day aristocracy with a way of life elevated to a different world than that of "ordinary folks," and with a sense of entitlement that gives them an unquestioning right to use their wealth to buy themselves ownership of the nominally democratic political game. American democracy has always been rough. Inequality is nothing new. Cultural wars have been a constant. But now it's *different*. Over the past fifty years or so, various trends have been moving side by side and intertwined, gradually, steadily, inextricably, to be now coming together into a predicament that is *new*.

No one has explained the predicament better than President Barack Obama. He chose to do that in his final State of the Union address in 2016. He was delivering one of the most trenchant presidential speeches ever and, an academic must concede, as sharp a political analysis as anyone could muster, and in simple and elegant language to boot. It is a sign of the sad state of American political culture that a shocking message from the outgoing president, speaking before Congress on the occasion of the State of the Union address, to the nation, that democracy itself is in peril, passed by unappreciated and hardly noticed.

President Obama called on his fellow Americans to "fix our politics" to prevent "democracy from grinding to a halt." The last time a president warned the country in such stark terms was when Eisenhower, in his farewell speech,

THE AMERICAN PREDICAMENT

The new inequality. It is not new that American capitalism creates inequality, but it is new that it creates an inequality that is exclusive of the mass of the population. "Part of the US success," writes Odd Arne Westad in *The Cold War*, with reference to the early period after the Second World War, "was how its massive economic power intersected with the daily lives of American citizens. Other rising powers in history had seen their rise mainly benefit their élites, while ordinary people had to be satisfied with the scraps left at the table of empire. The United States changed all that. Its economic rise created a domestic consumer society that everyone could aspire to take part in." So it did, but it has not lasted. From the last decades of the twentieth century, the experience of Westad's "ordinary people," deep into the middle class, has been stagnation in their standard of living, while at the extremes, the poorest have become even poorer and the rich, and in particular the very rich, have accumulated additional richness on a monstrous scale.

The new organization of monied interests. Big money has turned from relying on economic power to working through a combination of economic and organizational power, as I've explained in Book One, so as not only to influence public policy but to rig the political game itself. Politics have been made mega-expensive for the purpose of making money the ultimate political resource. That may to some degree be by deliberate design—there are big and influential players at work—but it is not dependent on any orchestrated conspiracy. It is enough that transgression is deregulated and that a fair number of people with enough money come to think of politics as a good investment.

The new distrust in government. The revolution of Franklin Roosevelt started to build a new foundation of trust in government as a force for good. That came to an end with the counterrevolution of Ronald Reagan. The proportion of Americans reporting (in Pew Research Center polls) trust in government institutions is down from a top of above 70 percent in the late 1950s to less than 20 percent by 2015.

The new culture of polarization. Americans used to live in reasonable comfort together across political disagreement. No longer. Majorities of Americans now, on both sides of the political divide, report in surveys, as they did not fifty years ago, that they live in fear of government under the other party and that they consider the other party a danger to their way of life. Marriage across party lines is increasingly seen, from both sides, as abhorrent. Conversation across political divides has ceased.

raised the specter of the military-industrial complex whose "economic, political, even spiritual" influence was "felt in every city, every statehouse, every office of the federal government." Had America listened to its wise leader then, it might have saved itself from the emergence later of an even more powerful politico-corporate complex.

Washington is dysfunctional. The tax system is broken and does not get repaired. So also criminal justice and immigration. The infrastructure is left to deteriorate. High-speed rail is but a pipe dream. The budget is running a roaring deficit. America is not getting the elementary governance it needs. But why?

President Obama answered that question as well. Washington is dysfunctional because elected representatives are "trapped" by "imperatives" and in "rancor," which they dislike but cannot get out of.

The imperative is that of raising money, "dark money," he had called it in his 2015 address. That pulls everyone into the rancor of having to out-shout each other. When Washington is unable to act and turns into a shouting match, the next bastion to fall is trust. "A better politics doesn't mean we have to agree on everything, but it does require basic bonds of trust between its citizens." The reason trust breaks down is that "those with money and power gain greater control over the decisions" that are made in Washington. "And then, as frustration grows, there will be voices urging us to fall back into our respective tribes." Further: "Democracy breaks down when the average person feels their voice doesn't matter; that the system is rigged in favor of the rich or the powerful or some special interest. Too many Americans feel that way right now."

In America's mega-expensive politics, what candidates and representatives are trapped into is dependency on the money of the spiders in this web. Organized money holds the strings and decides, before elections, who the deciders will be and, once they are in office, what they can decide. Again, the president was direct and radical. Since their representatives in Washington are trapped, "it's not enough just to change a congressman or change a senator or even change a President. We have to change the system. We have to reduce the influence of money in our politics, so that a handful of families or hidden interests can't bankroll our elections."

Another weak link in my chain of advantages is in the claim to effectiveness in democratic rule. That depends on how representatives turn power into effective rule, the difficult matter of statecraft that I have given the full treatment in Book Two. But before that, there is the question of what hands power is put into. Have we chosen representatives who are inclined to and capable of managing power for, in the words of George Washington again, the "discernment and pursuit of the public good"? If we choose the wrong ones, we may end up with leaders who abuse the power they have been given, even to the extent of making themselves autocrats, or with incompetent leaders who just make a mess of it.

One advantage of democracy is that it should make for selection of leaders by meritocratic competition, but that does not necessarily work in practice. Voters can choose between the candidates that are on offer. The candidates that are on offer are those who have been nominated. In theory, nomination is competitive. Voters can trust that all the candidates that have made it through to being nominated are competent and that they can safely choose between them on the basis of the policies they are offering. Potentially improper leaders have been shot down in the process. Or should have been shot down. But James Madison, reflecting on the early experience with the American Constitution, thought this form of government contained a particular source of instability: that the people might be deceived.[17] Quite so, today's observer might say, looking out over the contemporary democratic landscape.

There are various ways for candidates to be nominated. Political parties play a key role. Candidates make it through to nomination for high office by working their way up within their parties, for example, from experience in local government to candidacy for national office. Parties then serve as gate-keepers to shut out candidates that are not up to it or not well intentioned and to filter through the better ones. In the British system of single-representative constituencies, local party committees have traditionally been in charge of rejecting nonserious candidates and would usually interview the serious ones before making the final nomination.

Another way is through primaries, in which typically party members (although sometimes not only party members) vote directly for candidates, which means that nominations are more or less taken out of the hands of party officials and put to citizens. This has become the standard method of nomination in American democracy and seems to becoming used more broadly, including in Britain.

Unfortunately, bad leadership is a fact of life in contemporary democracy, as are dishonest leaders, as is manifest in an epidemic of corruption.* It

*In *The Global Age*, Ian Kershaw lists entries in the index under "corruption" for Albania, Bulgaria, the Czech Republic, Greece, Italy, Romania, Slovakia, Spain, Ukraine, and elsewhere. Indeed, one of the many merits of that history is to show, in a way that may surprise even the informed reader, how saturated European democracy has been with corruption. In France, allegations of financial malpractice have been a constant, leading (in 1993) to the suicide of the former prime minister Pierre Bérégovoy, to the conviction and a suspended prison sentence (in 2011) of former president Jacques Chirac for embezzlement and breach of trust while he was mayor of Paris, and the conviction (in 2021) of former president Nicolas Sarkozy on a charge of bribery. In Italy, "an enormous scandal was exposed [in 1992] in which corruption ran through the entire political system in a huge web of corruption and criminality of politicians and public officials.

happens not only sometimes but often that representatives and leaders are elected who turn out to be ill suited, either because of incompetence or because they disrespect democratic norms and sometimes the law. This happens not only in make-believe democracies, such as in Russia in which an autocratic leader like Vladimir Putin can give himself a sheen of respectability through rigged elections, but also in established democracies such as in Britain and America where there has recently been a run of disastrously bad leaders, such as David Cameron, Theresa May, George W. Bush, Donald Trump, and Boris Johnson. There is also good leadership, including in those two same countries, but even reasonably good leadership is not even reasonably assured.[18] This book was finished in the shadow of Britain's Brexit crisis. That was mainly a constitutional crisis, a misfortune made possible by a constitution unable to protect the polity from the breakdown of orderly governance. At the same time, it is unavoidable, even for someone like myself who wants to think that most politicians most of the time are of pretty good standing, to not see contemporary Westminster as a display of an unfortunate combination of shabby irresponsibility and absence of leadership material.

The exposure to bad leadership in contemporary democracy is a result of inadequately competitive procedures of nomination. Candidates for political office are not properly tested. We protect the process of voting very carefully with detailed rules and regulations, but we have paid no similar attention to the process of nomination. In the age of the internet and social media,

---

A thousand politicians and almost 1500 civil servants and businessmen were accused of taking bribes. The former socialist Prime Minister Bettino Craxi was later sentenced in absentia—he had fled to Tunisia in 1994—to twenty-eight years of imprisonment. [Former Prime Minister Giulio] Andreotti was finally in 2002 given a sentence of twenty-four years of imprisonment, only to be acquitted finally on appeal" (p. 434–35). In Germany, former Chancellor Helmut Kohl had much of his reputation destroyed when it was revealed (in 1999) that his party under his leadership had received and kept illegal funds and operated illegal financial arrangements for hidden donations, including secret bank accounts. In Britain, party and campaign funding remains notoriously opaque, with regular scandals erupting about secretive money in more or less contravention of established law, most recently in the Brexit campaign. Under former prime minister Tony Blair, the Labour Party obtained large loans from private sources (until the secrecy of it was uncovered, since "loans" did not have to be declared as "donations"). There was a suspicion, in the "cash for honors" scandal, that lenders had been promised seats in the House of Lords. In 2006 the House of Lords Appointments Commission rejected several of the prime minister's nominees who were among those who had made loans to the Labour Party. A complicated police investigation followed, resulting however in no charges being brought since there was no solid evidence of cash for honors collusion prior to loans being promised. In 2009 Parliament was hit by the "claims scandal" in which was revealed a culture of cheating on claims for expenses in the conduct of members' business.

political parties are lessened as institutions of democracy and now pretty unable to manage the role of gatekeeping. Nomination through primaries is wide open to manipulation. As a result, we have here a serious weakness in electoral democracy as now constituted. There are good reasons to think that more demanding testing at the stage of nomination might increase the likelihood not only of good leadership but also of more respect for political leaders.

A further weak link is in the assumption of inclusive citizenship. In her history of the United States, *These Truths*, Jill Lepore shows that the problem of citizenship—who is to be included and in what meaning—has plagued American democracy from its inception and continues to be unresolved. African Americans were, while slavery persisted, denied citizenship by a flawed Constitution. That was rectified by emancipation during and after the Civil War, but still African Americans continued to be denied full citizenship in many parts of the country by secondary law. That has also been rectified, but still, again, African Americans continue to suffer from exclusion as a result of entrenched racism in the political culture. Immigration has produced another dilemma of inclusion-exclusion. White immigrants have been treated in one way, Asian and other nonwhite immigrants often differently. Who gets to be citizens and on what terms continue to be unsettled questions. The inclusion of women was a long time coming. Above, I have argued that children remain unrecognized as a political group and that we have yet to recognize that they, as other groups, have interests that should have representation. Inclusive citizenship is an unfinished journey, not only in fact but also in imaginative ability.

Yet another weak link is in the assumption of freedom of information, from its grounding in a free press and upward. Press freedom exists when the media— print, broadcasting, and internet based—are pluralistic, competitive, dedicated to informing society, and managed under editorial autonomy, when, in Dahl's necessary conditions, citizens have access to alternative sources of information.

These ideals are realized to different degrees in different democracies. One problem has been and is that of editorial autonomy. Newspapers, magazines, and radio and TV stations are not only media but also businesses. They have owners. Owners may restrict editorial autonomy in the interest of business priorities or use their power of ownership to make their outlets instruments for their own political influence. Britain's culture of press management has been and is notoriously indulgent to the machinations of outrageously meddling press barons.

The internet and social media are changing the nature of the power game. On the one hand, we have better access to information than we have had and are more informed, can get at information more easily and quickly, can more easily check information against other sources, and are more connected than we have been. One dimension of the internet revolution is more people power.

But there are downsides. Social media can be used as instruments of harassment, persecution, and manifold and often vicious violations of privacy and dignity. Their use in this way is widespread, causing not only individual distress, harm, and danger, but also cultural polarization and distrust.

They can also be used, with an effectiveness hitherto unknown, to manipulate information. Big data analytics, targeted and carefully designed information campaigns, willful disinformation—this is now part of the reality of democratic politicking. The internet is borderless. It has made it possible for operators anywhere in the world to meddle to effect in public life where they have no business to operate.

The world of social media is dominated by a few big providers and is as a result inadequately competitive. It should be simple enough: those providers should be broken up. That is just a matter of good old antimonopoly trust busting. The big trusts were once in steel and rail; now they are in information and data.

The managers of social media outlets claim to be technicians who provide platforms on which others can publish information and to be without responsibility for what information their often millions of users choose to dispense. We who use the platforms to great benefit and pleasure are dazzled by the brilliance of the technological geniuses behind Google, Facebook, Twitter, Instagram, and such and defer to their ingenuity. We should not. It is ugly, harmful, and manipulative in the extreme what platforms allow and encourage to be posted and spread around. Platform managers are publishers, every bit as much as those who run newspapers are publishers, and the fact that they operate electronically, on the internet, and worldwide does not make them nonpublishers. If I write an article for the *Los Angeles Times* that it publishes, those who run the paper have editorial responsibility. If I post an opinion on Facebook, those who run Facebook should have editorial responsibility. They will claim that they cannot take that responsibility because of the scale of the operation, but that is not correct. Many worldwide internet platforms are edited. Wikipedia, for example, was started on the idealistic view that editing would be unnecessary but found that to be unworkable and devised editorial routines. Amazon has routines in place to block book reviews from being posted that contravene their standards. Facebook and the like should operate filters to catch questionable postings and expose them to editorial controls *before* they are published. It's the easiest thing in the world if the technical geniuses are made to put their minds to it. It is not enough that they promise to remove objectionable postings after the fact or put warnings on postings that spread untruths and rumors. They should, as newspaper editors do, operate routines to prevent what is not fit to be published from getting published in the first place.*

These weak links are much in evidence in the American Predicament. President Obama confronted the fragility of democracy and called on Americans to "fix our politics." Under his successor, however, things went from bad to worse, finally to an attempted coup d'état by mob violence. The next election brought in a new administration, that of President Biden, with a radical agenda. Is what is now unfolding in Washington the "fix" President Obama called for?

There is much promise. There is again competence, decency, and dignity in the presidency. There is again a will to deal with the big issues of the day, from climate change globally to poverty locally. There is again an acceptance of government as an instrument of good. There is determination to repair previous neglects, such as in infrastructural decay. There is again engagement with the world and with allies. There is again a clear voice in defense of democracy and its values. There is again a readiness to take on the responsibility of leadership.

But it is too early to celebrate. The inequality, the force of monied interests, the polarization—none of this has been overcome. The new policy of family and child support is a milestone in the American welfare state, but still not a determination to eradicate poverty. There is no basis of consensus to enable that commitment. The new seriousness on global warming is laudable, but much remains in turning intention to action. Again, there is a failure of underlying consensus. The re-embrace of leadership in the world is welcome, but assertive authoritarian regimes, China in particular, remain successful in driving divisions between democratic countries and regimes.

It is not enough to change a president, observed Obama, we have to change the system. There is a new president in office and new policies are being rolled

---

*During the attempted coup d'état in America following the 2020 elections, Twitter and Facebook blocked President Trump from using their platforms. That was interpreted as an acceptance on the part of Twitter and Facebook of editorial responsibility. This was possibly a step forward for the principle to be accepted, but editorial responsibility is not an established principle if it remains at the discretion of platform managers.

out. But prevailing power relations are robust. Inequality may be dented at the bottom of the distribution—no mean achievement—but hardly in the upper echelons. Monied interests are not de-organized and can still "bankroll our elections." The Supreme Court remains "an aberration" and continues to undermine checks and balances. Social media remains destructively unregulated. Beneath it all, the culture of polarization persists. In Washington and state capitals, there is not even consensus around democracy itself and basic democratic principles. Voting rights are being deliberately curtailed. The power to cheat with strategic gerrymandering of voting districts is protected and exercised. Mutual distrust is such that truth fails to be authoritative and lies become good currency.

The smartness of representative democracy

Democracy now is mostly done in the well-known way: citizens elect representatives to make laws and oversee public policy on their behalf. Even in Switzerland, with its routine of referendums, laws are made in a representative assembly, only with the additional provision that what the representatives decide usually needs to be ratified by the voters.

This design, for all its simplicity, is a very smart arrangement, unexpectedly smart since those of us who are used to it take it for granted. It solves four problems in one go: a problem of power, a problem of manageability, a problem of size, and a problem of quality.

Power. Since representatives are elected by citizens and can be deselected by them in the next election, they govern under popular control. We can let the governors have the power they need because we retain the power to control them. The problem of power is solved.

Manageability. The problem of power is solved and governance gets done with next to no burden on citizens. The Athenians had no notion of representative democracy. If the people were to have power, they would also have to accept the chore of decision-making. For all the romanticism that is attached to Athenian direct democracy, their system came with an awful load on citizens of tedious participating in never-ending debates in council and assembly meetings from dawn to dusk. In a representative system, we can vote, leave the tedium to a few representatives, and get on with life.

Size. When the American republic was created, a way needed to be found to govern a large territory. The previous republican experience was that of cities governing themselves, such as in the Italian city-states of the Renaissance. The previous democratic experience was that of direct democracy. Some of this could be replicated in America on the local level, and there was experience of town democracy before the consolidation of the federation, but a new model was needed for national and state government. The Founding Fathers, building on prior experimentation with elected legislatures in the colonies, settled for representation: localities send representatives to the capital to manage public affairs in the place of citizens themselves. We may take this for granted now, but without the invention of popular representation, we could not today have had national democracies.

Quality. It is a big deal to make and implement timely, good, and workable decisions and to shape policies so that they have a chance of actually resolving the problems they are supposed to deal with and to do this without too much of unanticipated cost. This job should be in steady hands and done by ordered procedure so as to maximize the chance of good decisions and minimize the risk of mistakes.

Quality governance is, as is clear to see, not assured, but the method of citizens electing representatives to make policy in assembly decision-making is designed to protect against, in Eisenhower's words, "misinformed mistakes." Representatives working in assembly, when things work reasonably as they should, have more and better information to draw on than is available to other citizens. There will be routines to provide representatives with relevant information and services on which they can draw to gather information on matters before them. We citizens can seek to make ourselves informed, but representatives have the advantage that information is brought their way and put in front of them professionally and systematically. It is elementary: if difficult decisions are to be made, it is in everyone's interest that they are made by well-informed decision makers. I should not want to make myself the decision maker when my representative can do it on the basis of more and better information.

Assemblies are, furthermore, arenas of competition. Candidates compete to be nominated, those nominated compete for votes, and those elected compete over policies and for votes again in the next election. Even the Athenians, whose system was committed to selecting officials by lot, opted for elections when they were particularly concerned to get quality officials: the boards of ten generals and ten treasurers, who were in charge of military and financial affairs, were chosen in elections. Competition does not always look edifying; the game may seem shortsighted and opportunistic; it may get rough and nasty. But if you think that looks bad, be careful what you wish for.

National assemblies generally work so that policies are debated in several stages and reassessed and confirmed several times before the final decision is made. Such rules force the representatives to take the time that is needed and to consider all relevant evidence so as to avoid decision-making by rush and wishful thinking. Procedures are shaped to avoid the traps of haste and convenience that Kahneman and Tversky warned of as perils of careless decision-making. A democratic assembly will be composed of representatives from different parts of the country, with different backgrounds and experiences and who will be elected on different political platforms, all of which improves the likelihood that decisions will be tested by robust debate. One reason autocratic rule is likely to be of lesser quality is that decision-making is by the few, typically a self-appointed junta whose men (usually men) are on the committee because they are of the same persuasion.

Finally, the representative method offers citizens the opportunity to elect competent representatives. Most of us know (or should know) that we ourselves are not cut out to be governors and that it is in our interest to elect those among us who are the more able. This, it is true, depends on nominations and elections being genuinely competitive—one of the weak links in my list of democratic advantages—but provided that assumption holds, we should be able to trust that we are putting the ship of state into the hands of able officers.

Advocates of "participatory democracy" want a different method of decision-making in which citizens participate directly as decision makers. That is an idea to be resisted. Only a minority of citizens would be able and inclined to spend their time in such participation. We should no more give people with an inkling for evenings of political meetings an extra say in the formation of public policy than we should give it to people who happen to have more money than others. It is not advisable to shift decision-making power from elected to self-selected decision makers. It is not advisable to shift decision-making from more to less informed decision makers. It is not advisable to shift decision-making out of assemblies designed for the purpose.

My analyses lead me to reject the call for a reinvention of democracy. Reform, yes; reinvention, no. The reinventors underestimate what we have. We should not turn our backs on the brilliant invention of representative democracy, not belittle it, not talk it down. Gimmicky alternatives, such as "participatory democracy," are not only vacuous ideas but also offer no value added to the combined smartnesses of the simple way of citizens electing representatives to govern on their behalf.

Tocqueville and Dahl again

The problem of democracy is that it comes with many and big advantages when it works well but that it is not easy to make it work well. We might think that there is some ideal constitutional recipe that would make for the good democracy, but when we look to different democratic countries, we find that they are arranged very differently and that there is no single design that is *the* workable one. Constitutions can do only so much. It is people, leaders and followers, who make them work. The main teaching of Tocqueville and Dahl is to look deeper than to the constitution, to look into the political culture.

I offer a new definition of democracy, which, again, goes deeper than to the constitutional setup. I pull culture directly into the definition, not just as a condition but as a component of democracy. The secret of a democratic culture lies in a pact between us down here and those up there.

The democratic way of managing joint affairs rests on an acceptance of disagreement. There is never agreement in a free population about political matters, certainly not important matters. With luck, we can find consensus, but if so, always across disagreement. That is why the representative method is so unexpectedly smart, because the representative assembly is the best possible setting for the forging of fair consensus. There is no "will of the people." The job of our representatives is not to implement what we the people will but to find the ground for fair compromise in the many things we the people want. That is difficult for them to do because it is difficult for strong-willed citizens to accept that they often cannot get their own way, really never fully get their own way. We are helped in that acceptance if we can see that governance, even if not as we want it, is fair. A democratic culture rests, finally, on *tolerance*, which is to say the understanding that things do not always work out perfectly. Democracy comes with advantages, which, however, present themselves with much imperfection. The quest for George Washington's "public good" is a collaborative game of trial and error.

From the acceptance of disagreement, imperfection, and tolerance follows the embrace of reform. When we know that we can only progress by trial and error—so argued Karl Popper—we also know that we can only progress step by step. If we insist on utopia, we abandon tolerance. If we hold on to tolerance, we know that we are never at ways end. Democracy is a work in progress and will so ever remain. We who think of ourselves as defenders of liberty and good government, should, as Robert Dahl showed the way, defend democracy by criticizing democracies.

We Need to Talk about Democracy

"They said, some men are too ignorant, and vicious, to share in government. Possibly so, said we; and by your system, you would always keep them ignorant, and vicious. We propose to give all a chance; and we expect the weak to grow stronger, the ignorant, wiser; and all better, and happier together. We made the experiment; and the fruit is before us."
ABRAHAM LINCOLN, 1854

It looked so good. Democracy held the moral high ground in the world. The harmony (of sorts) between government and people that Tocqueville had seen in early America was never more a reality than in the West in the second half of the twentieth century. Looking back now, this stands as a magnificent achievement.

Into the twenty-first century, those gains have been lost. Democracy is not respected. Social harmony has evaporated. The task before us is to restore and repair.

In 2020 the democratic world was hit by two catastrophes. The COVID epidemic fell down on governments as the ultimate stress test. Some democratic governments, the most prominent ones, failed to give their populations such protections that they could have provided. Toward the end of the year, American democracy was brought to near death when a sitting president who failed to win reelection tried a coup d'état to cling to office and refused to participate in the orderly transition of power, in an outrage for which he was not universally censored and in some measure praised.

Repair is urgent.

Restoring freedom

To see what is finally at stake, look to Hong Kong. There, a way of life grounded in rule of law, an independent judiciary, liberty of speech and assembly, and government under a legislature that had been reasonably pluralistic and accountable is being crushed before our eyes. It is being crushed by a junta of self-righteous men in Beijing who happen to have power that happens to be free from control. Does it matter? Life will go on. People will continue to go to work and bring their pay home to support their families. Business will progress, and investors and entrepreneurs will still get rich. There will be Sunday picnics in the park. As it is for many people in mainland China. But it will not be the same; it will be a lesser way of life. It will be life bereft of the dignity of freedom. As it is for people in mainland China.

We who have been used to living in freedom have, under the cloud of COVID, experienced life without it. That loss turned out to be heavy, and twofold. We could not ourselves arrange our daily lives, and we were limited from living socially in togetherness with others. We have had a taste of the alternative, and we have felt, personally, the truth in Aristotle's wisdom that we humans are social animals.

I *recommend* that we hold on to freedom as the supreme guiding principle that gives meaning to democracy.

Citizens enjoy liberty, to come and go as they please. They use their liberty in their daily lives. They engage with others in deliberation and thereby contribute to reason for themselves and in public life. The final blessing of liberty is not to have it but to live it.

Isaiah Berlin has explained that ideas matter, that there are different ways of understanding freedom, and that if we misunderstand, we may pervert what we wish for. He wanted to strip the idea down to the essentials of the individual being free from coercion. I have found that to be a necessary condition of freedom—the "fundamental sense"—but not a sufficient condition. As the purpose of democracy is not to be democratic, the purpose of freedom is not to be free. It is to enable people to achieve their human potential. We need to be able to make our own choices, but also to make good choices in our own interest. We are not free unless we are in control of, in Adam Smith's language, our passions.

Reason is cultivated in togetherness. The free person has free choice and then leans on others in the use of choice.* It is the idea that he is free who is unbound that perverts. That perversion runs through this treatise as a warning. It is the idea that stimulated the free market ideology that unleashed the financial crisis of 2008. It is the idea that justifies indifference to exclusion on the ground that the poor have after all had the freedom to make something of themselves. It is the idea that has caused the welfare state to fall into

---

*"Leans on" is from the blues song "Lean on Me" by Bill Withers, written, composed, and recorded in 1972, in reaction to the chilly individualism of life in Los Angeles. Millions of people since then have appreciated this song for its simple human wisdom: "We all need somebody to lean on." No one has any difficulty in grasping that wisdom in a song, but then along comes the philosopher and says that in freedom, we should just forget what we know from our own experience and go by the cold logic that it is all about the individual who leans on no one.

disregard. It is the idea that has, sometimes, enabled the healthy to do their own thing up against an epidemic that threatens other people's lives.

I *recommend* that we shun the too-good-to-be-true idea of freedom as just free choice and revive the Aristotelian idea of freedom as access to human dignity.

Restoring power

When global capitalism crashed in 2008, democratic governments were unprepared. The state had been rolled back and markets allowed free rein. Market institutions, banks, and others turned to reckless gambling and brought themselves to ruin and the economies they were supposed to serve to chaos. Lessons have been learned. State power has been restored and regulations reimposed.

When public health crashed in 2020, democratic governments, at least many of them, were again unprepared. Lessons were learned with overnight speed. State power has been restored as never before in peacetime.

I *recommend* that we listen to Max Weber and accept it as fact that governments are and must be wielders of vast powers.

The experiment of small-power states up against globalization in economic and social life is over. If we want, as we should, the new normal to be democratic, we should start by asking to what repairs state powers should be turned. I have used the metaphor of a house: a constitutional architecture that sits on a foundation of culture. There are repairs to be made in the architecture, but for that to be realistically possible and for those repairs to work, we must strengthen the foundations.

The cracks in the foundation are in the form of polarizations. People stand against each other in hostile inability to communicate and collaborate. A stable house stands on solid ground. Cracks appear when the ground shifts. The democratic house stands on a ground of social structure. That ground has been shifting with recurring, widening, and ever more pernicious deprivations and exclusions. The first call on repair goes to the social underpinning of democratic government. Inequalities have been neglected to such a degree that citizens have turned to revolt. If polarizations cannot be overcome, or at least noticeably modified, not much else will work. But if they can, if neglect can be turned to attention, those who now feel disenfranchised will have reason to feel that they are listened to. There will be less reason for polarization. There would be hope that social relations might turn from mutual hostility and toward, in President Obama's words, "basic bonds of trust between citizens." It is not much to ask in civilized societies that people can see each other as fellows. They do that if they are not wrenched apart by winnings floating to the top while those already dispossessed are left dispossessed again and again. Pull back runaway inequality, and we can restore the three C's of democracy: culture, conversation, and contract.

I *recommend* that we put state powers to work to deal with the problem of inequality.

The way to deal with inequality is with the tried-and-tested method of the welfare state. The way to mobilize the welfare state is to reconnect with the beginnings of neoclassical economics and the moral imperative that inspired its original champions, under Alfred Marshall's banner, to rid affluent economies of the evil of poverty.

I *recommend* that we determine not only to control or modify poverty but to *eradicate* it.

Not all exclusions are in material deprivation, but many are, the most severe ones, and most others have a dimension of want to them. Not all problems of inequality are located at the bottom of the distribution, but it is here, going back to Marshall again, that we find "the chief cause" of the "physical, mental and moral ill-health" of exclusion. If democratic governments now determine that it is part of the necessary repair that they deal with inequality, they will need strong arguments to fight down the resistance of monied interests. It is in the commitment to eradicate poverty that we can find that moral force. Poverty is that which is unacceptable. We have the means. It is necessary to repair democracies that are torn apart by polarizations. It is not defendable to let fester that which is unacceptable.

What then follows are economic and labor market policies for jobs and decent pay whereby the excluded are integrated into the pride of fending for themselves. What follows further are protections in the form of pensions, health and social care, family support, and decent poor relief. This is hardly a radical program. These are all matters that are established on the political agenda in all democratic countries. It is now a question of mobilizing determination. We have seen in the experience of epidemic management that determination can be mobilized. There was a salutary lesson in Britain's policy response when poor relief (Universal Credit), for years inadequate and ineffective, was overnight ramped up to a decent level of support and made to operate without friction.

I *recommend* that the way to deal with inequality is to remobilize the welfare state.

The welfare state is not in fashion. That is not because of economic deadweight. The Scandinavian countries are the most successful of any in both economic performance and social protection, arguably economically successful because they are socially successful. Nor because welfare state arrangements are cumbersome and ineffective. That we know from Britain's National Health Service, the survivor from the great reforms of the 1940s that has miraculously escaped the rolling back of state power. This service provides free and universal access to high-quality care, with no hassle for users, and at uniquely low cost. It was the branch of the state that stood up to the test of the epidemic, in sharp contrast to, for example, the neglected sector of social care. It was the service British people in the first lockdown came out of their houses for once a week to applaud in appreciation. So much for people not valuing public service when they get it. So much for apathy and "malaise." So much for the welfare state not feeding into trust and community.

The welfare state is out of fashion for the most elementary of reasons: it is tax-costly. It does not drain the economy, but it does ask for sharing, for, going back to Marshall again, "economic chivalry."

During the second half of the twentieth century, the level of taxation in advanced economy countries has increased to pretty much its social maximum. There have been significant differences between countries, even between the advanced economies, but those differences have during the past few decades been more or less leveled out to a tax extraction of plus or minus 40 percent of national income.[1] There are still differences and still, no doubt, somewhere, some scope for some increase in tax extraction, but a continued trajectory toward steadily rising tax levels is no longer available. The reason is not only that the tax level just cannot continue to rise forever but also a loss to national governments in their power to tax. There is not much that is clear in economic globalization, but the challenge in taxation to national governments is. Businesses, the larger corporations in particular but also smaller operators, have obtained the power, more than previously, to credibly threaten to move capital and jobs to more hospitable domains if they find their home turf unfriendly. Businesses see all taxes, including personal taxes, as ultimate costs to themselves. The tax regime is therefore an important component in the equation of localization and relocalization. No government can now entertain notably more costly taxation than any other, and all governments live under intense pressure, backed up by real power, to cut taxes and certainly not impose new ones.

Channeling economic resources to public causes via taxation is a pretty crude method. If we could find more imaginative ways, more might get done by way of public service, while tax capacity could be reserved for causes that cannot be funded in any other way, such as welfare state redistribution.

I *recommend* that what governments cannot extract, they encourage citizens to give up voluntarily.

This, as it happens, is already being done. People do voluntary work and make financial contributions to charities that do good works, and do so under the encouragement of tax exemptions. This is a magic form of nontax taxation. Effort and money flow to public purposes, while those who work and pay do not think of it as extraction.*

More could be done. Let all contributions to good works from citizens be recognized, in the form of both money and voluntary work. Let the government commit not only to tax exemptions but to matching the contributions of citizens so that what citizens provide, either in money or labor, would trigger an equivalent provision from the government. Say a group of parents think the local school should offer pupils more physical education. They raise half the money to employ a teacher for the purpose, knowing that the government is obliged to put up matching funds. Or say you do volunteer work one night a week at a local shelter for the homeless. You would be able to bring to the shelter your labor, plus a matching government grant. For every £10 worth of volunteer work you do, the cause of your choice benefits to the effect of £20.

There would be much in it for the government. As a result of its facilitation, it would see useful services being provided for only half the cost to itself. Or for less than half the cost. In the school example, the money goes into a salary on which the school pays social insurance contributions, and the new teacher pays taxes on her income and VAT on her spending. That spending in the next round stimulates further economic activity, which generates further public revenue.

There should also be much in it for citizens. I do not subscribe to the responsibility of representatives to make public policy decisions being diluted by participatory decision-making. That seems to me a waste of everyone's time, or worse. But a subtext in what I am suggesting here is participation in a different

---

*Ahead of Christmas 2019, the British government announced a fund of £1.15 million in support of community groups around the country who were engaging to save local pubs in rural and remote areas that were threatened with closure, often by bringing them into community ownership. An estimated one hundred initiatives were expected to receive support from the fund. In early 2020, in the London Borough of Richmond (where I live), the local council launched the "Richmond upon Thames Voluntary Fund" to "give the community an opportunity to donate to local organisations who make a big difference to the lives of vulnerable people." The reason for the initiative, it was explained, was that, because of constraints in tax funding, "it is not possible [for the council itself] to provide all the support needed." Voluntary donations to the fund would benefit from national tax exemption, known as Gift Aid, whereby every £100 donated to the fund would trigger an additional £25 as a tax rebate. In mid-year 2020, the British government allocated £85 million (out of a £750 million fund in support of charities) for a monthlong "community match challenge" in which funds raised privately for selective COVID charities would be matched pound for pound by government money.

meaning: the opportunity for citizens to make consequential decisions by their own actions. Decide on some purpose, put some effort or money into it, and you can see that purpose realized under your own agency. That's real participation, not just the talking shop kind.

Imagine thousands and thousands of initiatives throughout the land and you have a democratic structure of participatory social justice. You have democratic culture in motion. Doings are in response to needs identified by citizens and under their authority. Citizens massively decide on the provision of public goods, in a decentralized pattern. Ordinary people make decisions. They take power and accept responsibility. The government facilitates and supports.

I have had in mind a country like Britain, which is relatively poor in the provision of public service but rich in nonpublic institutions of public provision. There are charitable associations across the board, large and small, national and local. These are run and supported by people eager to do more work. They represent an underused capital. With more encouragement, it would be meaningful for citizens to engage and to get together and create more institutions of their own to work for causes of their interest.

REFORM AND REALISM

Is it realistic to make recommendations for new directions in constitutional and public policy in an age of polarization and political gridlock? Many observers are despondent about the possibility of reform.

For my part, I am eclectic about "realism." We cannot know the future, and we cannot know what will turn out to be possible. Ideas matter. Even ideas that are not immediately acted on have life and may continue to do work in future deliberations. Circumstances change, and ideas that were once farfetched are suddenly pertinent. After the triple blow of economic crash, a deadly pandemic, and an attempted antidemocratic coup d'état in America, the democratic world is not the same. The ground has been shifting in ways of thinking about government and regulation. There is, hopefully, an understanding that the future cannot be business as usual. Democracies are always unfinished and always need to adapt and evolve. We who care about democracy must always encourage reform and ways of improvement.

The recommendations given here reach broadly. I make recommendations for constitutional and legislative reform. I recognize that such recommendations have poor prospects unless the political culture is receptive to ideas and disposed to acting on them. Culture cannot be reformed from above but must repair itself from inside. But we can do something about the conditions that might enable cultural self-repair. I therefore start with the tensions in social structure that cause polarizations in the political culture that again cause gridlock in constitutional procedures. I think there must be reason to hope that it may now be realistic to propose that we must deal with the problem of inequality, that if we do, there will be less cause for polarization and more cause for trust and confidence, and that, if so, we should be able to move on to repairs in the constitutional architecture. I think there must be reason to hope that such repairs will feed back into improvements in trust and confidence.

Restoring leadership

State power sits in government offices. The use of power is in the hands of holders of office. We want representatives and officials to be competent. We need their leadership. We want it to be meaningful that we implore them, following Machiavelli, to be effective.

It is one of the virtues of electoral democracy that we can elect competent leaders. We know how to conduct free, fair, and frequent elections. We have the theory, and we have the procedures. The attempted coup against the 2020 elections in America failed because they were conducted according to established standards so that the authority of the outcome could not be undermined.

However, before elections there are nominations. Here, we have neither theory nor safe procedures. The question of how to nominate meets only a big black hole in democratic theory. The methods of party screening and primaries are not robust, are easily corrupted, and easily allow unsuitable candidates through. There is a big job for the theoreticians waiting to be done toward a theory of nominations of similar dignity to the well-developed theory of elections.

I *recommend* to the political scientists that they make the study of nominations a priority.

In many walks of life, it is now established convention that candidates for high office are subject to some kind of "fit and proper person" test.* In the

---

*In 2003 Brian Mawhinney, a retired member of Parliament and cabinet minister, became chairman of the English Football League, which was in the grip of financial mismanagement. The next year he pioneered a "fit and proper person test" to ban from directorship in or major ownership of a club any person who had competing interests in other clubs, who was disqualified from holding business directorships, or who had a serious criminal conviction or a history of insolvency. This is recognized to have contributed to a cleaning up of mismanagement in the league during Mawhinney's seven years at the helm.

British judicial system, magistrates' courts are the lowest level criminal and family courts that hear, in the first instance, all cases in these areas and rule on all but the heaviest ones. Cases are usually heard by three magistrates, with the assistance of a legally trained adviser. Magistrates are lay judges and serve on a voluntary and part-time basis. To become a magistrate, you apply to the advisory committee of your local magistrates' court, which nominates candidates to the Lord Chancellor and Lord Chief Justice, who make the appointments. As in politics, any citizen (between nineteen and sixty-five years of age) is eligible to be a magistrate. There are no specific educational requirements, but there are certain other criteria. Nominees must be without serious criminal convictions and without a record of bankruptcy. The committee needs, further, to be satisfied that you have certain personal qualifications, such as maturity and a good sense of fairness, the ability to understand documents and think logically, and that you are a person of "good character."

There are two qualities to be noted in this experience. The first one is the serious attention given to nominations. The method is elaborate, and much work and attention go into ensuring that candidates are proper and qualified. Second, it is a method that has made for legitimacy. Magistrates make serious and consequential decisions in complicated matters and are trusted to do so well and fairly. There are roughly 330 magistrates' courts in England and Wales, served by just over 16,000 magistrates. This system churns on effectively day in and day out without a whiff of scandal. No one speaks despairingly of "the magistrates" as they do freely of "the politicians." It works to require of candidates that they be of good character.

Something similar applies to the selection of juries in court cases. All citizens have a right and duty to do jury service, but there are mechanisms of vetting to block unsuitable candidates. In the British system, for example, you cannot serve if you have been convicted of a serious crime, nor if a conflict of interest might arise, nor if the judge considers you unsuitable for other reasons in a specific case. If you misbehave during the case, you can be dismissed. Court service is a democratic duty, or privilege, if you will. It is not "undemocratic" to test candidates' suitability.

In the British National Health Service, one of the world's biggest corporations by personnel, Parliament has imposed a fit and proper person test of potential directors of health trusts. Here candidates are exposed to pre-appointment vetting for both qualifications and "good character." The Bank of England operates (as of 2016) a "Senior Management Regime" according to which institutions must apply to the Financial Conduct Authority for the clearing of candidates for board position or directorships according to criteria that include competence and "fitness and propriety." The European Central

Bank operates a similar fit and proper person test of candidates for management bodies of credit institutions, to ascertain both that the candidates are qualified and that they are of good repute.

It should be obvious that we should want our political leaders to be qualified and to be of good character and capable of commanding respect and exercising leadership. If so, it should be obvious that those who aspire to office should be tested. Universal eligibility is a democratic principle on a par with the universal right to vote. However, "universal" does not mean absolutely no infringement. Citizens can in certain circumstances lose the right to vote and to stand for office by court order, for example, in response to electoral fraud or treason. In Britain, civil servants, judges, and members of the police and armed services are excluded from standing for Parliament, as are, in certain circumstances, persons who are subject to bankruptcy restrictions. If a sitting member of Parliament is sentenced for crimes under certain criteria, a recall petition is triggered, which, if signed by at least one in ten voters in the constituency, will result in a by-election.* To ask of candidates that they have a certain minimal suitability to act as their fellows' representatives is not to negate the principle of universal eligibility.

I *recommend* the introduction of a fit and proper person test for candidacy to local and national elected office. At a minimum, a candidate should be obliged, as a condition for standing, to file with the relevant electoral authority a formalized self-declaration that he or she (1) does not have a history of (serious) criminal convictions, (2) does not have a history of (serious) insolvency or bankruptcy, (3) does not have a history of having withheld (serious) income or property from taxation, and (4) authorizes the electoral authority to check the veracity of the self-declaration and commits to providing the authority with relevant documentation. If unwilling to file, the candidate would be disqualified from standing. If it later emerges that the candidate had filed falsely, he or she should be dismissed from office.

Restoring constitutional order

The constitutional architecture is built around, let's call it, the People's Assembly (sometimes known as Congress, sometimes Parliament, sometimes National Assembly, sometimes by other names). Assemblies do the citizens' work, allocate powers to the executive, and control the exercise of that power

---

*As happened in the case of Labour Party MP Fiona Onasanya, who in 2019 was found guilty of perverting the course of justice by having lied to the police in order to avoid prosecution for speeding.

on behalf of citizens. I have concluded that the best way to safe and effective rule is through well-functioning assemblies that answer to citizens. For example, if we are going to deal with the problem of inequality, it is a People's Assembly that must mobilize the necessary determination. While we wait for a big-bang invention for better democracy, we should hold on tight, very tight, to the simple but unexpectedly smart method of electoral representation. No better way is so far known, and it is going to take some invention.

I *recommend* restored confidence in governance in the hands of assemblies of elected representatives.

Assembly democracy is not an impressive sight across the democratic world. Assemblies often perform poorly, under pressure from executive branches in want of unchecked powers and from nonparliamentary actors, in particular organized monied interests. I have given warning that my attention drifts to the American and British cases. If democratic government is in a bad way, much comes down to dysfunction in the People's Assemblies, certainly in the American Congress and British Parliament.

Well-functioning assemblies depend on well-functioning nominations and elections. Nominations I have dealt with above. The running of elections was put to the test in America in 2020. It is gratifying that no general recommendation is called for.*

Assemblies should be representative of the citizenry. In his review of the American Constitution, Robert Dahl concluded that a major fault is the lack of representativeness in Congress. In the British case, elections are designed deliberately for Parliament to be composed in a way that is poorly representative. That is under a theory that an electoral system that gives the winning party overrepresentation makes for strong governments, which, again, is thought to make for effective governance. I have found this to be a false theory—the English Delusion. A theory that has been falsified should be discarded.

I *recommend*, in Britain, America, and elsewhere, that election systems that perform poorly in representativeness be scrapped in favor of systems of proportional representation.

Democracy should be grounded in inclusive citizenship. There is some considerable way to go to complete this march. It is no longer contested that all adults have a right to representation through the vote, but it remains to be accepted that children should have the same right. Like other citizens,

---

*But there is the American scandal of "gerrymandering." It is so obvious that the drawing up of electoral districts should be in the hands of relevant expertise, as it is in many states, that it is an embarrassment to have to recommend it.

children have interests, and like other citizens their interests should have the backing of voting power.

I *recommend* extending voting rights to children, using the tested method of proxy voting. That would improve the quality of electoral democracy and in the process put more voting power behind the carriers of long-term interests.

Once the assembly is constituted by well-functioning elections, its effectiveness depends on well-functioning internal procedures. Here, the British Parliament offers a case study in how not to do it. There is the oddity of the House of Lords, which many British reformers think should be reformed away. In fact, however, and this is a curious concession from someone writing in defense of democracy, the Lords are by and large a positive influence in legislation. It is in the elected House of Commons that reform is urgent.

The House of Commons is one of the most ineffective organizations known to man. The job it is unable to do in any proper way is to provide adequate predecision scrutiny of legislation and budgetary proposals. Most members of Parliament simply have no idea in any detail what legislation they put their name to or what budgets they allocate the government. When then prime minister David Cameron in 2015 put to Parliament a proposal for a European Union referendum, the House of Commons was without procedure for subjecting this proposal to scrutiny. The Referendum Act, on a monumental decision for the country, passed through Parliament on a nod without Parliament doing any work to inform itself about and deliberate over implications and consequences.

I *recommend* that the House of Commons takes control of its own agenda. The post of leader of the House of Commons, the government's commissar in Parliament, should be abolished and the business of the Commons put under the authority of a Committee of Speakers.

I further *recommend* that select committees be put in charge of scrutinizing government proposals in the first instance.

It would work like this: The government makes proposals to Parliament in the form of bills and budgets. Proposals are received by the Committee of Speakers, which decides how they are to be dealt with and with what priority, or returns them to the government for further preparation. When accepted to be dealt with, proposals are allocated to the relevant select committee to be turned over in detail. The committee may again return the proposal to the government for further preparation, or report to the House with its recommendations, which may contain amendments to the government's proposals and may come with majority and minority recommendations. The committee will be obliged to have scrutinized the matter according to specified procedures, such as to assess constitutional, legal, administrative, and economic implications, and to report to the House with a written recommendation. Only at this stage is the matter considered by the House in plenum, which can then debate in the knowledge that it has been under the scrutiny of the competent committee and with full information on the merits, demerits, and implications of the proposal. Brits might be surprised to learn that this, radical to their ears, is to propose no more than is standard in better performing People's Assemblies in many other countries.

As the House of Commons now works, too much business is conducted in plenum and not enough in committee. This impedes the capacity of the House and disables it from considering policies with adequate care. The above proposal, magically, puts more work to the House while at the same time increasing its capacity. When more work is done in committee, the Commons can work effectively with more matters at the same time. The House of Commons has 650 members yet so little capacity that it can give most legislation only scant attention, does next to no work on budgets, and still regularly runs out of time in dealing with matters before it.

In recent years, as it happens, select committees have taken on more work and responsibility than they have had, in the form of scrutinizing policies after the fact. That has given them and Parliament a new and more active role in policy oversight. The committees and their members have risen to the challenge and are now doing eminent oversight work, in evidence of the quality of work that is done in Parliament once Parliament is given serious work to do. If the House of Commons were given similar responsibilities in predecision scrutiny, Britain would be a better governed country.

Once People's Assemblies are constituted in well-functioning elections and have well-functioning working procedures, their effectiveness depends on balanced relations with other institutions and actors that operate in various ways in their environment. Above, I have dealt, in the British case, with assembly-government relations. It is part of the English Delusion that it is conducive to good government that Parliament does not get in the way of governmental expediency. I have recommended balanced relations so that Parliament be in a position to give governmental policies adequate scrutiny. Other potential predators are courts, media, and organized monied and corporate interests.

People's Assemblies are under court oversight. This relationship, to be productive, depends on a fine balance. Court oversight is a valuable check on legislatures and executive agencies, but may, and may easily, pervert to sucking capacity away from those who do the governing. Courts that get a taste of power tend to reach for more. The problem is acute in America with, following

Robert Dahl, the "aberration" of excessive Supreme Court power. The problem is judicial activism.

I *recommend* that People's Assemblies stand guard against judicial activism and take measures to temper such activism when it rears its head.

Court moderation depends primarily on judicial culture. Lawmakers can, and should, contribute to court moderation by subjecting the temptation to activism to reasoned criticism. In the case of the United States, Congress should reclaim its rightful position in the system of checks and balances by pulling the Supreme Court down to earth and weaning it off its excessive activism and its inflated opinion of its own eminence. The lack of willingness in Congress to stand up to a court that is destroying the constitutional system of checks and balances is difficult for an observer to reconcile with. Congress has the means but has been unable to mobilize the resolve.

I *recommend* that the number of justices be increased to ten, with a six to four majority being required for judgment.

Social media have opened up a marvelous world of connectivity and exchange of information that is enriching the lives of people around the world. But there is a downside in uncontrollable power, distortion, and manipulation. As usual, unregulated markets pervert. The new economy of information technology, social media, and big data analytics is woefully underregulated and dominated by a few gigantic cartels. This sector straddles economic and political markets and, as now constituted, operates so as to undermine efficiency on both accounts. A few providers are in control, and normal consumer behavior is without impact. It is time to impose order on the Wild West of social media.

I *recommend* the breaking up media and data trusts.

I *recommend* that normal editorial responsibility be imposed on those who manage social media sites.

When President Obama warned Americans about democracy "grinding to a halt," he warned specifically about reducing the "influence of money in our politics" so that "a handful of families or hidden interests can't bankroll our elections." He was right to warn. If organized monied interests are in control in the metagame of power, assemblies are not of the people, nominations are not open, elections are not fair, and power is not under popular control. We *must* draw back the unregulated use of money as a political resource. We *must* find a way of paying for politics that is compatible with basic principles of political equality.

The United States Supreme Court has decided that it would be a suppression of freedom of expression to deny citizens the right to support political causes and candidates of their liking financially, and this principle now has broad support in jurisprudence in America and elsewhere. However, it does not follow that there is a right to unregulated political use of private money. Such a right does not exist in economic markets, where monopolistic practices are generally, if not always effectively, unlawful. That should be the case all the more in political markets, where the principle is, as it is not in economic markets, that each participant should have the same influence. It bears being repeated: the use of economic power to undermine the reality of political competition is destructive of democracy, not only damaging but *destructive*.

There are arguments for public funding of political parties and campaigns. Democracy is a public good and should not depend on private funding. Some European democracies do have extensive public funding, which to some degree does discourage some forms of private funding, for example, from business. But there are drawbacks. One is that it is rarely consistent. For example, the ability of trade unions to fund social democratic parties has usually not been restricted in the way other forms of private funding has. Another drawback is that public funding has tempted established parties to fund themselves lavishly from the public purse in ways not available to up-and-coming parties. This has been visible in, for example, Germany and Scandinavia.

Some of us have for some time been suggesting alternative ways of arranging public funding, mainly some variation of letting public funds be distributed through the hands of voters in the form of vouchers for parties or candidates of their choice. That might, it has been thought, both shut down transgression and put a new power of equality into the hands of voters. This may have some theoretical merit, but, in truth, it is not an idea that has found much favor or attracted much interest outside of a small community of politico nerds.

Monopolistic power in the political market arises if one or a few donors are able to obtain decisive influence, or collude to give themselves such influence, and when there is a direct connection between donor and recipient so that the donor can extract favor from the recipient on the threat of withholding funding. In the American Predicament, and not only there, monopolistic power in this form is rampant. Since Adam Smith, it has been known that if monopolization is possible, it will happen. In *The Wealth of Nations*: "People of the same trade seldom meet together, even for merriment and diversion, but the conversation ends in a conspiracy against the public, or in some contrivance to raise prices." In recognition of which, in business, in civilized economies, there are laws against such conspiracies and contrivances. If the managers of supermarket chains agree to raise the price of milk and not to challenge each other on the agreed price, they are breaking the law. We should be no more naive and no less prudent in politics than in business.

Political monopolization does not have to be. It could be prevented in ways that are compatible with antimonopoly principles in economic markets. That could be done, first, by capping rules. There should be upper limits on the size of any individual donation and standard antimonopolistic regulation against collusion. Mega-expensive politics, as now in the United States, is a way of making money the ultimate resource of political power. Upper limits on donations would not need to be draconian, only enough that an individual donor could not make himself dominant.

Furthermore, it could be prevented by regulations whereby recipients would not know the identity of donors, as suppliers and consumers in economic markets generally do not know each other. A donor who wants to support a group or candidate does not for that purpose need to make himself known by name to the group or candidate in question. That is only needed if his intention is to purchase influence, which is what should be prevented.

I *recommend* a fiscal clearing house between citizens and political groupings and candidates to raise the funds to pay for politics.

It would work like this: Citizens put money into the clearing house earmarked for groups or candidates they wish to support. That money would come out of the clearing house to the groups or candidates in question, but without the name tag of the donor. No donor should be able to demand that his identity or donation be made public, and no recipient to know who the donors are. With the clearing house the only or main source of political funding, parties and candidates would be competing for money in a fair market.

If we think people make political donations in order to buy influence, why would anyone under such regulation put up any money at all? The first answer is that most people who make political donations are not out to buy influence. That may be the case for big donors but is not the thinking behind smaller donations. It is common enough that people support causes they are interested in, political as well as nonpolitical, without any idea of return to themselves.

With antimonopoly regulations in the political market, we should not only allow but encourage citizens to donate politically. Citizens would hold the power of money in much the same way they hold the power of the vote, not anyone or any small group individually but collectively and with equality. It would sharpen our representatives' attention to know that they have to satisfy us citizens enough to get us to give up not only our vote but also some of our money. If this were the way to pay for politics, citizens would have to contribute in order to have a working democracy. We want democracy; it needs money to run; we have to put it up.

To ensure that, I recommend additional stimulus behind the encouragement, fiscal stimulus (much as I've recommended above for the cause of nontax taxation). Let each private donation release a matching alloca-tion from the public purse. My personal donation would be worth twice as much as I myself put in. Matching public monies could follow private dona-tions to the intended recipients. Or, as would be my preferred arrangement, they could go, in part, into funds to support local civil society activities and thereby feed into the preservation of democratic cultures. Political party–like activities would be eligible for funding, which would facilitate the formation of new political groupings and relax the grip of established parties on political money. My contribution, then, would first support a group or candidate of my choice, including with a matching donation in addition to my contribu-tion, and then, in addition, civil society activity in my community. The distri-bution of local funds would be in the hands of an appropriate local committee under local government authority, breathing additional life into local democ-racy. This should all be a pretty good deal for politically and socially minded citizens. Indeed, it should be a good deal for all concerned—citizens, parties and candidates, civil society activists, the government—except for those who are in the business of advancing their own interests by way of perverting po-litical equality.

Between the people down here and their assembly up there is local govern-ment. Much of what is delivered in public services is delivered locally. Local authorities tie up the chain of control between people and power.

The study of local government is peripheral in democratic theory, some-thing that ambitious theorists have not seen to be sexy enough to be worth dirtying their hands on. In a recent and ambitious review of democratic theory—*The State of Democratic Theory* by Ian Shapiro—local government and local democracy get exactly zero mention.

I *recommend* to the political scientists that they turn their attention and energy to the neglected study of local governance and lift the study of local democracy out of the theoretical shadows.

Tocqueville found that democracy worked well for the Americans in part because of the strength of local communities. In Book Four, I explained that the Scandinavians have had the good luck of shaping social protection on the model of locally based poor relief. That is in part because they have also had the good luck of maintaining a tradition of municipal government. In Book Three I have visited "the way of life among the folks in the valley," about cultural vitality in local communities. I ascribe that vitality in part to the tra-dition of high-responsibility local government in small-scale municipalities. As I believe the success of the Scandinavian welfare state owes more to local politics than is often recognized, I believe that the success of Scandinavian democracy rests strongly on the vitality of its local democracy. That vitality comes from the municipalities being small enough for genuine nearness and from those municipalities having real powers, including in taxation, and real responsibilities such as in social care, schooling, land management, and cultural life. No wonder two out of three voters, or more, find it worth their while to vote.

I *recommend* that units of local government be small in size and big in authority.

Britain has chosen the opposite way. Here, there is no municipal government at all. The lowest level political units are districts and urban boroughs with populations typically between 100,000 and 300,000, and even these units have next to no power and only very basic responsibilities. In *The British Constitution*, its most recent and comprehensive analysis, the late Anthony King concluded that "local government is no longer, in any meaningful sense, a part of the British constitution." That is a result of local units that are big in size and small in authority. No wonder two out of three voters, or more, do not bother to vote.

Beyond national governments are further centers of power in supernational authorities. The extent of supernational government, mainly an invention of the second half of the twentieth century, is much greater than often recognized. The United Nations family of organizations is a global government, complete with an assembly of lawmakers, the General Assembly, an executive, the Security Council, ministry-like agencies for health, agriculture, trade, refugee matters, and much more, central banking, courts, regional councils, and so on. The European Union is a supernational authority with the power to make decisions that are binding on nations, again, with the whole structure of government: parliament, executive, administrative departments, central bank, and its own court.

The experience of supernational governance is good. We have seen in Book Four the capacity of the United Nations to bring about concerted action of poor relief within the Millennium Development framework. The European Union has bound European nations together in mutual dependency in a way that is curing the continent, we must hope, of its centuries' old propensity to warfare.

There is, however, a democratic deficit in the shifting of political power upward and out of national institutions, principally elected People's Assemblies. Even in the European Union, with its directly elected parliament, there is a feeling that power is insufficiently accountable. But when Robert Dahl observed it as unavoidable that decisions of the international system are not made democratically, he, for once, slightly missed the point. The problem is, rather, that decisions of the international system are outside of democratic control.

Democratic control sits in a chain from citizens on the ground to decision makers up high. That chain, I have been suggesting, should start with citizens who are embedded in democratic cultures, move upward via local governments of nearness and authority, and tie down national decision makers with the powers that rest in the vote and in deliberation. Could that chain be extended beyond national legislatures to also tie down decision-making on the supranational level?

Not so easily, it seems. The experiment in the European Union with a directly elected parliament has not done the job. Voting participation is low, and the European Parliament is not widely seen by citizens as their agency for the holding of power to answer. It has not become an experiment that others are looking to for a model. It would be hard to see, for example, direct elections to the United Nations General Assembly or that anyone would suggest it. However, there happens to be another way in an underappreciated method: *indirect* elections.

I *recommend* a regime of indirect elections to supranational governing assemblies.

The democratic deficit arises because authority is sucked out of national parliaments and usurped by unaccountable bodies higher up. That deficit could be filled by those bodies being embraced into the control of national parliaments that in turn are under popular control.

The General Assembly of the United Nations, for example, could be constituted by national parliamentarians. The European Parliament could be made up of parliamentarians from member states. Other regional unions, now in the making, could do likewise. Supranational decision-making would be in the hands of elected representatives. There would be an unbroken chain of control from citizens on the ground to decision-making on the global level.

Practically, to take the case of the European Union, let the Parliament be elected by and among the elected members of national legislatures. European elections would then be wrapped into national elections, and European politics would figure in those campaigns. This would give attention to European issues, at least more than now with poorly attended elections fought with indifference, expose voters to one election instead of two, and enliven that election (something that is much needed in its own right). National legislatures, instead of being sidelined, would have a direct role in European governance. Members of the European Parliament would be accountable to their national legislatures and thereby to voters. The European Parliament would consist of elected members. A European Parliament does not have to sit continuously. It could meet, say, twice a year for one or two months at a time. It would pass European law, appoint the executive, adopt its budget, and undertake oversight. It would have the authority to hold the executive to answer, and also, importantly, to hold the European Court of Justice back from excessive activism. Parliamentary subcommittees could meet at other times. Members of the European Parliament would continue as members of national parliaments, which would ensure their accountability and overcome the feeling of distance from citizens to the European Parliament.

The use of indirect elections for this purpose is well known. The Council of Europe, established in 1949 as the first regional organization of postwar reconciliation, is managed under the oversight of a Parliamentary Assembly made up of members of the national assemblies of member states. The project of European integration started with the same method. The European Coal and Steel Community, formed in 1951, was set up under the management of a High Authority assisted by a Common Assembly whose members were drawn from national parliaments. When the European Economic Community was formed in the Treaty of Rome in 1957, it was under the management of a Commission, a Council of Ministers, and a Parliamentary Assembly, composed of delegates "designated by the respective Parliaments from among their members." The Assembly was renamed Parliament in 1962, and direct elections were introduced in 1979. The thinking was that a supranational parliament could not have real authority without being directly elected, but there is no reason that an assembly constituted by indirect elections should have less democratic legitimacy.

A similar arrangement for the United Nations could turn its General Assembly into a genuine global parliament that would have the democratically grounded final authority in what is in reality already a global government.

Would it matter? It would. It would make it possible to delegate power upward without a loss of democratic control. Such delegation has already happened in Europe, but at the cost of a democratic deficit. The British Brexit revolt against the European Union was driven, in no small measure, in a message that should be listened to, by a pretty widely shared feeling in a liberty-minded population that too much power had been shifted to Brussels, that that power was not properly accountable, and that it was starting to make itself autocratic. A United Nations under democratic accountability could be allowed powers it is now denied, and would be better equipped to deal with global matters, such as the gigantic challenge of threats to sustainability and environmental balance or, as is likely, the recurrence of health pandemics. It would have more authority to restrain international courts from creeping

SUMMARY OF RECOMMENDATIONS

I have recommended

- that we resolve to salvage democracy, not to reinvent it
- that we hold on to freedom as the supreme guiding principle that gives meaning to democracy
- that we revive the Aristotelian idea of freedom as access to human dignity
- that we accept it as fact that governments are and must be wielders of vast powers
- that we put state powers to work to deal with the problem of inequality
- that we determine not only to control or modify poverty but to *eradicate* it
- that the way to deal with inequality is to remobilize the welfare state
- that what governments cannot extract in taxes, they encourage citizens to give up voluntarily
- that the political scientists make the study of nominations a priority
- that a fit and proper person test be introduced for candidacy to elected office
- that we restore confidence in governance in the hands of elected assemblies
- that election systems be designed on the principle of proportional representation
- that voting rights be extended to children, using the tested method of proxy voting
- that, in Britain's Parliament, the House of Commons takes control of its own agenda
- that, in Britain's House of Commons, select committees be put in charge of scrutinizing government proposals in the first instance
- that People's Assemblies stand guard against judicial activism
- that, in the US Supreme Court, the number of justices be increased to ten, with a six-to-four majority being required for judgment
- that media and data trusts be broken up
- that editorial responsibility be imposed on those who manage social media sites
- that we pay for politics from contributions from citizens, channeled through a fiscal clearing house, and with the encouragement of matching contributions from the public purse
- that the political scientists turn their attention and energy to the neglected study of local governance and lift the study of local democracy out of the theoretical shadows
- that units of local government be small in size and big in authority
- that supernational governing assemblies be given democratic legitimacy by way of indirect elections

activism. It could enact law, such as much-needed supernational tax law, have some powers of taxation of its own, and be trusted with more money to do more work. There could be a United Nations police force, for example, to help in the execution of court rulings, and a standing army for better and more rapid peace-making and peace-keeping operations.

Restoring confidence

Up against the crumbling of confidence, I have sought remedies through the restoration of freedom, power, leadership, and constitutional order. Well and good, but we citizens are not innocent bystanders and not only consumers of democratic goods. We should make demands, but also take ourselves to task.

Democracy depends on us, as we depend on it. It needs to be wanted; to be wanted, it needs to be believed in; to be believed in, it needs to be understood. If we hold on to it, we will have it. If we let go, it will be lost. The Athenians understood this too late and were then unable to salvage their freedom. It is not too late for us if we engage now. We are finally in a battlefield of ideas. Ideas are made up of the ways women and men think about their condition. I have said to those up high: govern, lead, be effective. Now, I recommend to us down here: *think* about what you have, what may go lost, what you might get instead.

Think about freedom. The democratic way of arranging joint affairs is in respect and protection of freedom. We can be governed yet live freely. We can seek information and knowledge freely. We can meet up with others freely. We can discuss freely. We can express ourselves and deliberate freely. We can be the authors of our own lives.

Think about government. If we have order, it is from government we get it. We must hope that we can regain confidence in government as a force for George Washington's "public good."

Think about power. Democratic governments, no less than autocratic ones, must have power, and it is the power we allow them that enables them to deliver for us. To ensure the good use of power, we the people must retain the counterpower to control the power that is exercised over us. Governance starts and ends with power. Democracy solves the problem of power.

Think about effectiveness. It is hardly a radical recommendation to those who take on the responsibility of governing that they should govern with effect, but it is a recommendation worth making. We citizens need to see that those set to govern deal with the problems. If they do, they will have our loyalty; if they don't, they will forfeit it. Where governments fail in delivery, confidence and trust wither.

Think about culture. If the culture does not hold up, no constitutional fix will save the day. Orchestrated deliberation, for example, cannot be of much import if people do not trust each other and are not inclined to deliberate, and if they are so inclined, orchestration is needless. The bedrock is culture before constitution.

Think about autocracy. Governments *will* go autocratic if they can. When we citizens engage in the mundane business of voting and deliberating, we are, day in and day out, preventing tyranny.

Think about equality. Political equality coexists with social and economic inequalities. There is no escaping that uneasy cohabitation. But although embedded in societies of inequality, democracy does deliver remarkable equalities. These include equal rights, equality before the law, and equality in the access to the vote and to eligibility. The democratic problem is to prevent economic inequality from transgressing into the domain of politics in such a way as to erode the reality of political equality.

Think about reform. Democratic government is infuriatingly messy. We need tolerance of imperfection. We should open our minds to democracy being a venture, ever moving and evolving, never finished, always in need of improvement. Karl Popper's "open society" is built on self-critical awareness, the determination of modest achievements, step-by-step improvements, trial and error—a culture of reform. A democratic culture is one of values but also a love affair with a fickle and sometimes unassuming creation that we must be determined to improve on but can never make flawless.

Think about the vote. It's a miracle. It creates equality. It creates power. It controls power. We elect representatives; we dismiss them; we control them. It enables us to elect competent leaders and enables them to work competently. It forces representatives to compete for our goodwill. It ensures that our voices are heard and our interests heeded. It matters.

Think about competition. It is because citizens vote that candidates must compete, and that they must compete for the goodwill of ordinary people. It is through competition that candidates are tested and that we can have hope that the competent ones prevail and that we get leaders who respect our interests. The competition for votes may look cynical and opportunistic, but that spectacle, even when awful, is much to be preferred to governance that is free from the trouble of having to pay attention to the populace.

Think about representation. We citizens elect representatives and can safely, relatively safely, allow them power. We can have governors we can trust. We can be governed by those among us who know how. They in turn, working on the basis of consent, can back up their policy making with the authority to get decisions implemented.

Think about assemblies. Our representatives form national and local assemblies. These are the custodians of the power we delegate upward, not any individual or small clique but a collective. Working in assemblies, representatives control each other. They work in settings and under rules that are conducive to good decision-making. When democratic government is dysfunctional, that is often because assemblies perform poorly, as presently, for example, the British Parliament and the American Congress.

Think about deliberation. As government runs on power, culture runs on deliberation. Deliberation is made up of a running conversation between citizens and citizens and leaders and is made possible by the freedoms of expression, association, and information and by free and pluralistic press and media. When citizens use these freedoms, deliberation creates a buzz of people discussing, asking, quarreling, demanding, pushing, resisting. If citizens are not vigilant in this way, all the more danger that rule perverts into soft, or not so soft, despotism.

Think about participation. There is no such thing as nonparticipatory democracy; hence "participatory democracy" is a misnomer. But there is a question of where and how citizens should participate. They should vote; they should make their voices heard; they should deliberate. But once they have elected representatives, there are good reasons for leaving public policy decision-making to them, albeit under pressure from below. Outside of voting, the value of participation is as an input into deliberation and culture.

Think about obedience. If leaders are to deliver, followers must obey. Romantics may have it that women and men of free spirit obey only themselves and their own reason. But democracy is a demanding contract that comes with commitments on citizens. We citizens need to accept that if we want a functioning democracy, we cannot only insist on rights, we must also accept duties. In Henry Brooks Adams' Washington novel *Democracy* (1880), the moral is that citizens who wallowed in disgust at the unedifying sight of political competition must finally face the truth that fault lies in themselves.

Think about leadership. The translation of power into governance depends on skillful leaders. Governance is personal, in the hands of those who happen, for a short while, to hold the offices of government. Persons matter, notably their ability to extract that all-important authority from the governed.

Think about poverty. For governments to merit loyalty, their governance must be fair. That means that their protection should reach everyone and that no one should be left neglected, even the most humble citizen, in particular the most humble citizen. The final test of fairness in material conditions is in protection against poverty, all the more since we know how to institute such protection.

Think about money. The principle of political equality is that each citizen is the same, including with the same influence, and that no one is more than the other. That, obviously, is not the way money and the power of money are distributed. Here, some have little, the many some, and a few much. It follows from democratic principles that the power of money should not be at work in the democratic competition. The transgression of monied power into democratic politics is destructive of fair and equal political competition.

Think about taxation. It is sad but true: the most direct participation most of us have in government is as payers of taxes. None of us want to pay, yet we must, and our governments must have the capacity to extract it from us, so much so that the business of government can be summed up, in the title of a memorable book (by Geoffrey Brennan and James Buchanan), as "the power to tax." What must be paid is always more than anyone wants to part with. Hence, taxation is an arena of duel between citizens and governments and the meeting ground of power, authority, legitimacy, compliance, obedience, and more. What governments demand and citizens give up, and with what grace on both sides, is a manifestation of the settlement of order that prevails, or not, in your polity.

Think about variations. Democracy comes in many shapes and forms. This pluralism is wondrous. Democracy is flexible; it can be made to work under diverse conditions and experiences. It does not have to be according to a single recipe and should not be forced into any straitjacket of *the* right kind of democracy. Every democratic country does it in its own way, and nowhere has the enterprise found its final form.

Think about tolerance. Since perfect democracy is an unknown, we must live with uncertainty about the democracy we get. It may not be as beautiful as it presents itself in our dreams; it may not be as ethical as ideal principles prescribe; it may not be as dignified a performance as it ought to be. We should work to make it better, certainly, but also really understand that we cannot have perfection. We must protect ourselves from the delusion that democracy with flaws is democracy not worth having. If we give up on tolerance, we start down the road of certainty, ideology and ultimately tyranny.

Think about the advantages. Democracy, for all the imperfection and mess that is clear to see, has a lot going for it, *a lot*. From freedom, rights, citizenship, and autonomy, via rule of law, effective governance, and prosperity, to the advancement of world peace, democracy has it. Up against all of this, autocracy can promise only more effectiveness, and even that turns out to be a propagandistic boast on which no known autocracy has been able to deliver.

Think about the alternative. The alternative to imperfect democracy is not perfect democracy but autocracy. Some democracies are solid, some flimsy; some have more quality than others; some deliver better than others. Autocracies are also of many kinds, on a range from more or less benevolent to more or less tyrannical, some more effective in delivery than others. But for all the fuzziness on both sides of the divide, there is a divide. Life for most people is better where they live under democratic rule, however imperfect, than where rule is autocratic, even more so if it is perfect in its autocracy. Robert Dahl, again, with elegant brevity and simplicity: democracy is a far better gamble than any attainable alternative.

The short answer

Democracies live as long as their governments deal with the problems and deliver. That enables citizens to be confident that their interests are in trustworthy stewardship.

What democratic governments need to deal with at the present juncture, and with urgency, is the problem of inequality. That is tearing democratic cultures apart in destructive polarizations and driving the excluded to revolt.

To deal with the problem of inequality, we need to restore faith in government as an instrument of good. In that interest, we must block inequalities in economic markets from transgressing to the destruction of equality and competition in political markets.

Acknowledgments

This project has had a hospitable home at King's College London, in its excellent Department of Political Economy. I am grateful to Jeremy Jennings, Mark Pennington, Andrew Blick, and other colleagues for support and companionship.

The essays at the core of the book pull together main threads from years, indeed decades, of scholarship. I am grateful to Oxford University for having given me a base for that work. I wish to acknowledge also a big debt of gratitude to the Wissenschaftszentrum Berlin für Sozialforschung, to the Ash Center for Democratic Governance and Innovation of the Kennedy School at Harvard University, and to Lillehammer University College for years of affiliation, collaboration, and friendship.

The book owes much to research on nondemocratic and predemocratic systems. I am grateful to Huck-ju Kwon, Ilcheong Yi, Taekyoon Kim, and Jooha Lee for our collaborative study of South Korea's transition from authoritarianism to democracy. During five years of research on the Chinese political system, resulting in *The Perfect Dictatorship*, I had the privilege of fruitful collaboration with a range of colleagues in China, whose names now cannot be mentioned. I am in debt to Hong Kong University Press for handling that book with excellence, in particular to its then publisher, Malcolm Litchfield. Today it is unlikely they would have been able to publish it.

At University of Chicago Press I am grateful to my editors Chuck Myers, who commissioned the book, and Chad Zimmerman, to anonymous readers for helpful guidance, to Holly Smith, Jenni Fry, and Michaela Luckey for getting the book out there in good order, and to The Froebe Group for copy editing. My agent, Peter Bernstein, has been unfailingly supportive and helpful in the making and handling of the book.

Many friends have tolerated long discussions and given generously of criticism and guidance, for which here a big and collective thanks. My wife and writing companion, Mary Chamberlain, has been, as always, a marvelous moral and intellectual support.

Notes

Preface

1. The first comprehensive historical analysis of the crash and the magnitude of its fall-out is in Kershaw, *The Global Age*.

2. John S. Dagpunar, "Sensitivity of UK Covid-19 Deaths to the Timing of Suppression Measures and Their Relaxation." *Infectious Disease Modelling* 5 (2020): 525–35.

3. Vasilis Kontis et al. "Magnitude, Demographics and Dynamics of the Effect of the First Wave of the COVID-19 Pandemic on All-Cause Mortality in 21 Industrialized Countries." *Nature Medicine* (2020).

4. Huntington, *The Third Wave*; Diamond and Plattner, *Democracy in Decline?*

5. Jacques, *When China Rules the World*; Bell, *The China Model*.

6. Snyder, *The Road to Unfreedom*; Clover, *Black Wind, White Snow*; Medvedev, *The Return of the Russian Leviathan*.

7. Applebaum, *Twilight of Democracy*.

8. Mounk, *The People vs. Democracy*.

9. https://www.kingsfund.org.uk/blog/2020/04/ethnic-minority-deaths-covid-19.

10. Piketty, *Capital in the Twenty-First Century*.

11. Khanna, *The Future Is Asian*; Frankopan, *The New Silk Roads*.

12. Miller, *Can Democracy Work?*

13. Deneen, *Why Liberalism Failed*. Mishra, *Bland Fanatics*.

14. Levitsky and Ziblatt, *How Democracies Die*; Runciman, *How Democracy Ends*; Diamond, *Ill Winds*.

15. Albright, *Fascism*.

16. Hertie, *The Governance Report 2017*; Gamble and Wright, *Rethinking Democracy*; Gutman and Thompson, *Why Deliberative Democracy?*; Ackerman and Fishkin, *Deliberation Day*; Fishkin, *Democracy When the People Are Thinking*; Keane, *The Life and Death of Democracy*; Crouch, *Post-Democracy*.

17. Hertie, *The Governance Report 2017*. For a similar analysis, see also Gamble and Wright, *Rethinking Democracy*.

18. Dahl, *On Democracy*, p. 145.

19. Keane, *When Trees Fall, Monkeys Scatter*.

20. On the great inventions in the march of government, see Finer, *The History of Government*, pp. 87–94.

21. See, e.g., Gutman and Thompson, *Why Deliberative Democracy?* and Fishkin, *Democracy When the People Are Thinking*.

22. Dahl, *On Democracy*, p. 46.

23. Ringen, *The Perfect Dictatorship*.

24. Ian Johnson, "What Holds China Together?" *New York Review of Books*, September 26, 2019.

Book One

1. Weber, *The Theory of Social and Economic Organization*, p. 152. Weber's own term in German was *Chance*. *Probability* is Talcott Parson's translation. An alternative might be to stick with *chance* (as do Gerth and Mills in *From Max Weber*), or perhaps *opportunity*. It does not matter much for my purpose since whatever version, it pulls power down to earth in the way I describe.

2. From Aron, *Peace and War*; Parsons, *Sociological Theory and Modern Society*; Coleman, *Foundations of Social Theory*; Dahl, "The Concept of Power."

3. Lukes, *Power*; Bourdieu, *Language and Symbolic Power*; Nye, *Soft Power*.

4. Kołakowski, *Freedom, Fame, Lying and Betrayal*, p. 1.

5. My *Jungle Book* reference is to the excellent 2016 Hollywood version.

6. In a ranking of thirty countries on an index of soft power by the Portland consultancy, China has the bottom rank (www.softpower30.portland-communications.com).

7. Steinmetz, *The Richest Man Who Ever Lived*.

8. Frankopan, *The Silk Roads*, p. 22.

9. These Italian, German and French examples are from Kershaw, *To Hell and Back*.

10. As explained in Berlin, *Many Thousands Gone*.

11. Havel, *The Power of the Powerless*.

12. Frankopan, *The Silk Roads*, p. 160.

13. As reported by the *New York Times* on March 12, 2016, based on South Korean intelligence sources.

14. Montefiore, *The Romanovs*, p. xxiii.

15. Ewald, *Eisenhower the President*.

16. On "followership," see Kellerman, *The End of Leadership*.

17. Dahl, *On Democracy*, p. 158.

18. Ringen, *Nation of Devils*.

19. Montefiore: *The Romanovs*.

20. Chernow, *Washington*.

21. Steinberg, *Bismarck*.

22. Machiavelli, *The Prince*, iv.

23. Weber, *The Theory of Social and Economic Organization*, p. 153.

24. This example is inspired by a biographical portrait of the conductor Sir Simon Rattle on BBC Television on February 14, 2015.

25. Suetonius, Divius Augustus, p. 48.

26. Davies, *Europe*, p. 841.

27. Ringen et al., *The Korean State*.

28. Davies, *Europe*, p. 760.

29. Kershaw, *The Global Age*, p. 302.

30. MacMillan, *The War That Ended Peace*.

31. Zuboff, *The Age of Surveillance Capitalism*.

32. Clark, *The Sleepwalkers*.

33. For a rich program of research on trends in global governance, see https://www.wzb.eu /en/research/international-politics-and-law/global-governance/.

34. Keynes, *General Theory*, last page.

35. Nye, *The Powers to Lead*.

36. Snyder, *The Road to Unfreedom*, p. 249.

37. Ringen, *Nation of Devils*.

38. On the newness of this configuration, see Hacker and Pierson, *Winner-Take-All Politics*.

Book Two

1. For an elegant management of the difficult art of interpreting *The Prince*, see Benner, *Be Like the Fox*.

2. Such as Jacques, *When China Rules the World* and Bell, *The China Model*.

3. From the big relevant literature, see, e.g., Bemelmans-Videc, Rist, and Vedung, *Carrots, Sticks and Sermons*.

4. Pressman and Wildavsky, *Implementation*.

5. Rose, "On the Priorities of Government."

6. In "Politik als Beruf," a lecture at Munich University in 1919. Gerth and Mills, *From Max Weber*, p. 78.

7. Ziegler, *Edward Heath*.

8. Webster, *The NHS*.

9. Powell, *The New Machiavelli*, p. 184.

10. Finer, *History of Government*, pp. 295–96.

11. But not in China, where bureaucracy had been invented centuries before, for it to be reinvented in Western Europe much later, cf. Finer, *History of Government*, pp. 78–94.

12. Hamilton, *American Caesars*, p. 98.

13. Ringen, *The Economic Consequences of Mr. Brown*.

14. Herzberg, "One More Time."

15. Pink, *Drive*.

16. Sumption, *Trials of the State*.

17. Hart, *The Concept of Law*.

18. I here again lean on Hirschman, *Exit, Voice, and Loyalty*.

19. On "new governance," see, e.g., Salamon, *The Tools of Government*.

Book Three

1. Aristotle, *Politics*, 1310a12.

2. By, e.g., Keyt, "Aristotelian Freedom."

3. Berlin, *Liberty*, p. 172.

4. Parijs, *Real Freedom for All*.

5. Mill, "On Liberty."

6. Berlin, *Liberty*, pp. 340, 336–37.

7. Raz, *The Morality of Freedom*.

8. Nussbaum and Sen, *The Quality of Life*.

9. Aubié, *Liu Xiaobo's Struggle for Human Rights*; Liu, *No Enemies, No Hatred*.

10. Berlin, *Liberty*.

11. Berlin, *Liberty*, pp. 35, 48. See also, e.g., Jahanbegloo, *Conversations with Isaiah Berlin*, in which Berlin is challenged to clarify his view on negative and positive liberty and refuses to discard positive liberty as such.

12. Berlin, *Liberty*, pp. 322–28.

13. Mesure, *La rationalité des valeurs*.

14. Boudon, *Raisons, bonnes raisons*; *La rationalité*; *Renouveler la démocratie*.

15. Kahneman, *Thinking, Fast and Slow*; Lewis, *The Undoing Project*.

16. Becker, *A Treatise on the Family*

17. Ringen, *Citizens, Families and Reform*.

18. Diogenes, *Lives of the Eminent Philosophers*, p. 540.

19. Sen, *Rationality and Freedom*, p. 5–7.

20. Offer, *The Challenge of Affluence*.

21. Berlin, I think, was caught in the middle. His philosophy was the freedom of the citizen but his politics the freedom of the consumer.

22. Evans, *The Pursuit of Power*.

23. Boudon, *Renouveler la démocratie: eloge du sens commun*.

24. *The Economist*, April 12, 2014.

25. Ringen, *The Perfect Dictatorship*, pp. 148–49.

26. Harris, "Berlin and His Critics," in Berlin, *Liberty*. See also Schmidtz and Pavel, *The Oxford Handbook of Freedom*.

27. Kołakowski, *Freedom, Fame, Lying and Betrayal*, p. 101.

Book Four

1. Marshall, *Principles of Economics*, p. 594.

2. Marshall, *Principles of Economics*, p. 596–601.

3. Robinson, *Economic Philosophy*.

4. Layard, *Happiness: Lessons from a New Science*.

5. Sen, *Inequality Reexamined*; Atkinson, *The Economics of Inequality, Inequality*; Piketty, *Capital in the Twenty-First Century*.

6. Ringen, *The Perfect Dictatorship*, p. 121ff.

7. Ringen, *The Perfect Dictatorship*, pp. 147–48.

8. Marshall, *Principles of Economics*, pp. 598–99.

9. I first reviewed this research, theoretically and empirically, in *The Possibility of Politics*.

10. Marshall, *Principles of Economics*, p. 595.

11. Stedman Jones, *An End to Poverty?*

12. Townsend, *Poverty in the United Kingdom*, p. 31.

13. Ringen, "Direct and Indirect Measures of Poverty."

14. The work that more than any other triggered the "rediscovery" of poverty was Harrington, *The Other America*.

15. On the relative theory and criticism of Rowntree's methodology, the pioneering work was Abel-Smith and Townsend, *The Poor and the Poorest*.

16. Judt, *Postwar*.

17. Atkinson, *Incomes and the Welfare State*.

18. But see Baldwin, *The Politics of Social Solidarity*.

19. Ringen, *The Possibility of Politics* and *Citizens, Families and Reform*.

20. As argued in possibly the most influential work in Scandinavian social policy thinking, Myrdal and Myrdal, *Kris i befolkningsfrågan* [Crisis in the population question].

21. Parijs and Vanderborght, *Basic Income*.

22. MacMillan, *War*, p. 40.

Book Five

1. Dahl, *On Democracy*, p. 155.

2. Dahl, *How Democratic Is the American Constitution?*, p. 1.

3. Dahl, *On Political Equality*, p. 94.

4. On the many forms and variations of democracy, see Held, *Models of Democracy*.

5. On "democratic quality," see Ringen, *What Democracy Is For*.

6. Dickson, *The Dictator's Dilemma*.

7. Dahl, *On Democracy*, p. 61.

8. For a detailed examination of the idea of rule of law, see Bingham: *The Rule of Law*.

9. Clover, *Black Wind, White Snow*.

10. Holmes, *Passions and Constraint*.

11. Kershaw, *The Global Age*.

12. Ringen et al., *The Korean State and Social Policy*. Choi et al., *The Korean Government and Public Policies in a Development Nexus*.

13. This is one interpretation of the problem of "social choice," following Arrow, *Social Choice and Individual Values*.

14. Weale, *The Will of the People*.

15. Berlin, *The Crooked Timber of Humanity*.

16. Farrell, *Billionaire Wilderness*.

17. Lepore, *These Truths*, p. 144.

18. On the shifting quality of political leadership in America, see Nye, *Presidential Leadership*.

Postscript

1. Organisation for Economic Co-operation and Development, *Revenue Statistics*, https://www.oecd.org/tax/tax-policy/revenue-statistics-2522770x.htm.

References

Abel-Smith, Brian, and Peter Townsend. *The Poor and the Poorest.* London: Bell, 1965.

Ackerman, Bruce, and James S. Fishkin. *Deliberation Day.* New Haven, CT: Yale University Press, 2005.

Adams, Henry Brooks. *Democracy: An American Novel.* 1880.

Albright, Madeleine. *Fascism: A Warning.* New York: HarperCollins, 2018.

Applebaum, Anne. *Twilight of Democracy: The Failure of Politics and the Parting of Friends.* Allen Lane, 2020.

Aristotle. *Politics.* (ca. 330 BCE).

Aron, Raymond. *Peace and War.* New York: Praeger 1967.

Arrow, Kenneth J. *Social Choice and Individual Values.* New York: Wiley, 1963.

Atkinson, A. B. *The Economics of Inequality.* Oxford: Oxford University Press, 1983.

Atkinson, A. B. *Incomes and the Welfare State: Essays on Britain and Europe.* Cambridge: Cambridge University Press 1995).

Atkinson, A. B. *Inequality: What Can Be Done?* Cambridge, MA: Harvard University Press, 2015.

Atkinson, A. B. *Poverty in Europe.* Cambridge: Cambridge University Press, 1998.

Aubié, Hermann. "Liu Xiaobo's Struggle for Human Rights." PhD diss., University of Turku, Finland, 2017.

Baldwin, Peter. *The Politics of Social Solidarity.* Cambridge: Cambridge University Press, 1990.

Barber, Michael. *Instruction to Deliver: Tony Blair, Public Services and the Challenge of Achieving Targets.* London: Politico's, 2007.

Becker, Gary S. *A Treatise on the Family.* Cambridge, MA: Harvard University Press, 1981.

Bell, Daniel A. *The China Model: Political Meritocracy and the Limits of Democracy.* Princeton, NJ: Princeton University Press, 2015.

Bemelmans-Videc, Marie-Louise, Ray C. Rist, and Evert Vedung, eds. *Carrots, Sticks and Sermons: Policy Instruments and Their Evaluation.* New Brunswick, NJ Transaction, 1998.

Benner, Erica. *Be Like the Fox: Machiavelli's Lifelong Quest for Freedom.* London. Allen Lane, 2017.

Berlin, Ira. *Many Thousands Gone: The First Two Centuries of Slavery in North America.* Cambridge, MA: Harvard University Press, 1998.

Berlin, Isaiah. *Liberty*. Edited by Henry Hardy. Oxford: Oxford University Press, 2002.

Berlin, Isaiah. *The Crooked Timber of Humanity*. Edited by Henry Hardy. London: Murray, 1990.

Bingham, Tom. *The Rule of Law*. Allen Lane, 2010.

Blair, Tony. *A Journey*. London: Hutchinson, 2010.

Boudon, Raymond. *Raison, bonnes raisons*. Paris: Presses Universitaires de France, 2003.

Boudon, Raymond. *La rationalité*. Paris: Presses Universitaires de France, 2009.

Boudon, Raymond. *Renouveler la démocratie: eloge du sens commun*. Paris: Odile Jacob, 2006.

Bourdieu, Pierre. *Language and Symbolic Power*. Cambridge, MA: Harvard University Press, 1991.

Bourquin, Pascale, Jonathan Cribb, Tom Waters, and Xiaowei Xu. *Living Standards, Poverty and Inequality in the UK*. London: Institute for Fiscal Studies, 2017.

Brennan, Geoffrey, and James M. Buchanan. *The Power to Tax*. Cambridge: Cambridge University Press, 1980.

Caro, Robert A. *The Years of Lyndon Johnson: Master of the Senate*. New York: Knopf, 2002.

Chernow, Ron. *Washington: A Life*. New York: Penguin, 2010.

Choi, Jongwon, Huck-ju Kwon, and Min Gyo Koo, eds. *The Korean Government and Public Policies in a Development Nexus: Sustaining Development and Tackling Policy Changes*. New York: Springer International, 2017.

Clark, Christopher. *The Sleepwalkers: How Europe Went to War in 1914*. Penguin, 2012.

Clover, Charles. *Black Wind, White Snow: The Rise of Russia's New Nationalism*. New Haven, CT: Yale University Press, 2016.

Coleman, James S. *Foundations of Social Theory*. Cambridge, MA: Harvard University Press, 1990.

Crouch, Colin. *Post-Democracy*. Cambridge: Polity, 2004.

Dahl, Robert A. *On Political Equality*. New Haven, CT: Yale University Press, 2006.

Dahl, Robert A. *How Democratic Is the American Constitution?* New Haven, CT: Yale University Press, 2001.

Dahl, Robert A. "The Concept of Power." *Behavioral Science*, Vol. 2, Issue 3 (1957), pp. 201–15.

Dahl, Robert A. *On Democracy*. New Haven, CT: Yale University Press, 1998.

Dahl, Robert A. *Who Governs? Democracy and Power in an American City*. New Haven, CT: Yale University Press, 1961.

Davies, Norman. *Europe: A History*. London: Pimlico, 1997.

Deneen, Patrick J. *Why Liberalism Failed*. New Haven, CT: Yale University Press, 2019.

Descartes, René. *Discours de la méthode* (1637).

Diamond, Larry. *Ill Winds: Saving Democracy from Russia, Chinese Ambition and American Complacency*. Penguin, 2019.

Diamond, Larry, and Mark F. Plattner, eds. *Democracy in Decline?* Baltimore: Johns Hopkins University Press, 2015.

Dickson, Bruce J. *The Dictator's Dilemma: The Chinese Communist Party's Strategy for Survival*. New York: Oxford University Press, 2016.

Diogenes Laertius. *Lives of the Eminent Philosophers*. (ca. AD 220). Edited by James Miller. New York: Oxford University Press, 2018.

Durkheim, Emile. *Le suicide, étude sociologique* (1897).

Evans, Richard J. *The Pursuit of Power; Europe 1815–1914*. Penguin, 2016.

Ewald, William B. Jr. *Eisenhower the President: Crucial Days, 1951–1960*. New York: Prentice Hall, 1981.

Farrell, Justin. *Billionaire Wilderness: The Ultra-Wealthy and the Remaking of the American West.* Princeton, NJ: Princeton University Press, 2020.

Finer, S.E. *The History of Government.* Vols. 1–3. Oxford: Oxford University Press, 1997.

Fishkin, James S. *Democracy When the People Are Thinking: Revitalising Our Politics through Public Deliberation.* New York: Oxford University Press, 2018.

Frankopan, Peter. *The New Silk Roads: The Present and Future of the World.* London: Bloomsbury, 2018.

Frankopan, Peter. *The Silk Roads: A New History of the World.* London: Bloomsbury, 2016.

Friedman, Benjamin M. "Brave New Capitalist's Paradise." *New York Review of Books,* November 7, 2013.

Friedman, Benjamin M. "Work and Consumption in an Era of Unbalanced Technological Advance." *Journal of Evolutionary Economics,* Vol. 27, Issue 2 (2015), pp. 221–37.

Gamble, Andrew, and Tony Wright, eds. *Rethinking Democracy.* Political Quarterly Monograph Series. London: Wiley, 2018.

Gerth, H. H., and C. Wright Mills., *From Max Weber: Essays in Sociology.* New York: Oxford University Press, 1946.

Gutman, Amy, and Dennis Thompson. *Why Deliberative Democracy?* Princeton, NJ: Princeton University Press, 2004.

Habermas, Jürgen. *The Theory of Communicative Action.* Vols. 1–2. Cambridge: Polity Press, 1984/87.

Hacker, Jacob, and Paul Pierson. *Winner-Take-All Politics: How Washington Made the Rich Richer and Turned Its Back on the Middle Class.* New York: Simon & Schuster, 2010.

Hall, Edith. *Aristotle's Way: How Ancient Wisdom Can Change Your Life.* London: Bodley Head, 2018.

Hamilton, Nigel. *American Caesars: Lives of the US Presidents from Franklin D. Roosevelt to George W. Bush.* London: Bodley Head, 2010.

Harrington, Michael. *The Other America.* New York: Macmillan, 1962.

Hart, H. L. A. *The Concept of Law.* Oxford: Oxford University Press, 1961.

Havel, Vaclav. *The Power of the Powerless: Citizens against the State in Central-Eastern Europe.* Edited by John Keane. London: Hutchinson, 1985.

Hawes, James. *The Shortest History of Germany.* London: Old Street, 2017.

Held, David. *Models of Democracy.* Cambridge: Polity Press, 2006.

Hertie School of Governance. *The Governance Report 2017.* Oxford: Oxford University Press, 2017.

Herzberg, Frederick. "One More Time: How Do You Motivate Employees?" *Harvard Business Review* 46, no.1 (1968): 53–62.

Hirschman, Albert O. *Exit, Voice, and Loyalty.* Cambridge, MA: Harvard University Press, 1970.

Holmes, Stephen. *Passions and Constraint.* Chicago: University of Chicago Press, 1995.

Hood, Christopher C. *The Tools of Government.* London: Macmillan, 1983.

Huntington, Samuel P. *The Third Wave: Democratization in the Late Twentieth Century.* Norman: University of Oklahoma Press, 1991.

Jacques, Martin. *When China Rules the World.* London: Penguin, 2012.

Jahanbegloo, Ramin. *Conversations with Isaiah Berlin.* London: Peter Halban, 1992.

Judt, Tony. *Postwar: A History of Europe Since 1945.* New York: Vintage, 2010.

Kahneman, Daniel. *Thinking, Fast and Slow.* New York: Farrar, Straus & Giroux, 2011.

Kant, Immanuel. *Zum ewigen Frieden* [Perpetual peace]. (1795).

Keane, John. *The Life and Death of Democracy.* New York: Simon & Schuster, 2009.

Keane, John. *When Trees Fall, Monkeys Scatter: Rethinking Democracy in China.* Singapore: World Scientific, 2017.

Kellerman, Barbara. *The End of Leadership.* New York: Harper Business, 2012.

Kershaw, Ian. *The Global Age: Europe 1950–2017.* Penguin, 2019 (published in the UK as *Roller-Coaster*).

Kershaw, Ian. *To Hell and Back: Europe 1914–1949.* Penguin, 2015.

Keynes, John Maynard. "Economic Possibilities for Our Grandchildren." *Nation and Athenaeum*, October 11 and 18, 1930.

Keynes, John Maynard. *The General Theory of Employment, Interest and Money.* London: Macmillan, 1936.

Keyt, David. "Aristotelian Freedom." In *The Oxford Handbook of Freedom.* Edited by David Schmidtz and Carmen E. Pavel. New York: Oxford University Press 2018.

Khanna, Parag. *The Future Is Asian: Global Order in the Twenty-First Century.* London: Weidenfeld & Nicolson, 2019.

King, Anthony. *The British Constitution.* Oxford: Oxford University Press, 2007.

Kołakowski, Leszek. *Freedom, Fame, Lying and Betrayal: Essays in Everyday Life.* Penguin, 1999.

Layard, Richard. *Happiness: Lessons from a New Science.* Penguin, 2005.

Lepore, Jill. *These Truths: A History of the United States.* New York: Norton, 2018.

Levitsky, Steven, and Daniel Ziblatt. *How Democracies Die: What History Reveals about Our Future.* Penguin, 2018.

Lewis, Michael. *The Undoing Project: A Friendship that Changed the World.* Penguin, 2017.

Lipsky, Michael. *Street-level Bureaucracy; Dilemmas of the Individual in Public Services.* New York: Russell Sage, 1980.

Liu Xiaobo. *No Enemies, No Hatred: Selected Essays and Poems.* Edited by Perry Link, Tienchi Martin-Liao, and Liu Xia. Cambridge, MA: Harvard University Press, 2013.

Lukes, Steven. *Power: A Radical View.* London: Palgrave Macmillan, 2005.

Machiavelli, *The Prince* (1532).

MacMillan, Margaret. *War: How Conflict Shaped Us.* London: Profile Books. 2020.

MacMillan, Margaret. *The War that Ended Peace: How Europe Abandoned Peace for the First World War.* London: Profile Books. 2013.

Marshall, Alfred. *Principles of Economics.* 8th ed. 1920.

Medvedev, Sergei. *The Return of the Russian Leviathan.* Cambridge: Polity, 2019.

Merkel, Wolfgang, and Sascha Kneip, eds. *Democracy and Crisis: Challenges in Turbulent Times.* Berlin: Springer, 2018.

Mesure, Sylvie, ed. *La rationalité des valeurs.* Paris: Presses Universitaires de France, 1996.

Mill, John Stuart. *On Liberty and Other Essays* (1859).

Miller, Fred D. "Platonic Freedom." In *The Oxford Handbook of Freedom.* Edited by David Schmidtz and Carmen E. Pavel. New York: Oxford University Press 2018.

Miller, James. *Can Democracy Work?* London: Oneworld, 2018.

Mishra, Pankaj. *Bland Fanatics: Liberals, Race, and Empire.* New York: Farrar, Straus & Giroux, 2020.

Montefiore, Simon Sebag. *The Romanovs, 1613–1918.* London: Weidenfeld & Nicolson, 2016.

Mounk, Yascha. *The People vs. Democracy.* Cambridge, MA: Harvard University Press 2018.

Myrdal, Alva, and Gunnar Myrdal. *Kris i befolkningsfrågan.* Stockholm: Bonniers, 1934.

Nussbaum, Martha S., and Amartya Sen, eds. *The Quality of Life.* Oxford: Oxford University Press, 1993.

Nye, Joseph S., Jr. *The Powers to Lead*. New York: Oxford University Press, 2008.

Nye, Joseph S., Jr. *Presidential Leadership and the Creation of the American Era*. Princeton, NJ: Princeton University Press, 2013.

Nye, Joseph S., Jr., *Soft Power: The Means to Success in the Modern World*. New York: Public Affairs, 2004.

Offer, Avner. *The Challenge of Affluence*. Oxford: Oxford University Press, 2006.

Okun, Arthur M. *Equality and Efficiency: The Big Tradeoff*. Washington, DC: Brookings, 1975.

Parijs, Philippe Van. *Real Freedom for All*. Oxford: Oxford University Press, 1997.

Parijs, Philippe Van, and Yannick Vanderborght. *Basic Income: A Radical Proposal for a Free Society and a Sane Economy*. Cambridge, MA: Harvard University Press, 2017.

Parsons, Talcott. *Sociological Theory and Modern Society*. New York: Free Press, 1967.

Peters, B. Guy, and Frans K. M. van Nispen, eds. *Public Policy Instruments: Evaluating the Tools of Public Administration*, Cheltenham, UK: Edward Elgar, 1998.

Pierson, Paul. *Dismantling the Welfare State? Reagan, Thatcher and the Politics of Retrenchment*. Cambridge: Cambridge University Press, 1994.

Pigou, A.C. *The Economics of Welfare* (1920).

Piketty, Thomas. *Capital in the Twenty-first Century*. Cambridge, MA: Harvard University Press, 2014.

Pink, David H. *Drive: The Surprising Truth about What Motivates Us*. New York: Riverhead, 2009.

Popper, Karl. *The Open Society and its Enemies*. Vols. 1–2. London: Routledge, 1954.

Porter, Michael. *Competitive Strategy*. New York: Free Press, 1980.

Powell, Jonathan. *The New Machiavelli: How to Wield Power in the Modern World*. London: Bodley Head, 2010.

Pressman, Jeffrey L., and Aaron Wildavsky. *Implementation: How Great Expectations in Washington Are Dashed in Oakland; or, Why It's Amazing that Federal Programs Work at All*. Berkeley: University of California Press, 1973.

Rand, Ayn. *Atlas Shrugged*. New York: Random House. 1957.

Rawls, John. *A Theory of Justice*. Cambridge, MA: Harvard University Press, 1985.

Raz, Joseph. *The Morality of Freedom*. Oxford: Oxford University Press, 1986.

Ringen, Stein. "Direct and Indirect Measures of Poverty." *Journal of Social Policy* 17, no. 3 (1988): 351–65.

Ringen, Stein. *The Economic Consequences of Mr. Brown: How a Strong Government Was Defeated by a Weak System of Governance*. Oxford: Bardwell Press, 2009.

Ringen, Stein. "Levemåten hos dølafolket før og nå" *Årbok for Gudbrandsdalen* 2011.

Ringen, Stein. *Nation of Devils: Democratic Leadership and the Problem of Obedience*. New Haven, CT: Yale University Press, 2013.

Ringen, Stein. *The Perfect Dictatorship: China in the 21st Century*. Hong Kong: Hong Kong University Press, 2016.

Ringen, Stein. *What Democracy Is For: On Freedom and Moral Government*. Princeton, NJ: Princeton University Press, 2007.

Ringen, Stein, Huck-ju Kwon, Ilcheong Yi, Taekyoon Kim, and Jooha Lee. *The Korean State and Social Policy: How South Korea Lifted Itself from Poverty and Dictatorship to Affluence and Democracy*. New York: Oxford University Press, 2011.

Rose, Richard. "On the Priorities of Government: A Developmental Analysis of Public Policy." *European Journal of Political Research* 4, no. 3 (1976): 247–89.

Rowntree, B. S. *Poverty: A Study of Town Life.* London: Macmillan, 1901.

Runciman, David. *How Democracy Ends.* Oxford: Oxford University Press, 2018.

Sachs, Jeffrey. *The End of Poverty: Economic Possibilities for Our Time.* Penguin, 2005.

Salamon, Lester M. *The Tools of Government: A Guide to the New Governance.* New York: Oxford University Press, 2002.

Schmidtz, David, and Carmen E. Pavel, eds. *The Oxford Handbook of Freedom.* New York: Oxford University Press, 2018.

Sen, Amartya. *Development as Freedom.* Oxford: Oxford University Press, 1999.

Sen, Amartya. *Inequality Reexamined.* Cambridge, MA: Harvard University Press, 1992.

Sen, Amartya. *Rationality and Freedom.* Cambridge, MA: Harvard University Press, 2002.

Shapiro, Ian. *The State of Democratic Theory.* Princeton, NJ: Princeton University Press 2003.

Skidelsky, Robert. *Money and Government: The Past and Future of Economics.* New Haven, CT: Yale University Press, 2019.

Smith, Adam. *An Inquiry into the Nature and Causes of the Wealth of Nations* (1776).

Smith, Adam. *The Theory of Moral Sentiments* (1759).

Snyder, Timothy. *The Road to Unfreedom: Russia, Europe, America.* London: Bodley Head, 2018.

Stedman Jones, Gareth. *An End to Poverty?* London: Profile Books, 2004.

Steinberg, Jonathan. *Bismarck: A Life.* New York: Oxford University Press, 2011.

Steinmetz, Greg. *The Richest Man Who Ever Lived: The Life and Times of Jacob Fugger.* New York: Simon & Schuster, 2015.

Suetonius. *The Twelve Caesars.* (ca. AD 120).

Sumption, Jonathan. *Trials of the State: Law and the Decline of Politics.* London: Profile, 2019.

Tocqueville, Alexis de. *Democracy in America.* Vols.1–2. (1835, 1840).

Townsend, Peter. *Poverty in the United Kingdom.* London: Penguin, 1979.

Truman, Margaret. *Harry S. Truman.* New York: Morrow, 1972.

Weale, Albert. *The Will of the People: A Modern Myth.* Cambridge: Polity, 2018.

Weber, Max. *The Theory of Social and Economic Organization.* Edited by Talcott Parsons. New York: Oxford University Press, 1947.

Webster, Charles. *The NHS: A Political History.* Oxford: Oxford University Press, 1998.

Westad, Odd Arne. *The Cold War: A World History.* Allen Lane, 2017.

Wildavsky, Aaron. *Speaking Truth to Power: The Art and Craft of Policy Analysis.* New York: Little, Brown, 1979.

World Bank. *Poverty and Shared Prosperity: Taking on Inequality.* Washington, DC: World Bank, 2016.

Wu, Harry. *Re-estimating Chinese Growth.* New York: Conference Board, 2014.

Ziegler, Philip. *Edward Heath.* London: Harper, 2010.

Zuboff, Ahoshana. *The Age of Surveillance Capitalism: The Fight for a Human Future at the New Frontier of Power.* London: Profile, 2019.

Index

About the Author

Stein Ringen is a Norwegian political scientist of states, governance, and democracy. He has published scholarly books and other works on topics ranging from the Scandinavian welfare state via constitutional matters in Britain and the US to dictatorship in China, and on inequality, poverty, income distribution, social and public policy, and comparative government. He is Visiting Professor of Political Economy at King's College London, Emeritus Professor of Sociology and Social Policy at the University of Oxford, and Emeritus Fellow of Green Templeton College, and has been an associate of Nuffield and St Antony's Colleges in Oxford. Before joining the University of Oxford, he was Professor of Welfare Studies at the University of Stockholm. He has held visiting professorships and fellowships in Paris, Berlin, Prague, Brno, Barbados, Jerusalem, London, Lillehammer, Sydney, Hong Kong, Guangzhou, and at Harvard University. He has held various research and government posts in Norway, including as Assistant Director General in the Ministry of Justice and Head of Research in the Ministry of Public Administration. He has been a consultant to the United Nations, and a news and feature reporter with the Norwegian Broadcasting Corporation. His journalism has appeared in the *Financial Times*, *The Washington Post*, the *Los Angeles Times*, the *South China Morning Post* (Hong Kong), ChinaFile (New York), *El País* (Madrid), *Aftenposten* (Oslo), openDemocracy, *The Times Literary Supplement*, and elsewhere. He lives in London with his wife, the novelist and historian Mary Chamberlain.